THE THEATRE OF LOUIS NOWRA

The Theatre of
LOUIS NOWRA

Veronica Kelly

Currency Press • Sydney

First published in 1998 by
Currency Press Pty Ltd
PO Box 2287, Strawberry Hills, NSW 2012, Australia
email: currency@magna.com.au
website: www.currency.com.au

National Library of Australia CIP Data

Kelly, Veronica, 1945-.
The theatre of Louis Nowra.

Bibliography.
Includes index.
ISBN 0 86819 572 3.

1. Nowra, Louis, 1950-. —Criticism and interpretation.
I. Title.

A822.3

Cover design by Robyn Latimer
Production by Dean Nottle
Printed by Star Printery

FRONT COVER PHOTOGRAPH: Damon Herriman and Sara Zwangobani as Lewis and Dulcie in *Summer of the Aliens*, Sydney Theatre Company, 1993. (Photo: Robert McFarlane)
BACK COVER: Melita Jurisic as Betsheb in *The Golden Age*, Playbox Theatre Centre, 1985. (Photo D.B. Simmonds / Sterio Stills); Kylie Belling as Roma in *Byzantine Flowers*, Sydney Theatre Company, 1989. (Photo Branco Gaica); David Ngoombujarra and Claudia La Rose Bell as Vince and Ruth in *Crow*, State Theatre Company of South Australia, 1994. (Photo: Hugh Hartshorne)

Publication of this title was assisted by the Commonwealth Government through the Australia Council, its arts funding and advisory body.

Contents

Acknowledgments

I would like to thank the many people whose generous co-operation has made this book possible: Kate Richter and Danielle Cullen at Hilary Linstead & Associates; Rose Wilson at the State Theatre Company of South Australia; Emma Toohey and Marian Vickery at Opera Australia; Damien Hodgkinson at Belvoir Street Theatre; Sydney; Nick Broun at Black Swan Theatre Company; Raymond Omodei at the Hole in the Wall; Perth; Trish Latham at Darwin Theatre Company; Adam Bennett at Melbourne Theatre Company; Tania Angelini at Playbox Theatre Centre of Monash University, Melbourne; Rosemary Herbert at La Boite; Brisbane; Julie Geiser at Opera Queensland; Hannah Jamieson at the Queensland Theatre Company; Mark Radvan and Jamie Maclean at Queensland University of Technology; Wesley Slattery at the Sydney Theatre Company; Peter Derrett at Theatre North, Lismore; the Fryer Library of the University of Queensland; Currency Press, William Yang, Louis Nowra.

To my colleagues at the University of Queensland, Joanne Tompkins and Helen Gilbert, I owe much for their interest and support, and the inspiration afforded by their ground-breaking scholarship in the fields of contemporary Australian and post-colonial theatre. My students' interest in, and critical engagement with, the plays of Louis Nowra over the years have provided a constant source of stimulation.

My affectionate gratitude is above all due to Toni Johnson-Woods, whose friendship, tireless efficiency and enthusiasm made possible the writing and documentation of this book.

NOTE

To Juanita Catherine Oates, née Kelly
(13 June 1899–22 February 1998)
this book is dedicated with love

Introduction

In the quarter-century since 1973, in a career spanning writing for theatre, television, opera, film and fiction, Louis Nowra has established himself in the forefront of Australian theatre both in cultural prestige and, increasingly, commercial success. In a decentralised Australian theatre industry, and amid many brilliant contemporaries, Nowra has over this vigorous period sustained a prolific output and is even now only in mid-career. His theatre has both charted national concerns and challenged mainstage aesthetic practices. Over thirty original dramas and translations of European plays theatricalise modern Australia's creative energies, comedy and nightmares, combining passionate and often idiosyncratic personal visions with the articulation of deeper communal concerns. The crises of a settler nation—Aboriginal dispossession, and Australia's involvement in imperial wars from the Western Front to Vietnam—are expressed in plays of comic energy and disturbing potency. Ironic Celtic yarn-spinning contextualises his portrayals of savage mutilations and shattered cultures wherein characters bear witness to the pressures of unfinished historical business. Recently *The Temple* (1993) and *The Incorruptible* (1995) have examined contemporary public figures: respectively the eighties business entrepreneur and the populist politician.

Although his drama has been held in high critical esteem from the outset, this increasing commercial visibility would even a decade ago have appeared both surprising and unlikely. Initially Nowra was hailed—or lamented—as an 'internationalist' writer of dark and difficult high-culture parables; an idiosyncratic and austere theatricaliser of the violent and confronting rather than a celebrator or affirmer of comfortable local imagery. The early full-length plays were set in remote times and places—eighteenth-century Russia, nineteenth-century Paraguay, among the warlords of 1920s China—and appeared perversely to ignore the spirited theatrical recuperations of Australian events and personalities so significant to an enthusiastically nationalist period of playwriting. *Inside the*

Island (1980) set in far western New South Wales before the Great War, confirmed that Australia's heterogenous spiritual history was always Nowra's main theme. *The Golden Age* (1985) confirmed Nowra as our foremost dramatic non-naturalist and anatomist of the complex interconnections and cross-identifications of Australian colonised and colonisers.

After a brief hiatus in stage writing Nowra returned to the theatre with *Capricornia* (1988) displaying a looser and more narrative-driven style; still epic and critical in its intentions but with a more transparent emotional texture. A fresh stylistic path is recently evident in the popular semi-autobiographical works *Summer of the Aliens* and *Così* (1992), which seem to confirm the emergence of a new approachable, popular and user-friendly Nowra. This accessibly confiding and 'autobiographical' manoeuvre exhibits a sophisticated fictional game of comic invention and romantic self-revelation. *Così*, Nowra's most celebratory play cannibalising aristocratic culture, is perversely set in a 1970s Melbourne madhouse.

Nowra defines his theatrical aesthetic as 'detachment', a term with affective no less than methodological implications: 'being removed from people at the same time as liking them'. Towards evil and suffering, of which his plays show many examples, Nowra's 'detachment' likewise precludes easy horror and easy judgements alike. The urbane poise of the high comic vision is celebrated amidst the improvisational chaos of *Così* wherein obsessional and over-medicated asylum inmates rehearse and produce Mozart's opera:

> Happy is the man who calmly takes life as he finds it
> And through the vicissitudes of life
> Lets himself be ruled by reason
> What makes another weep
> will make him laugh
> and despite the tempests of his life
> he will find serenity and peace.

Nowra's early characters are typically the oppressed, the underdog, the racially marginalised and the mentally damaged. His theatre explores the rich and frightening 'jungle' of the human mind: its wilful intensity, its blinding visions, its creative adaptability, its terrors, suffering and its durability. The sense of the awesome expanse of Australian nature and the fragility of its white human occupation provides his characteristic background to an exploration of the tenuousness of what is called normality. For *Inside the Island* he adapts Patrick White's phrase 'the country of the mind' as being the proper homeland of his landscape-oriented theatre. Such plays deal with the survivors of post-colonial Australia's legacies of class inequality, imperial racism, indigenous dispossession and the cultural displacements and hybridisations of a multicultural migrant society. Invasion, adaptation, resistance, renewal, metamorphosis and the amoral and transformative power of love are constant themes, typically figured through images of fires, exile, disease, madness and imprisonment. Countering these dynamic but dangerous forces is the isle of Cythera, Nowra's ambiguous image of ideal fulfilled love, whether lost or to be won. For *The Golden Age*'s lost 'tribe' of white Australians, descendents of refugees from the convict hell of Van Diemen's Land, Nowra devised a syncretic and concretely sensual language made up of archaic British dialects, while the physical energy characteristically demanded of his performers is at its most intense. Within its story of a resilient oral culture all but destroyed by contact with 'civilisation', a story is discernible of the dispossession and shattered 'dreaming' of indigenous people. Nowra's vision of national history is a distinctively post-colonial one, where tragedy, romance and farce can collide in magic realist mode; where the inarticulate and marginalised possess strengths inaccessible to their oppressors; and where the traumas of the past erupt into the present to be rehearsed, replayed and refigured.

More consistently than any other mainstream Australian playwright, Nowra has written characters and created roles for a wide variety of ethnic and sexual identities. Non-English-speaking and Aboriginal characters and performers have had major implication and input in this theatre-making. Gay characters range from the warlord Bao of *The Precious Woman*, the camp ironist David of *Sunrise*, the dynastic Terry of *The Temple*, the passionate central relationship of *Deceit*, to the many urban inhabitants of *The Jungle*'s gay scene. Lesbian love structures the relationships of *Spellbound* and unites the central couple of *The Widows*. Although Aboriginal experience can be understood as mutely informing the complex narratives of *Visions*, *Inside the Island* and *The Golden Age*, after the 1988 *Capricornia* adaptation Nowra created specifically Aboriginal roles. Along with *Byzantine Flowers* (1989), the play sequence *Capricornia*, *Crow* (1994) and *Radiance* (1993) forms an important narrative tetralogy of historical Aboriginal stories: a black version of

Nowra's projected 'Empire' sequence (see below). Violent colonial history and the black heroine also occur in the Mozartian Bicentennial opera *Whitsunday*, set to music by Brian Howard. More powerfully than any other white Australian playwright, Nowra has traced the impact of the hybridised contemporary Aboriginal experience on the white imagination. His central characters, whether the powerful or the marginalised, are frequently women. Complaints of lack of good female roles do not apply within Nowra's dramaturgical practice; his casts are typically of equal gender distribution or predominantly female.

Dominant male roles appear in *The Temple*'s ebullient crook Laurie Blake and *The Incorruptible*'s Robespierre figure Ion Stafford. Through the former character Nowra revisits and ironises a middle-class icon; appropriately in a farce satirising the fall of corporate Australia's deregulated financial idols. Laurie is a deliberate quotation of the male 'larrikin' or 'ocker' figure; a kind of national comic mask hybridised for middle-class consumption from parodies of working-class masculinist social styles. Through its ambiguous celebration and anxious interrogation of this pugnaciously demotic and masculinist mask figure, new-wave Australian theatre rose to national prominence in the late 1960s. By contrast, Nowra's plays embody with an unillusioned respect the historical and class consciousness of an older Australian working-class formation; of mostly Irish and other British-descended peoples whose tough realism and sardonic resilience survived the batterings of social marginalisation, imperial wars and economic depressions with a fair amount of their own vision and disrespect intact. However, Nowra is far from being a purist conservative. His theatre, screen work and fiction are deeply interested in international culture and postmodern fluid social identities, and particularly in the experience and impact of the newer Australian peoples; the migrants from over one hundred different countries who have altered the social texture of post-war society. Asian and European characters figure in his dramas, and indeed comic and tragic communication between peoples of different cultural traditions is central to his plays from the outset. 'You eat like a bird', Ly the Vietnamese migrant is told in *Sunrise*, a remark which aptly bewilders him.[1]

Nowra maintains strong demotic and popular tastes which draw upon an eclectic field of cultural reference. His subversive rewriting of international popular and pulp-fiction narratives and motifs is complemented by postmodern textual appropriations of sources ranging from Wagner to Kleist, Ovid to Daffy Duck, from Quentin Tarantino's lowlife dystopias to the outback folk ballads of Ted Egan. While the Australian mainstage of government-subsidised theatre which he has successfully colonised remains basically a preserve of middle-class sentiment, Nowra's plays maintain the outsider's compassion, dark comedy, violence, irony and questioning political vision. 'Australian culture' in Nowra's theatre is a dynamic and richly-textured hybrid of competing stories and styles. The visions of the marginalised, the damaged and the survivor assume disruptive and questioning agency; acting as metamorphic and comic forces in the theatrical transactions between social power and imaginative transformation.

This study presents a comparative interpretation of the cultural thematics of Nowra's theatre, with supportive reference where required to his prose, screen-writing or radio work. Biographical and theatre-historical material may be found in Chapter 1, to which the reader is referred for understandings of the immediate performance conditions of individual plays, their receptions, and their places within the industrial framework of Nowra's writing career. Chapter 2 outlines a framework for reading the basic relationships and theatrical dynamics of these plays, wherein teaching and learning operate as metaphor for the performative and transactional nature of culture. The analytical focus of this section is on the 'teacher' characters and the family dynamics of their relationships with their 'pupils'. The male teacher characters in their various manifestations are examined first, then the female ones, advancing a reading which sees these dramatic transactions as realising responses to Empire within the Australian post-colonial condition.

Chapter 3 more closely analyses and picks apart the plays' rich cultural subtexts, using various theoretical perspectives which help us to see more clearly the contemporary cultural and political discourses in which Nowra's theatre is a significant intervention. These readings are advanced through consideration of the gothic (particularly the Frankenstein myth), historical theories of scientific hybridity, Mikhail Bakhtin's carnival, Ovid's metamorphosis, and postmodern camp and kitsch. Key thematic concepts here are the hybrid and the survivor, and, related to these, the paradoxical relationships of the 'real thing' and the 'fake'. The textual and theatrical strategies evolved for the oblique or the explicit exploration of the Aboriginal condition from a white Australian perspective are noted throughout Chapters 2 and 3. While these chapters explore considerations of theatrical style and live performance signifiers, particularly the powerful extra-linguistic and somatic displays of the colonised 'pupil' characters, a fully developed and detailed analysis of Nowra's forceful theatrical motifs occupies Chapter 4. These include rituals, embedded performances and metatheatre, use of dance and music, self-authored display, mimicry, transvestism (gendered, class or cultural), and significant usages of costume and masquerade. A sustained analysis of costume and self-performance in *Radiance* is given to show how even Nowra's more recent naturalistic-seeming dramaturgy foregrounds the dynamic and performative nature of the post-colonial character, while a concluding reading of *Così* outlines the carnivalesque and re-integrative functions of performance.

The author of his life. Louis Nowra (standing) with Tamblyn Lord (kneeling) and Kylie Belling in *Summer of the Aliens*, Melbourne Theatre Company, 1992. (Photo: David Parker)

Chapter 1

Author of his life

A Victorian childhood

Louis Nowra was born in Melbourne on 12 December 1949 as the eldest child of a working-class family; a younger sister arrived within two years. It was his mother Gloria Mary Herbert's second marriage; her first husband was a handsome Indonesian whom she met in 1945 when based in northern Queensland. Gloria subsequently lived in Java with her pro-Dutch husband during the turmoil of the War of Independence and the overthrow of the Dutch colonial regime. Two aunts, Marg and Pearl, also married Indonesians, who had to remain in Australia after the War of Independence as political exiles. 'From both uncles I understood the pain of exile and the important decision of what side you choose during violent political times.'[1] These Australian aunts and his Indonesian uncles surrounded the young Nowra with Javanese cooking and exotically beautiful cousins. One cousin tried to enter the Miss Australia beauty competition but was rejected as being a 'half-breed':[2] this is the purist version of Australian 'identity' which Nowra's theatre writing was later to challenge. Gloria Herbert was a young woman whom the social and gender mobility of the war years had assisted in her determination to shift for herself and lead a cosmopolitan life. Twins were born to her early marriage, but died in infancy. Before Gloria's husband returned to Java he gave his wife a loaded American .45 automatic pistol to 'protect herself'.

At the end of 1945 Gloria Bruyn, as she then was, used this pistol to shoot dead her father Robert Francis Herbert, then a postal linesman, in the St Kilda flat in which they were living with her mother Myrtle, brother Robert Charles just discharged from the Royal Australian Air Force, and other siblings. Gloria had intervened in a routine but violent row between her parents, incurring verbal abuse from her father, whom she with spirit told to watch his language. As the quarrel escalated the nineteen-year-old Gloria fetched the pistol from her bedroom and shot him. He dropped dead instantly with a bullet in the neck. She then phoned the police and was charged with murder. At the trial her defence was that she believed she had emptied the gun and had used it only to frighten her father and prevent him from hitting her mother. Both her mother and brother stressed the violent temper, physical assaults and drinking, with which the Great War veteran Robert Herbert had made family life a misery since the marriage in 1922. On 27 February 1946 a jury took fifteen minutes to acquit Gloria of both murder and manslaughter. Family legend has it that she shot her father because he said he was glad of her twins' death, since he didn't want 'niggers' in the family. The shooting occurred on 12 December 1945, four years to the day before the birth of Gloria's first surviving child. It was years before the young Nowra learnt why his birthday was never celebrated by family parties.[3]

Gloria Doyle, as she had become, possessed social aspirations which eventually included sending her son to university; a common ambition in this post-war economic period when many Australian families saw tertiary education for their children within their grasp for the first time. 'Instead of having Bizet's *Carmen* to play on our record turntable, we had its Hollywood version in *Carmen Jones*: instead of having Borodin's *Prince Igor*, we had *Kismet*. It was as if I were receiving art through a plastic sieve.'[4] Through his mother Nowra acquired exposure to that peculiar lower middle-class cultural formation of 'accessible aesthetics' characterised as kitsch; and Nowra's own writerly response is frequently that of camp—that detached yet passionate perspective which typically adopts an ironic viewpoint both to the earnest manifestations of kitsch and to the self-constructions of high and low culture alike.[5] Nowra has written briefly of his mother's autocratic nature and her 'brilliant and savage tongue which would pick out the weaknesses in anyone'.[6] These traits were later to be bestowed on the imperious matriarchs Eliza Lynch of *Visions* and Lillian Dawson of *Inside the Island*, and the acid-tongued glamour queens of *Miss Bosnia* and *The Jungle*. Lillian Dawson he describes as a portrait of Gloria: 'a wonderful intelligence but a very destructive attitude towards other human beings.'[7] The personalities of Nowra's parents, both of strong but opposing temperaments, are obliquely diffused throughout his writings.

Nowra's father Clarrie Doyle was a truck-driver of Irish descent 'in love with distance' who drove interstate on the Hume Highway and was an infrequent visitor in his children's lives. One day when Nowra was nine years old, he states, his father left to get some parts for the truck and didn't return for two years.[8] From him Nowra derived a very Irish sense of fantasy, a gift of yarn-spinning and an appreciation of the strategic functions of bullshitting. 'He had that great ability to turn pain into humour, and so caught up did he become in his autobiographical stories that he laughed at his own outrageousness as he told them.'[9] Clarrie Doyle also possessed a 'black Irish temper' and a pronounced anti-authoritarian streak: traits his son was to inherit.[10] Nowra's story 'The Father' characterises its semi-fictionalised subject as 'full of schemes. He often talked about bank robbers, con-men and illegal schemes.' He informed his children, to their mother's disgust, they were related to the Kelly Gang, and of his admiration for big crooks who robbed the government and got away with it.[11] The career of *The Temple*'s Laurie Blake, working-class hero, self-made man and irrepressible big-time schemer, seems a fictional amplification of Nowra's understanding of the dreams and energies of Clarrie Doyle. Clarrie's visits home occasioned jokes and presents for his children, but also fear-filled tension as the parents quarrelled violently aided by a loaded .303 rifle. These were highly-charged incidents, more so since Gloria informed her various husbands (she was later to marry a seaman) that she had already killed one man and could do so again. Nowra recounts a more mundane incident of domestic warfare wherein his steak-and-egg eating father, home late from an interstate trip via the pub, was in retaliation served bullock's eyeball on rice as a 'Javanese delicacy': his father, 'eyes gleaming dangerously with beer and speed', hurled the offending morsel down the hall.[12]

Gradually Clarrie Doyle left his children's lives and remarried, founding his own transport firm and other ventures with chequered success. Contact was sporadic between the young Nowra and this enigmatic figure as they increasingly became inarticulate strangers; yet he continued to intrigue his son through hints of an intense if concealed inner life. Memory, fiction and family legends create for a child a penumbra of desire and emotional mythology where objective truth remains elusive. 'The Father' includes a detail of its subject's serving a jail term for a savage knife attack on a gay man who approached him, attracted by his 'exceptionally handsome and sweet-looking' appearance. Clarrie's fictionalised character first appears as the autodidact ex-truckie magnate of the 1985 short story 'Instructions to a Painter'. Here 'Sir Laurie Blake' commissions a series of paintings of vivid moments of his life; images with 'the precise clarity of a dream' yet hyper-real in their emotional intensity. 'He was a man who had come to me, and all his children, perhaps even his wives, in fragments... Fragmentary as a man, the word "father" had given us, and perhaps even him, a purpose.' Fragmented personalities may be endowed with some form and cohesion through imaginative acts of fiction, and after all, 'we forgive fathers everything.'[13]

Since the production in 1992 of *Summer of the Aliens* Nowra has been increasingly articulate about the imaginative stamp his childhood has left on his theatre. In a biographical article concerning memories of Anzac Day he recalls the family legends of his maternal grandfather Robert Herbert's experiences fighting in both Gallipoli and France, where he was buried alive three times by exploding shells. He never recovered from his third burial under tons of dirt and mud, and upon repatriation became insomniac for fear of nightmares about live entombment. The violent mental agonies of the soldiers of *Inside the Island* figure forth history searing itself into the human imagination, and *The Song Room* shows how such literally unspeakable experiences can isolate war-traumatised soldiers from their families. Nowra recalls himself as a youth marching in the St Patrick's Day Parade,[14] yet is ambivalent about his class and Irishness. He tends to be dismissive about both, and changed his name to prove it. 'I hate being considered Irish... they are a maudlin, sentimental group of people with only one shining ability, which is to tell a story.' Refusing to identify as a multicultural 'hyphen-person',[15] he rejects tribalised identities—as ethnic minority or game economic battler—as marginalisation gambits fit only for buying credit with the well-meaning middle class. 'I'm not interested in any wounds I carry, nor should an audience be. I can't stand an author parading their own pain on stage or in novels.'[16] Declaring the only good thing about being born working-class is getting out of it, he yet despises the blindness of social privilege: 'The middle class likes to believe that Australia is an egalitarian, classless society. A working-class boy knows that is totally untrue.' This sharp class analysis carries over into the epic scope of his plays. 'I try to write about the three classes: working class, middle class and upper class. When you're working-class poor you know that's what it's about. Who has the power, who doesn't; who has the economic base, who doesn't.'[17]

The Doyles grew up in the then new and raw outer-suburban housing commission estate of Fawkner, strung out along the Hume Highway opposite the New Melbourne General Cemetery. Details of this environment are evoked in *Summer of the Aliens*: the clayey earth resistant to exotic flowers, the flickering black and white televisions, the concrete housing slabs which dripped condensation during Melbourne's damper moods. So too are the rolling expanses of dry wheat-coloured grass crisping under the expansive summer skies, inviting a lighted match and ideal for mucking about in the intensely tribal and territorial children's packs of those times. Fawkner, now a well-groomed and prosperous suburb, is today no further from central Melbourne than is Tullamarine Airport via its freeway. In the 1950s, well beyond the tramlines at the city's then northern edge, it must have appeared an imposed hybrid milieu of neither country nor city; isolated toy houses dropped into an ancient landscape from some kitsch flying saucer.

The young Nowra, born with a rare blood condition, suffered from asthma and hence insomnia: he would bang his head on the wall to gain insensibility; or else, like the child narrators of the radio plays *Widows* and *Summer of the Aliens*, roam the streets after dark, peering into windows and trying to make sense of the inmates' lives and behaviour. In Fawkner behaviour could be violent and extreme. 'There is no fun in being brought up in an area where two doors down the guy is in jail because he has committed incest with his two daughters and one is pregnant.'[18] At age four he was sent to St Mark's and taught by Irish nuns whom he remembers with little affection, and state primary schooling in Fawkner followed with Nowra as the perpetually youngest child of his group. At home the boy was surrounded by females: his mother, sister and grandmothers, and there were many girl cousins who teased and coddled him. Boys, and school, were a different matter, and the child felt less at ease with both. Gender definitions were severely policed: the greatest

Shooting cats after school. Damon Herriman and Mitchell Butel in *Summer of the Aliens*, Sydney Theatre Company, 1993. (Photo: Robert McFarlane.)

school punishment was to have to sit with the girls. To prefer the company of girls was to be awarded the dreaded title of 'sissy'; and in this tough neighbourhood where disputes were settled by physical force the outward markers of masculinity had to be quickly mastered. Sport, especially cricket, glued the community together; Collingwood was the Doyle's football team.

Nonetheless, childhood also contained free escapades with a scattered family among whom he spent holidays in the country towns of Seymour, Broadford and Avenal. In his 1985 'Autobiography' and subsequent writings these childhood adventures emerge with sunlit clarity and later found expression in *Summer of the Aliens*.[19] After the domestic tensions of Fawkner, the rural sojourns were like a release from prison. Not that 1950s country towns were idyllic: their stifling social and cultural restrictions rapidly became apparent to an acute and imaginative child yearning for larger possibilities. The stagnant country-town milieu is one from which the sensitive and talented— *The Misery of Beauty*'s celebrated and beautiful dancer Straub, *Spellbound*'s Annie, or the opera star Cressy of *Radiance*—typically flee in a driven trajectory towards metropolitan sophistication and imaginative self-creation, but which retain those originary domestic secrets which define identity forever. The far-western wheat country setting of *Inside the Island* picks up the flat sunburnt expanses of the north Victorian landscape which overwhelm and frame the human figure. Nowra credits this early exposure to various forms of Australian nature as a factor influencing the characteristic outdoor settings of his plays with their insistence on the power of physical environment: 'If my characters are indoors then it becomes claustrophobic for me. I want to run out of the rooms and take my characters with me.'[20]

Besides the monochrome marvels of late-fifties television, and trips to the suburban movie theatre with his mother to wallow in *Picnic* or *Written on the Wind*, live metropolitan theatre and its denizens entered the young boy's life. His paternal grandfather ran a hotel behind the Melbourne Tivoli in whose bar the visiting Nowra could encounter variety artistes: 'ice skaters, exotic dancers, clowns, comedians and musicians' not to mention seven actual dwarfs from *Snow White* who appear remembered in the dwarf Peter of *Inner Voices*.[21] In this last era of Australian live vaudeville, the future playwright was fortunate to have such contact before television and the clubs dispersed these entertainers from the mainstage theatres. His mother's brother, the playwright Bob Herbert, returned serviceman and pacifist, was stage director and stage manager for the J.C. Williamson theatrical chain, then famed for its lavish and devoted remounts of Broadway musicals.[22] In his trips to Melbourne the young Nowra was enchanted by such shows as *Camelot, My Fair Lady, Hello Dolly, Mame* and *Can-Can*. An outstanding memory was *The Cherry Blossom Show* with its exotic Japanese dancers in colourful kimonos.

Nowra attributes his sustained dislike of mimetic naturalism to the early impact and open dramaturgy of these productions with 'the concise scenes, the songs, the colour and the dancing'. He came to understand theatre as 'an act of the imagination' which could be set anywhere. Alas, backstage the magic vanished, and unglamorous people and fake gorilla suits took its place. The early passages of *The Misery of Beauty*, where Frogman works in a sleazy Carlton cabaret as the magician Earl's assistant, expose the tragi-comic paradoxes of artistic illusion: the beautiful vision conjured up from the tacky, the interdependence of the real and the fake. Bob Herbert, with his long career in commercial theatre, encouraged the boy's confidence to be different, and demonstrated that a professional career in Australian theatre was possible. Herbert's play, *No Names... No Pack Drill*, fictionalises his sister Gloria's wild life and blackmarket deals in wartime Sydney. When in 1980 it shared the Sydney Theatre Company's inaugural Opera House season with his nephew's *The Precious Woman*, it was a cause of particular satisfaction to them both.

In 1962 the Doyles, now moderately prosperous, moved from Fawkner to the leafy middle-class suburb of Macleod. Close by were numerous large institutions such as the just-founded La Trobe University and the Plenty and Mont Park mental hospitals, in which both his grandmothers were to spend their last years in senile dementia. His paternal grandmother collapsed into mental twilight after his grandfather ran off with a barmaid half his age: going mad can sometimes seem the sanest course of action. Nowra recalls being sent as a young boy on a visit to Granny in Geelong, only to have her take all his clothes overnight to burn them next morning in a huge backyard bonfire. The child realised she had gone mad, smiling her smile of 'exquisite pleasure' in the firelight much as Doug the pyromaniac was later to do in *Così*.[23] Years later, when Nowra was in his twenties, he would visit Mont Park where this grandmother believed herself living in 1948, seeing her grandson as her own son about to marry Gloria. His maternal grandmother, the widowed Myrtle Herbert, an ex-primary teacher who respected gentility and culture, slipped more slowly into dementia. Her bizarre behaviour and shocking anger thoroughly terrified and puzzled her grandson; uncomprehending, like all children, of the inexplicably extreme behaviour of adults. Nowra's writing was to contain numerous monomaniac characters whose visions are held with tenacious and usually destructive certainty: Earl the magician, Lopez, Lillian Dawson, Bao, Ion Stafford the 'incorruptible'; or, in comic vein, Roy the madhouse impresario of *Così*.

Nowra was relocated to the local school in Macleod where the rough physical manners he had learnt in Fawkner were seen as inappropriate to middle-class behaviour: once again the boy had to remake himself. Then in the summer of 1962–63, at the end of his first year of High School, he met with a severe accident whose effect on his life was incalculable. 'He was delivering newspapers with a friend [Greenie] one day when they decided to go exploring in a storm drain. Sitting down in a pile of leaves, they had a smoke; the cigarette fell, the leaves caught fire and Nowra, his clothes alight, rushed out of the drain without noticing a low concrete pipe with a razor sharp edge' projecting overhead. What felt like warm rain poured down his body as the boys sought help at the railway station. 'Jeez', said an awed Greenie, 'your mum's really going to hit you now.'[24] The head wound completely scalped Nowra, cracked his skull across and embedded pieces of concrete in his brain. After surgery, with five per cent vision remaining in his left eye, he returned to school adrift in a shadow land, blanking out, unable to connect sound with words and finding the simplest language and spellings incomprehensible. He eventually retaught himself to speak by 'writing' sentences on a mental blackboard and then reading them off. With the language centres of his brain in trauma, 'I was a bit of a drongo for the next four years.' He compensated by becoming the class clown: disruptive but popular. This enforced submersion in the arcane connections between language and the rich jungles of consciousness bore remarkable fruit in the invention of the hybrid poetic argot spoken by the lost white tribe of *The Golden Age*. Trips to psychologists and speech therapists left their satiric marks in *Albert*

Names Edward, Inner Voices and *The Song Room*, while the theme of the spiritual endurance of the 'unteachable' character, or colonised culture, is one of the most persistent of his theatre writing.

Nowra was lucky in a sense that his brain was damaged while still growing, as the neural pathways were able to join up again just as a dire fate as an agricultural worker was being proposed in family councils. Suddenly, in fifth form, the fog lifted and Nowra came top of his class; the brain had reorganised itself around the traumatised area and learning was seen to have been unconsciously occurring. However life was still frightening and uncertain, and movies and hallucinogenic drugs enhanced visual perception and helped reorient a shattered world. During a final year at high school he recalls being underwhelmed by *Death of a Salesman*, his first legitimate live theatre production. Realism, he decided presented a 'shrunken, mean-spirited world'[25] with 'whingeing men in grubby cardigans and women shouting at their husbands.'[26] The visual style and imaginative sweep of Orson Welles' *Citizen Kane* or even JCW's colourful *Camelot* were lacking, and furthermore the actors were clearly only pretending to be real; a shabby sleight of hand after the confident theatricalism of the musicals. To the youthful Nowra, it was naturalism's paradox of verisimilitude that appeared truly 'surreal'.[27] As Ruth remarks in *Così*, 'I can handle something being an illusion or real but not at the same time' (26).

In 1967, at the age of seventeen, Nowra enrolled in English Honours at La Trobe University, merely because it was close to his home. The social ferment of the late sixties, of which Melbourne with its huge moratorium rallies and union activism was a pre-eminent site, focussed on opposition to Australia's increasing involvement in the Vietnam War. For the growing social and political opposition to the conservative and insular ethos of a long-lived Liberal-Country Party Coalition government, the rising star of Labor's Gough Whitlam focussed various hopes for change and renewal. Genuine radicalism was expressed in such outcomes as anti-conscription and Aboriginal civil rights activism, union green bans and the women's movement, and culturally by a vigorously nationalist vaudevillian-influenced theatre 'renaissance'. The post-war tertiary generation, however, benefiting from free education and including many first-generation children of Australia's extensive post-war immigration program, remained predominantly liberal-bourgeois and masculinist in their preferred sentiments and cultural expressions. Separating himself from those of his socially confident student peers, Nowra claims that he never attended a Don's party.[28] That middle-class radicals were wankers was an impression strongly formed by this working-class boy, later reconfigured in the acerbic portrait of the student leader Nick in *Cosi*. The social ethos of university study suited the still emotionally unsettled Nowra not at all on either temperamental or social grounds; but while not enforcing assiduous application to formal studies, the expansive pace of university life gave the recalcitrant student time to read widely off-course and form his own tastes: Nowra favoured the aristocratic writers Martin Boyd, Nabokov and Proust.

One year he and a friend produced *Trial by Jury* for the patients and staff of Plenty Mental Home where he worked part-time as a wardsman. This involved adapting to the patients' needs and capacities through extensive rewriting; Bee Gees and Beatles songs proved a popular substitute for Gilbert and Sullivan's music, and in their one performance the patients blossomed in self-confidence. This was Nowra's first hands-on experience of theatre-making and was drawn upon for *Cosi*, his 1992 homage to the healing madness of theatre. Nowra stayed at La Trobe until 1970 but never finished that undergraduate degree: in March 1996 however he received an honorary Doctorate from Griffith University for his 'distinguished contribution to literature'.

Early Melbourne writing

In 1971 Louis Nowra spent a miserable period as an untrained teacher and in the subsequent two years held down all manner of odd jobs such as meat cookery, loading and driving trucks for his father, and stewarding on the trans-Tasman ferry at the behest of his mother's new husband. In the heyday of the Vietnam protests Nowra and his friend David Riley started a street theatre group, and being its sole typist Nowra found himself writing the scripts as well. In 1973 he sent a revision of one such street theatre piece, *Kiss the One-Eyed Priest*, to Melbourne's experimental theatre La Mama. Since 1967 La Mama and its offshoot the Pram Factory had been a home for new Australian scripts. Such new wave classics as Jack Hibberd's *White With Wire Wheels*, *A Stretch of the Imagination* and *Dimboola*; David Williamson's *The Coming of Stork* and *The Removalists*; and plays by John Romeril and Barry Oakley received their premières there. In 1971 at the Pram Factory the Australian Performing Group had premièred *Don's Party*, Williamson's iconic lament for Labor's lost 1969 federal election and the unstable social cohesion of mateship and radicalism. Nowra recalls he liked the 'roughness, the energy and the Australian bias' of the APG, but not its preoccupations with beer, cars, women and sport. 'I found this aggressive Australian maleness and its middle-class sensibility off-putting.'[29]

Nonetheless at this period La Mama was the self-evident choice for a tyro Melbourne playwright. La Mama in Melbourne, the Jane Street and Nimrod theatres in Sydney, La Boite in Brisbane, Troupe in Adelaide and the Hole in the Wall in Perth were vibrant forums of Australian cultural nationalism and artistic experiment, scorning both the mainstage performance styles of the new state-subsidised companies and the studious cloning of the West End or Broadway repertoires. When in 1984 Nowra gave the keynote speech at the Australasian Drama Studies Conference at his old campus La Trobe, he pondered the state of writers' opportunities a decade after his debut. He understood his own historical good fortune in commencing playwriting six or seven years behind the vanguard, able in the wash of this 'first wave' to benefit from the alternative performance networks built in the 1960s with their experimental daring and pugnacious cultural-nationalist agenda.

> These theatres were in opposition and good theatre always comes out of opposition... Opposition also implies a struggle to find new styles, a new language. But where are these theatres now? Where can a young playwright, director or actor go to be adventurous without having to worry about economic failure?[30]

Nowra's own professional career can be read as a determined project to negotiate these tensions.

La Mama accepted *Kiss the One-Eyed Priest* and in July 1973 a season was directed by Darryl Wilkinson. Nowra found his first produced script 'dismal' and not for the last time resolved never to write for the stage again. However he persisted with a three-hander tribute farce *The Death of Joe Orton*, eventually to be staged in 1980. Nowra is a committed fan of Orton's self-consciously ornate language, camp-oriented gay sensibility and strong sense of structure; and Ortonesque comic violence was later to inform the ingenious survival scams of *The Jungle*. In 1974 his short play *Albert Names Edward*, written in a two-day burst, was sent to ABC radio and accepted, only to be broadcast in mid-1975 in such a cut and stilted form that Nowra determined forthwith that writers should have a larger input into radio drama production—a resolve he was subsequently to make good. An unproduced four-hander comedy 'Dreamhouses' was selected for development by the 1974 Australian National Playwrights' Conference; but after the first meeting with his director he withdrew the play. This experience may have confirmed Nowra in his strong advocacy of close personal contact between writer and director as the best development mode for new plays, and he tends to shun the various workshopping and dramaturgical services which since the 1970s have supported Australian theatre. With its theme of rural eccentricity and isolation, its violent deeds and intense family relationships—not to mention its junkyard set and gunshot ending—'Dreamhouses' might well have won attention in its moment. It is comparable in mood to *Backyard*, Janis Balodis's first play of 1980. In an remote piece of bushland, George—a kind of outback *facteur* Cheval[31]—takes as unwilling apprentice the shady and violent Arch to work as handyman on his disturbed daughter Lillian's 'city' of naive and jerry-built 'dreamhouses'. George eventually loses both his daughter and his dream city, rather as Nelson Taylor loses his Doruntine Hotel in the 1993 radio 'screenplay' *Sydney*. The structure of 'Dreamhouses'—twelve scenes punctuated by blackouts—exactly presages that of *Inner Voices* written two years later; the names 'Lillian' and 'George' reappear in *Inside the Island*.

At the end of 1974 Nowra married the composer Sarah de Jong with whom he was deeply in love; a beautiful and gentle woman whose musical talents have placed her high amidst Australian theatre composers. Sarah with her talent and creative energy was a loving and humane influence on Nowra and also collaborated with him on many mutually-conceived projects; his theatre remains notable for its high musical content. His first novel *The Misery of Beauty* was written in the couple's modest flat in bohemian Carlton and sent to the Australian specialist publishers Angus & Robertson. There it gained its author a $2,000 Fellowship and publication in 1976, the same month as the short play *Albert Names Edward* was produced at La Mama. *The Misery of Beauty* drags its characters through a typically

Collaborating on *The Widows*. Nowra, Sarah de Jong and Howard Gelman at the ABC studios in 1985.

Australian odyssey from inner-city bohemia to the rural outback in search of the secrets of identity. Painfully comic in its dealing with deformity, gender and emotional pain, the novel also adroitly switches linguistic class registers and is possibly the first to use as its central enigma the figure of a gay Aborigine.

Nowra was now a rising Melbourne name. A series of Commonwealth Literary Fund Fellowships kept the financial pot boiling. Before the couple left for six months in Munich, courtesy of the Goethe Institut, *Inner Voices* was sent to Sydney's Nimrod Theatre, then under the directorship of John Bell, Richard Wherrett and Ken Horler. This same script had been pulled by John Sumner, the magisterial administrator of the Melbourne Theatre Company, a week before rehearsal: 'My boy', he is reported to have said, 'I have been looking at the number of people in the play and for the same number of people I could do *Othello*.'[32] The validity of local vision and questions of cast size would alike remain important factors in Nowra's negotiations with management structures.

In Munich, living in the artistic Schwäbing district, Nowra and de Jong immersed themselves in German culture both high and low. Bavarian kitsch, they discovered, could hold its own with the Australian variety any day: 'The strange ambiguity about Germany is how bad taste and good taste can reside in the same room.'[33] Nowra encountered the work of Heinrich von Kleist, whose *The Prince of Homburg* he would translate for the Lighthouse Company in 1982. Upon their return the couple co-wrote a cabaret show *Sleezee*, performed at the Last Laugh in February 1977, again directed by Daryl Wilkinson. In Melbourne, Australia's home of comedy and cabaret, a cabaret-revue mounted in John Pinder's famous Carlton venue was an appropriate move for young artists hot from a European city famous for this performance tradition. *Sleezee* garnered censure as a 'banal flop' with an unplayable script and a plot rambling like Brown's cows:[34] Nowra could only agree with this verdict. For this convinced anti-naturalist, surrealism or stylistic nonconformity for their own sake were not to be the path forward.

A success in Sydney

In the same month that *Sleezee* bombed in Melbourne, John Bell's darkly energetic production of *Inner Voices* in the claustral Nimrod Downstairs drew national attention. Performed by the company which had triumphantly naturalised Shakespeare in 'greengrocer

Italian' and furthered the seventies 'larrikin vaudeville' style of presentational acting and musical clowning, Nowra's tightly-constructed semi-expressionist play about a young prince imprisoned without access to speech, appeared to wilfully renounce celebration of the 'Australian identity'. With Sarah de Jong's dance and song music organically integrated into the action, *Inner Voices* disturbingly proclaimed its author's visionary originality and stylistic distinction. Viewed as a sardonic and proletarian musical history collage, *Inner Voices* can, however, be seen as in basic accord with the characteristic styles and concerns of new wave theatre. A confronting and violently comic historical pageant set in a story-book eighteenth-century Russia, the play recasts in an unmistakably Australian idiom such folklore motifs of the king for a day and the feral child. Since Nimrod's success of the previous year, Steve J. Spears' monodrama *The Elocution of Benjamin Franklin* with Gordon Chater as the resilient transvestite and speech-teacher, had also dealt with 'difficulties of verbal communication', thematic continuities in company focus were noticed.[35] For *Inner Voices* six actors doubled the ten-plus characters, with the young Tony Sheldon outstanding in the semi-mute role of the *enfant sauvage* Czar, Ivan. Productions at Perth's Hole in the Wall and Brisbane's La Boite soon followed. *Inner Voices* reached Melbourne in October 1979 in operatic form, produced by the Victoria State Opera with libretto by Nowra and score by Brian Howard.

Meanwhile one of Australia's senior theatre institutions was on the verge of collapse: Sydney's state company, the Old Tote Theatre Company, over-extended in its three venues including the Opera House and the forbidding Seymour Centre, shed its 'Australian season' in a doomed bid to remain afloat. This season was a bold nationalist statement consisting of pieces by the established writers Dorothy Hewett and Patrick White, plus the young newcomer Louis Nowra. Thus was born the short-lived Paris Theatre, named for its makeshift venue, a former variety theatre in Liverpool Street opposite Hyde Park. The Paris personnel included the writer and actor Steve J. Spears, the actors John Gaden, Arthur Dignam, Julie McGregor, Robyn Nevin, Jennifer Claire, Geraldine Turner and Kate Fitzpatrick, composers Sarah de Jong and Ralph Tyrrell, and directors Rex Cramphorn and Jim Sharman. At last Nowra was part of a team with a common project—albeit funded by hasty grants and donations from art sales, boosted by White's characteristic private generosity towards cultural causes about which he felt strongly.

The Paris gamely launched Hewett's lavish musical *Pandora's Cross*, a cabaret-style homage to Sydney's old-time bohemian denizens and denunciation of current criminal scandals like the disappearance of Kings Cross residents' action leader Juanita Neilsen. Nowra's 1993 radio play *Sydney* and his 1995 grunge epic *The Jungle* would in their turn memorialise and celebrate the harbour city's pageant of high and low life. *Pandora's* hugely praised—but huge—set by Brian Thomson made bankruptcy imminent, to impassioned notices of both condemnation and support.[36] With an emergency grant of $30,000 from the Australia Council Cramphorn fought to keep the Paris open long enough to première *Visions* on 17 August. Set in 1860s Paraguay during the genocidal War of the Triple Alliance, this play appeared as perversely determined to reject the tasks of mimetic Australia-reflection as *Inner Voices* had been, puzzling some observers but delighting those seeking a more stylistically expansive and allusive Australian dramatic repertoire. Gaden and Fitzpatrick were the principals, and in a letter to the *Australian* White commended 'the emergence of a new talent, a young actress called Judy Davis who is one to watch for the future.'[37] Luciana Arrighi's vast painted backdrop evoking European dreams of the Rousseauesque 'exotic' can be glimpsed in Branco Gaica's photographs published in the Currency edition.[38] But a twelve-person cast playing eighteen-plus characters exhausted company finances even after the actors forewent payment and the gas deposit was returned to pay for the props. *Visions* rapidly closed, but the enthusiasm created by the Paris venture contributed to the formation by the New South Wales State Government in 1979 of the Sydney Theatre Company, under the artistic directorship of Richard Wherrett. Its inaugural production was Jim Sharman's inspired revival of one of the Paris casualties, White's *A Cheery Soul* starring Robyn Nevin, which helped to re-establish White as a playwright. Filling the cavernous stage of the Opera House's Drama Theatre, as perversely wide as the Paris space had been long, was now the STC's responsibility.

During the Paris events Nowra and Sarah de Jong left Melbourne to settle in a modest house in gritty inner industrial Sydney, within sight and scent of a brewery. His agents were M&L Casting (later Hilary Linstead & Associates). Nowra became Associate Director in the new state company, giving him sustained experience in theatrical collaboration and with it the confidence to loosen his tight conceptual structures. His compositional system of using file cards for planning

Europeans in their paradise. Judy Davis as the Maid, Kate Fitzpatrick as Madame Lynch with Mary-Lou Stewart and Claire Crowther as the sisters Corina and Adelaide in the Paris Theatre Company production of *Visions*, Sydney, 1978. (Photo: Branco Gaica)

out his compact and strongly scenic-centred dramatic structures was being phased out.[39] Of those days, he later said, he hardly changed a word in rehearsal, being too scared to make a judgement about who was right or wrong. 'It made some of my early plays too tight, too airless. Only when I gained confidence did I allow a greater input from actor and director.'[40] After further experience he came to consider the brute economics of live theatre production as artistically enabling rather than compromising, and prided himself on being able to deal pragmatically with external constraints. '[Theatre's] practicalities force you to change, to adapt, to alter according to budget, the sort of actors you have, and even the very theatre your play is done in.' When viewed positively, professional constraints can only improve a work.[41] With Cramphorn he co-translated Alexandre Dumas' *fils' Lady of the Camellias* as the Sydney Theatre Company's second show in February 1979 starring the crystalline stylist Kate Fitzpatrick; and Edmond Rostand's *Cyrano de Bergerac* for the classical virtuoso John Bell in July 1980. That expansive stage in its prestigious landmark building had to be kept filled, and indeed the STC was to provide Nowra with more generous cast sizes than he was ever again to experience.

In the early months of 1979 Nowra was the Literature Board of the Australia Council's writer-in-residence at the University of Queensland, during which time he wrote his second radio play *The Song Room* and incidentally revealed himself as an acute and detached critic of his own writing practice.[42] While in Brisbane he was able to see John Milsom's production of *Visions* at La Boite. Queensland was caught up in the social turmoil surrounding the National Party Premier Johannes Bjelke-Petersen's suppression of strikes and civil liberties, resulting in anti-uranium marches countered by police action and mass arrests.[43] Stephen Sewell's first play *The Father We Loved on a Beach by the Sea* had received its première in the same theatre in 1977, and the apocalyptic turmoil of the Joh years thereafter informed his critical Marxist scripts denouncing Australian political and spiritual deformities. Nowra and Sewell together became identified as leaders of the 'second wave' of 'internationalist' playwrights, sharing a common project of protest and prophecy couched in epic styles with mythic underpinnings.[44] The Queensland National Party's memorable parade of public corruption, populist politics and crackpot fundamentalism found its place in Nowra's 1995 political drama *The Incorruptible*.

Nowra keeps hundreds of scrapbooks containing newspaper clippings of the bizarre and cruel events which befall ordinary people—oblique glimpses of extraordinary fates filtered through banal reportage. His compilation from this archive titled *The Cheated*, a 'coffee-table book for depressives', paid off his contract debt to Angus & Robertson. Many incidents in his plays appear developed from this collection: for example the postman Mr Pisano of *Summer of the Aliens* who goes mad and burns his hoard of undelivered letters.[45] In 1986 Kai Tai Chan created a dance version of *The Cheated* for Sydney's One Extra Dance Company. Olive of *The Jungle* is a late example of a character whose origin might well be found in the 'cheated' files.

In the latter half of 1980 Nowra had taken up his first professional theatre position with the STC, but it was the Nimrod Theatre that opened his next play, *Inside the Island*, in August, directed by twenty-five-year-old Neil Armfield fresh from the University of Sydney, with whom Nowra set up a warm artistic collaboration. Reviews were mixed. While most showed relief that Nowra was 'at last' writing about Australia rather than remote lands and eras, Sydney's senior critic H. G. Kippax described it as un-Australian. Again Patrick White intervened in support of a play sharply critical of the colonialist role of his own social caste. According to Nowra, he was awoken by an early phone call wherein a magisterial voice announced, 'He's a real cunt.'[46] White subsequently stormed to the *Sydney Morning Herald* office demanding they print his more tactfully phrased letter refuting his old enemy. They refused, whereupon White paid for the letter to be inserted as an advertisement throughout the play's season.[47]

Inside the Island was cast for twelve actors playing seventeen-plus named characters; but Nowra's most epic cast ever was to be the Sydney Theatre Company's production in November of *The Precious Woman*, dealing with apocalyptic civil strife in 1920s China and directed by Richard Wherrett with design by the later Oscar winner Luciana Arrighi. It starred Robyn Nevin in the titular role with fourteen actors playing thirty-seven characters. That Nowra was not yet entirely relaxed into the author-director relationship is evident in the severely formal epic style of *The Precious Woman*: its austere and even operatic style he was later to deem 'tight-arsed'. The play's enigmatic ending, in which the mother who has learned the brutal complexity of political action cradles the corpse of the monstrous son she has helped destroy, he insisted was his most optimistic yet. Kippax hailed it as Nowra's 'best play' while John Moses in the *Australian* saw it as his 'brave failure'. Brian Hoad in the *Bulletin* sceptically noted the production's affinity with STC 'color and movement'.[48]

A week after this opening, *The Song Room*, directed by Andrew McLennan with atmospheric outdoor recording and original music by Sarah de Jong, was broadcast on ABC-FM radio. Its outstanding production values and organic union of text with music earned it high commendation in the 1981 Prix Italia.[49] Nowra's STC period concluded with a pantomime-style *Beauty and the Beast* which opened on Boxing Day 1980. It was written in collaboration with Rex Cramphorn, and Kerry Walker and Janice Finn played the flash-trash Ugly Sisters. Subtitled 'Scenes of Horror and Enchantment', the show cannibalised the Cocteau movie and pleased small children, but was a rushed writing job with a perfunctory second act and a perhaps unsatisfactory attempt to develop the dialogue through rehearsal with contributions from the cast.[50] *Beauty and the Beast* was to be Nowra's last Sydney première until 1988. He and de Jong transferred to Adelaide, firstly to translate and adapt Wedekind's 'Lulu' plays for Jim Sharman at the State Theatre Company of South Australia. The compressed work was reset during the all-too-relevant financial scandals of Weimar Germany and starred the now-hot 'young talent' Judy Davis. *Lulu* premièred in June 1981, and the next year Nowra became resident dramatist. Sharman, artistic director of the Adelaide Festival in 1982, took over the state theatre for two years, renaming it the Lighthouse Company. This period provided the most sustained and congenial collaboration with a stable team of directors, artists, composers and designers that Nowra was to experience.

The Lighthouse family

In 1982 Nowra held his last Arts Council grant. He vowed to accept no further direct assistance and to make a professional career out of writing, reasoning that if he was any good he would survive—a decision his self-made father would doubtless have applauded. In this he has had to negotiate the shifting patterns of subsidy, economic change and sheer fashion which have made Australian theatre of the last decades a more established but tougher working environment than that effervescent nationalist upsurge in which the young writer had commenced his career in 1973. By 1984 he was gloomily considering that, despite the acclaimed 'second wave' writing renaissance of which he and Stephen Sewell were the major figures; and his collaboration with such creative directors and Armfield and Sharman; and even despite Australia Council policies requiring of their subsidised companies substantial Australian content, 'we have failed to make Australian drama necessary.'[51] The industry's energies were again shifting, both to the big commercial international musicals and more immediately to the local theatrical margins, where community, women's, Aboriginal, physical, youth and multi-lingual migrant theatre, along with comedy, performance and circus work, would prove the lasting initiatives of the eighties.

The Lighthouse venture was just such an experiment in making Australian drama both 'necessary' and moreover at home on the mainstage, treating new scripts with the lavish resources usually dedicated to classics.[52] These premières would not be consigned to an 'experimental' small studio space but played proudly mainstage, with eye-filling and elegant design by Geoffrey Gifford and Mary Moore. Showing its philosophical inspiration in seventies experimental groups, Lighthouse was conceived as an ensemble, but one with defined roles and structure. Moreover, in contrast to the demotic vaudeville performance modes of the collectively-minded APG or Nimrod, it was flamboyantly arthouse and auteurist in the current European style. Realising that his venture was not going to fulfil all those demands for repertoire 'balance' and subscriber satisfaction which weigh upon state companies, Sharman aimed to establish an Elizabethan-style acting ensemble with a deliberately short lifespan. Lighthouse would perform both European classics (in commissioned translations) along with new and—most importantly—large-cast Australian plays. These two years saw Armfield's productions of a carnivalesque *Twelfth Night* and Sewell's *The Blind Giant is Dancing*, and Sharman's *A Midsummer Night's Dream* and his two Patrick White premières, *Signal Driver* and *Netherwood*.

For Lighthouse Nowra wrote *Spellbound*, his 'country and western' play about country-town emotional suffocation, set to Patsy Cline music on a South Australian orange farm. He took as his underlying theme John Shaw Neilson's poem 'The Orange Tree', in which a young girl listens to hear what the tree might tell her of life. The play's 'young girl', Annie, grows to maturity and leaves for

Sydney and broader horizons, while the passionately romantic Sylvia kills herself in a flood. *Spellbound* is Nowra's first major stage play set in contemporary Australia and contains one of his disoriented and disillusioned returned soldiers, the one-legged Vietnam volunteer Chris.

Nowra also translated and directed Kleist's *The Prince of Homburg*, a version of *Inner Voices'* education-of-a-prince narrative but with a less catastrophic ending. To his bemusement, however, his popular success was an evocation of rural popular culture called *Royal Show*, produced at the end of 1982 with Sharman as director. Set in post-war Australia as American influence supersedes the British imperial bond, this was an amiable group-devised comic homage to the country agricultural shows round which Sharman's father had toured his tent boxing troupe. *Royal Show*'s script and press reception suggest a joyful and inventive collaborative working process. Lighthouse's thirteen actors, now confident in playing together, impersonated over sixty-one characters including a ghost; adults played children, men played nuns, a woman played a Japanese General, and all cast members impersonated sheep, cows, pigs, chooks and sheep dogs—these animal sequences were devised by the Jacques Lecoq-trained Geoffrey Rush. In July 1983 Terry O'Connell restaged the play for the New Moon Theatre Company on a tour of Northern Queensland but it has otherwise had surprisingly little exposure.

With Rush as the titular character, Nowra also directed Nick Enright's translation of *The Marriage of Figaro*, a play of formal high comedy which resonates intertextually in the later *Così* and more immediately in *Sunrise*, the company's farewell show in which the 'family' performed together for the last time. This skilful company tribute has sustained parts tailored to individual strengths: for once, thirteen actors played thirteen characters. Sharman was again the director. Technically it is a masterly exercise in fluidly orchestrated large-cast scenes, and the last of Nowra's scripts to explicitly call for end-scene blackouts; perhaps indicating an expanded perception of how stagecraft can complement and animate a writer's vision. *Sunrise* is a considerable and significant text, anatomising through the internal decay of a clever and cultivated bourgeois Adelaide family the spiritual state of the 'island' Australia. It addresses those large class issues which Nowra sees as his proper thematic territory, and

Above: The Lighthouse ensemble cast of *Royal Show*,
Adelaide, 1982. Below: 'An island of culture in the desert'.
Geoffrey Rush as David and Gillian Jones as Irene, with John
Wood and Belinda McClory in the background, in the
Lighthouse production of *Sunrise*, 1983. (Photos: David Wilson)

connects to immediate South Australian history in its evocation of the 1950s atomic tests at Maralinga. For the first time, too, Aboriginal concerns become openly voiced. However, as he states, theatre—like family—is essentially ephemeral and 'you have to keep moving'.[53] The Lighthouse experience echoes in the situation of the 1985 telemovie *Displaced Persons*: from a tightly-knit group of assorted people under crisis, some die; some survive, adapt and go on.[54]

The Golden Age and aftermath

In 1984 Nowra became writer-in-residence with Melbourne's Playbox Theatre Company, where Rex Cramphorn as artistic director was producing, along with Australian premières, experimental productions of such European classics as *Scapin, Britannicus* and *Measure for Measure*. When, in February 1984, Playbox lost its theatre to fire, the company played at St Martin's Theatre in South Yarra and the Studio of the Victorian Arts Centre. During this residency Nowra directed Stephen McDonald's *Not About Heroes* and on one occasion gave a talk at Monash University which turned out to have interesting consequences. In a staff-room chat he was told the story of an inbred argot-speaking family discovered in the south-west of Tasmania in 1939 and brought to Hobart, only to be imprisoned during the war for government propaganda purposes. Thus was born *The Golden Age*, which was to break the long performance drought existing in his home city, despite Nowra's now international profile with productions in North America and Europe.

However, different industrial constraints were now brought to bear which vitally affected cast sizes. Cramphorn, deeply sympathetic to Nowra's work, had considered mounting a 'trilogy' of *Inner Voices, Visions* and *Inside the Island*, but such a grand project was now impracticable. Nowra was philosophical. While the expansive STC and Lighthouse days were over, he maintained that 'playwrights have an obligation to adapt' to economic constraints and 'if I'm any good I ought to be able to write a play for eight or nine characters'. Before many years had passed, casts of eight or nine would in turn come to seem quixotically lavish. At heart Nowra still wanted to see Australian theatre producing 'large-scale plays; plays that are unsettling and disrespectful; plays that go beyond that hospital ward of emotions the Australian living room; plays born in a spirit of opposition, and plays of political commentary.' The 1983 accession as Labor Prime Minister of Bob Hawke, 'master of the lack of convictions', was not conducive to such writing, he believed. 'You can oppose an arch-radical or an arch-conservative. But how do you fight a marshmallow?'[55] There are no tyrants in Australia, he considered two years later, 'but we have spiritual ones like lethargy'.[56] It is provincial lethargy and colonial deference to big-nation dictates that help destroy the *Golden Age* characters.

The Golden Age was directed by Cramphorn and opened at the Studio of the Victorian Arts Centre on 8 February 1985, a year and a day after the fatal Playbox fire, with eight actors playing sixteen characters. Meanwhile the Melbourne Theatre Company repaired omissions by mounting a revised version of *Visions* with Kerry Walker and Frank Gallacher in the lead. Nowra was looking to develop deeper emotional richness in his writing, and found it in the perilous romantic love of the working-class boy Francis (who is 'absolutely me')[57] for the charismatic nature-figure Betsheb, written for the intensely physical actor Melita Jurisic. *The Golden Age*, with its sophisticated quotations from Euripides and Shakespeare and its ambitious cultural statements about Australia's convict and Aboriginal heritage, received worse notices than the frothy entertainment *Royal Show*—this seemed to indicate that critics couldn't tell scripts from production.[58] Critical reception of the uncut and rather overlong première (blackouts were back) was sometimes perceptive and respectful, but overall saw the production as an ambitious mixed success. Nowra perceived the criticism as hostile and uncomprehending of a play in which he had ventured his imagination further and more daringly than in any of his plays hitherto. He vowed never to read press reviews again. Later, in 1993, he was able to assess things more relatively. 'I saw a production of *Golden Age* recently and I thought, "That boy's trying too hard".' He subsequently claimed to have 'reached the point where I didn't care what other people thought. I decided that if I was going to write for the theatre I had to enjoy myself.'[59] This change of attitude, however, was in the future, after the commercial successes of *Summer of the Aliens* and *Così* had demonstrated that people did want to see his plays. For now, the hurt cut deep. In a later interview he reminisced: 'There's something about seeing in the newspaper articles summing up a whole year and seeing a giant picture of *The Golden Age* with "flop" printed under it! It gives you a perspective about the true

Melita Jurisic as Betsheb in the Playbox Theatre Centre's production of *The Golden Age* at the Victorian Arts Centre, Melbourne, 1985. (Photo: D.B. Simmonds/Sterio Stills)

reality of theatre!'[60] It seemed a hard fate for the play which was going to lose him 'the stigma of being known as a writer of art plays that are done, and perhaps appreciated, by a couple of university students.'[61] *The Golden Age* has proved one of his most widely performed plays, and (as he feared) 'appreciated' by countless students and commentators in Australia and abroad. Despite the initial disappointment the play has accrued sufficient esteem to place it in the forefront of the canon of contemporary Australian drama.

A restless time followed in which Nowra, with no secure base, moved about the country in various roles, turning his energy to novels and screenplays. Shortly after the Playbox opening he directed Peter Maxwell Davies' opera *The Lighthouse* for the Perth Festival, and for the second half of 1985 taught undergraduate drama students at the University of Queensland. During this second Brisbane period he wrote the short Rodopi 'Autobiography' and commenced his second novel *Palu*, a story of magic and revenge set in a developing country not unlike the Papua Niugini which he and Sarah de Jong had visited.[62] This turn of writing suggests that, while still scorning parades of bourgeois pain, he was becoming less reticent about details of his personal life. 'Autobiography' as a fictional mode can be diffused over a vast range of characters and themes, and Nowra sees all his plays as part of his 'inner, emotional autobiography'.[63] While *Palu* is narrated in the first person by a black woman, Nowra declares there is a lot of himself in her.[64] His interest was growing in the tropical north of Australia as a site for imaginative exploration. In this year mention was made of an aborted film project with Jim Sharman titled 'Red Nights': the genesis of the later radio play *Sydney* and the 1997 novel *Red Nights*,[65] the enigmatic origins of whose Gatsby-like hero lie in Cairns. About this time the marriage with Sarah de Jong broke up, though their artistic collaboration was to continue. She settled in Sydney with a new partner to continue her career composing original music for dance, film, theatre and radio.

Nowra typically views writers as forming a kind of hierarchical class system:

> Poets are the aristocrats. They toss off a little verse before breakfast and then bask in the sun of their own indolence for the rest of the day. Novelists are the middle class, hard at work from nine to five, duly cranking out a number of pages a day. Then there are the playwrights, the proletarians whose work

doesn't stop at writing. They get their hands dirty. They rewrite, rewrite in a constant dialogue with designers, directors and actors. There are the screenwriters, who are just the spittoons for others.[66]

Though he remains philosophical about the writer's comparatively lowly status in the film production process, this spittoon fate was not to be Nowra's in his ABC television collaborations. Here he worked with producers who demanded innovation and risk at a time when theatre was increasingly preaching caution.[67] The first fruit of his screenwriting was *Displaced Persons* on ABC television, produced by Jan Chapman and screened on 29 September 1985 as the fourth in a series of telemovies by Australian writers, the others being John Misto, Stephen Sewell and Frank Moorhouse. *Displaced Persons* drew critical praise through its use of actors of European background and languages, with English subtitling, to draw attention to incidents of wilful mistranslation and helpless incomprehension. Dasha Blahova, Steven Vidler, Annie Byron and John Wood headed a cast of actors whose bi-lingual talents had received little mainstream airing. It earned its director Geoffrey Nottage the 1986 Australian Film Institute Award for Best Telefeature. Filmed at the old North Head Quarantine Station with Martin Armiger's moody music, *Displaced Persons* is closely related to *The Golden Age* through their imprisoned communities, World War Two setting, use of disease as a metaphor for cultural difference, and insistence on love as the engine of survival.

The next ABC collaboration was *The Widows*, a gothic tragedy for voices set in the Northern Queensland canefields, and based on a 1920s Hungarian case of mass poisoning by village women of unwanted husbands. It is narrated through the partial perceptions of a young girl who is the uncomprehending witness of her community's accelerating 'disease'. Sarah de Jong's music is an outstanding feature of this radio work broadcast in April 1986, in which Nowra collaborated closely with producers Jane Ulman and the American Howard Gelman. The experience of *Albert Names Edward* had taught him that a writer needs to be involved in, and gain knowledge of, all technical aspects of production.[68] A residency in the same year at the University of Central Queensland in Rockhampton near the tidal mangrove mudflats at Emu Park seeded a lasting image that appears in the third act of the 1993 stage play *Radiance*. Melita Jurisic, along with Brendan Higgins, Paul Chubb and John Bell, performed in his next ABC telemovie *Hunger*, broadcast in October. Like *Displaced Persons* and *The Lizard King* it examines Australian-European relations, this time occasioned by the Romanian hunger strikers who used moral pressure, at appalling personal cost, to persuade the Ceausescu regime to release relatives to join them in Australia.

The Lizard King was filmed in early 1987 at Heartbreak Corner's Tibooburra in the far northwest of New South Wales, starring John Hargreaves and Marie Christine Barrault in a story of a mother's obsessive search for her son lost in the desert. This beautiful-looking film with its red expanses of landscape was screened in February 1988, and interestingly contains a brief theatrical travesty of Nowra's favourite image of perfect but impermanent love—Watteau's eighteenth-century pastoral canvas *L'île de Cythère*. The author as bit player can be glimpsed in the background of this scene. Other activities included the workshopping of a theatre script—a rare undertaking for Nowra but one justified by the particular nature of the project. *Radiance*, the play produced at Belvoir Street six years later, was being developed over a fortnight with Aboriginal actors and money from the Aboriginal Arts Board. By this time Nowra's partner was Justine Saunders, the pioneer Aboriginal film and stage actor with a distinguished record of promoting black actors and playwriting. Although his writing had long suggested Aboriginal history buried in metaphoric narratives, from now on Nowra was less tentative about writing roles directly for black actors. Justine, he said, gave him 'confidence to make mistakes in writing parts for Aborigines.'[69] But as yet there was no immediate occasion to do so: Nowra was widening his professional world, but still avoiding theatre.

August 1987 saw Nowra's name kept to the forefront as the fruits of his busy years were almost simultaneously in the news. *Palu* was published, and the revised version of *The Golden Age* was performed in Sydney directed by Egil Kipste for the Nimrod Theatre Company. In 1984 debt had forced this colourful agent of Australian dramatic nationalism to sell its Surry Hills home and move to the Seymour Centre in the grounds of the University of Sydney. The old theatre, about to fall to developers, was rescued by a syndicate of industry workers and became the Belvoir Street Theatre. Nimrod's move and the nature of their new space did not stop the decline; and this brave

Golden Age production marked the dying twitch of a once-oppositional company now following the Old Tote into extinction. In the chilly caverns of the York Theatre Jurisic re-created her Betsheb, and a cast of ten actors doubled eighteen characters. A striking production of *The Golden Age* had been Neil Armfield's direction for the NIDA 1986 graduating class with Richard Roxburgh as Francis and Rosemary Harris as Betsheb, for which Nowra added scenes and rewritten material on the strength of the Playbox première. Nowra's relationship with tertiary training institutions, which regularly performed his dramas to train or showcase their acting students, was to become closer.

Other projects undertaken that year included another collaboration with the composer Brian Howard: *Whitsunday*, a commissioned work for the Australian Opera. The 1988 Bicentenary of Australia's settlement was looming, and both official Hawke-led nationalist commemoration and spirited dissenting ripostes were on the cultural agenda. A further project with Howard was under way by 1987: an operatic version of Jean Rhys' novel *Wide Sargasso Sea* for the State Opera of South Australia with Marilyn Richardson as the intended lead. Howard, then Head of Music at the Western Australian Conservatorium, described the libretto as portraying 'the dilemma of someone growing up in a society accepted as neither white nor black.'[70] This very post-colonial project unfortunately came to nothing through the composer's over-commitment.

Nowra also reports at this time writing an opera libretto for Graeme Koehne 'about sex'[71]— this was to be the wry and sophisticated chamber opera *Love Burns*, premièred at the Adelaide Festival in 1992. For Film Australia he was researching a television mini-series on big business in Australia—a change in focus from this agency's usual 'furries' (nature documentaries) and indicative of how the brash flavour of the deregulated and privatising eighties was now turning sour in the public's mouth. Stephen Sewell's gothic melodramas *The Blind Giant is Dancing* (1983) and *Dreams in an Empty City* (1986) had exposed Australian public life in the mode of Jacobean heroic tragedy. 'I am fascinated by how quickly a man with no money can become extremely wealthy and powerful', Nowra claimed in 1987.[72] He was eventually fired from this 'Takeover' project, but his research was subsequently to be used in the farce *The Temple*, which, like *Sydney* and *Red Nights*, suggests that at the bottom of every great

Above: The true Australian culture. NIDA cast of *The Golden Age*, Sydney, 1986. Dennis Clements as Peter, Richard Roxburgh as Francis, Bruce Hughes as Mac, Jeanette Cronin as Ayre, Stuart Halcroft as Melorne, Rosemary Harris as Betsheb, Mark McAskill as Stef, and Victoria Eagger as Angel. (Photo: Peter Holderness) Below: Cythera. *Whitsunday*, Australian Opera, 1988. Marie Therese Driscoll, Fiona Janes, Christa Lehmann, Miriam Gormley, John Shaw and David Hobson. (Photo: Branco Gaica. Photo courtesy of Opera Australia)

fortune will indeed be found a great crime; but one assured of public adulation if carried off with the comic effrontery of a sideshow trickster. For the Sydney Theatre Company Nowra planned a grand cycle of five full-length plays entitled 'Empire' tracing the fortunes, Martin Boyd-style, of three generations of a powerful Australian family. The problems of writing an 'intimate epic'[73] were about to loom large.

Bicentenary and empire

For its 1988 bicentennial season the Belvoir Street Theatre scheduled an ambitious stage adaptation of Xavier Herbert's vast 1938 Northern Territory novel *Capricornia*, thus signalling two anniversaries at once. Herbert's savage Hogarthian epic of early-century race relations in the Top End was considered a fitting counter to complacent official memorialising of those two hundred years of white settlement which were hardly an occasion of celebration for Aboriginal Australians. This project went into crisis at the sudden illness of the intended director Geoff Hooke. Armfield appealed to Nowra as a favour to step in to write the script and also direct the already-cast show, whose scheduled opening on 23 April loomed barely six weeks away. Nowra, who had just collaborated with May-Brit Akerholt in her translation of Ibsen's *Ghosts* for Belvoir Street, accepted the literary part of the task. A young and untried Kingston Anderson, whose NIDA postgraduate production of *The Song Room* had brought him to attention, joined the team as director.[74] An air of derring-do pervaded the enterprise as the eleven actors energetically created forty-one characters while Colin Offord devised plangent bush-haunted music. Nowra carved a straight dramatic line through Herbert's exuberantly sprawling material, altering genders and conflating characters. *Capricornia* emerged as a three-act epic centred on the 'Javanese Prince' Norman Shillingworth's journey from Melbourne to 'Port Zodiac' (Darwin) and hence into the country's heartland, there to discover both his real identity and the nature of that Australian history which created him.

Asian and Aboriginal characters were perforce necessary to the story: Laurence Clifford played Norman, Justine Saunders doubled Sally the stockworker and Norman's nurse Fat Anna, and the augmented role of Tocky O'Cannon was made memorable by Lydia Miller's volatile and comic performance. Anderson's *Capricornia* was a critical and popular success, and Nowra's return to theatre writing was warmly welcomed. The Belvoir Street production toured Australia, including Brisbane for Expo 88's Australian theatre season and then the Northern Territory, where it was enjoyed by the descendents of the models for Herbert's characters. The folksinger and songwriter Ted Egan, who had known Herbert and the family upon whom he had based his novel, arranged an outdoor performance in the red dirt of Alice Springs. Egan's ballad about an Aboriginal woman whose children were taken from her during World War Two after the death of her Irish husband became the germ of Nowra's 1994 play *Crow*.[75]

In thematic terms the *Capricornia* adaptation was a breakthrough for Nowra: thrown into the hurly-burly of a collaborative enterprise, there was little time to entertain doubts about writing black characters. The Bicentenary produced equally ambitious plays questioning national self-definition: Michael Gow's savagely critical (and criticised) *1841* had opened at the Adelaide Playhouse, while in Melbourne Don Watson, John Romeril and Tim Robertson's ambitious musical *Manning Clark's History of Australia* played to near-universal execration at the Princess Theatre. However, along with Jack Davis's dignified protest *Barungin* and Sewell's savage dynastic drama *Hate* at Belvoir Street in November, *Capricornia* with its exposing of Australia's 'secret history' of 'interbreeding... murder and mayhem',[76] appears one of the lasting theatrical successes bred by Bicentennial cultural debate.[77]

Four days after *Capricornia*'s première ABC television commenced broadcasting a thirty-part one-hour weekly serial *The Last Resort*, from a story idea by Nowra and produced by Jan Chapman. The writers were Nowra, Gabrielle Lord, Bert Deling and Tim Gooding, who devised their own stories and scripts around the situation of 'three sisters forced to live with each other in a run-down Bondi hotel'.[78] The actors included Kate Fitzpatrick, Kris McQuade, Nell Schofield, Wyn Roberts and Paul Chubb in a quirky but uneven series which Phillip Adams aptly described as 'a cross between *King Lear* and *Fawlty Towers*'.[79] In it however the basic situation of *Radiance* may be discerned: three very different sisters, each facing a personal crisis or economic impasse, must return home at the behest of an omnipotent parent to find a viable way of transforming their lives.[80]

Whitsunday, Nowra and Howard's Bicentennial commission for the Australian Opera, opened in Sydney on 2 September 1988 directed by Neil Armfield, conducted by Stuart Challender and with singers

David Hobson as the young hero, Miriam Gormley as the Kanaka maid, and John Shaw as their nemesis the sinister blackbirder Johnson. The collaborators saw their brief as creating something not only set in Australia, but 'about Australia in a deeper sense'; an opera which rehabilitated for our times those operatic essentials 'love and passion'. Set on a tropical Queensland island in 1913, the libretto traces, in Magic Flute mode, the trials of the young lovers in an eerie nightworld and their resistance to the seductions of the Prospero figure, the evil Emperor of Darkness. Again Nowra's favourite image, Watteau's idyllic rococo 'Pilgrimage to Cythera', is realised in the action more fully than in The Lizard King: theatricalising a beautiful 'age of innocence passing before our very eyes' whose characters stand unwittingly on the brink of imperial conflict.[81] In his Sydney Morning Herald review Roger Covell describes the score's dissociation of vocal and instrumental material, with the latter creating the tropical fecundity of birdcalls and spirit voices which inhabit this magic isle.[82]

A few days after the Whitsunday opening Nowra and Saunders set off for the United States where he took up a two months' residency teaching Australian drama at Yale University. Work progressed on the first play of the five-part STC 'Empire' commission: this was to be titled 'Byzantine Flowers'. On their return to their Sydenham home Saunders organised the Black Playwrights Festival at Macquarie University in January 1989. The two split as partners during this year, and Nowra spent a lot of time abroad in Canada, Ireland, London, and principally in living with the Inuit on the remote island of Shishmaref in the Canadian Arctic.

The reason for this was the intervention of his friend Vincent Ward, the New Zealand film director whose Vigil had attracted international attention. Ward, whose intense and original vision— and childhood head accident—made him a temperamentally congenial collaborator, wanted Nowra to script his movie Map of the Human Heart, a romantic story with Inuit and Métis characters set in the Arctic and in wartime London and culminating in the firebombing of Dresden. Life with the Inuit consisted of dedicated drinking and hunting: 'males are much the same the world over, hunting, talking about women, it's all that male bonding stuff, death and sex.'[83] In the far Arctic, and in rainy Ireland and London, the idea developed of an autobiographical theatrical trilogy. Distance from Australia gradually altered Nowra's view of people and the past. 'I realised it is easier to feel antagonism and angst than it is to feel empathy and pleasure in people... I decided to become less judgmental... it was almost a conscious decision not to become stuck in hate but to look for the great things in human beings.'[84]

In fact the 'Aliens' material, the first part of this projected trilogy, already existed in radio form, having been recorded by the ABC production team headed by Jane Ulman with Sarah de Jong's music. The team wanted a production with distinctive outdoor atmospherics, and sought locations around Sydney with similar dry acoustics to the treeless and birdless Fawkner of Nowra's 1950s youth. The radio *Summer of the Aliens* is told from the partial viewpoint of the adolescent Lewis to whom human, and especially adult, behaviour seems so arbitrary and strange that he can only conclude that his family and neighbours are being invaded by creatures from a flying saucer. The gently ironic evocation of suburbia and of teenage sexuality, filtered through a young person's puzzled observations, allows the listener to understand that the forces which possess Lewis's neighbours are merely human emotions in all their odd or savage manifestations. *Summer of the Aliens* is a brilliant piece of stereo sound engineering with naturally-spoken performances. It was premièred on the BBC in October 1989 and garnered praise both for its allusive script and its innovative production values.[85] It won for Australia its first international Prix Italia for Radio Drama and was broadcast on the ABC in August 1990 as the culminating show in a Nowra radio retrospective. Next year it was broadcast in the Czech Republic, Slovakia, Norway and Germany.

By December 1989 Nowra was back in Sydney living out of suitcases and straight into the Sydney Theatre Company rehearsals of *Byzantine Flowers*. The projected generational epic sequence 'Empire' had now become a single tightly-focussed drama directed by Kingston Anderson with six actors playing just six characters. Kylie Belling created the half-caste heroine Roma—an appropriate name given the play's imperial theme, but this Roma was prosaically named after the western Queensland town. Other actors included Simon Chilvers, Justine Saunders and Shane Connor. Set on a North Queensland sugar plantation, the play compresses generations of settlement history into a few years around the Great War, dramatising the decline of empire and compressing its bloody origins into tight exposition. Some of the *Palu* thematic is present in the upward career of the spirited Roma who rises in the household of an elderly sugar magnate. Reviewers found it generically ambiguous,[86] but *Byzantine*

Flowers forms an important step in Nowra's overall development, and its analysis of the moral dilemmas of the indigenous dispossessed trying to regain a 'home' remains of strong contemporary relevance.

In his 1989 article 'The Shrinking Vision' Nowra pondered how a professional writer should respond to the 1980s constriction of subsidised theatre, an ironic corollary of the high-level deregulated economic afflatus of that decade. The break-even point of Belvoir Street, he wrote, was now five actors; the budget of most companies was eaten up in rent, salaries and grandiose sets to fill those monumental cultural complexes which now dominated theatre in capital and provincial cities alike. Audiences too were getting older and sought consolation, not challenge. New local work competed in the same repertoire with the cream of imported plays, increasingly to be greeted with impatience if its success was not immediately apparent. It seemed that the old colonial distortion caused by Australia as a cultural importer was re-establishing itself to the tunes of 'excellence' and 'internationalist' rhetoric. The greedy success-oriented times had left their mark on cultural attitudes, Nowra considered, and the writer had to deal with industrial limitations as best he could. *Hate*, Sewell's Strindbergian five-character Bicentennial riposte, he saw as a case where such restrictions focussed the writing; but the overall effect on dramatic style and theme endangered the political dimension of the epic vision; 'the relationship between classes and people caught up in events larger than themselves'. Broad visions would shrink to concentrate on the individual, or the 'nuclear family in a living room... instead of his or her relationships with others' as part of 'the grid of power, class and race.' Significantly this article considers how, if one were to attempt a small-cast play about a financier like Alan Bond, for example, the 'connections between money, class, power and political manipulation' could be adequately handled. Would such a character 'come out as just a rogue and not a robber baron who is a part of, and a creation of, an Australia that is becoming devoid of financial and moral responsibility'?[87] Driving for narrative clarity and emotional depth rather than the resonant allusiveness of such earlier drama as *The Golden Age*, the domesticated 'Empire' epic *Byzantine Flowers* for all its urgency had to negotiate the industrial constraints of this 'shrinking vision'. Indeed, for some commentators, Nowra's 1993 play *The Temple* was also generically compromised by its cartoon-scaled anatomising of broad national follies.

Melbourne and its aliens

The new decade saw Nowra returning to his home city, eventually to buy an attractive house in South Melbourne with his partner the Special Broadcasting Service journalist and film-maker Gerri Williams. In May 1997 they would be married in Sydney. These commitments, financial and emotional, to the city about which he was at best ambivalent, necessitated hard work on Nowra's part. For the National Institute of Dramatic Art graduating class in May he supplied *The Watchtower*, his 'Magic Mountain' play set during World War Two in a tuberculosis sanitorium in the Blue Mountains. In training institutions large casts were a positive bonus. Reshaping this script for the student actors, however, put back his writing of 'Boofhead', a commission for the Queensland Theatre Company which had to date never performed a Nowra play. This drought was eventually broken in February 1997 when the QTC co-produced *Radiance* with Kooemba Jdarra Indigenous Theatre. A distinguished revival of *Capricornia*, starring Bradley Byquar with eleven actors in thirty-eight roles again directed by Anderson, transferred from the State Theatre Company of South Australia to Melbourne in October 1990: touring and production-sharing were responses of subsidised companies to the new economic climate. In the first week of this month Patrick White died; and Nowra's team Collingwood at last won the Grand Final.[88]

During this Melbourne period, Nowra's friend Vincent Ward was brought in as director of the third Hollywood 'Alien' movie, the sequel to Ripley's two previous blockbuster encounters with ambiguous androids, voracious invasive life-forms and ruthless intergalactic corporate finance. Ward demanded Nowra as his scriptwriter, occasioning chauffeured visits to Los Angeles to encounter, not for the last time, the film industry's money men. Eventually they rejected Nowra's 'Alien' script, and Ward too departed the space-epic's troubled production, so the world never discovered what ultimate fate Nowra had in mind for the embattled Ripley, deep space's Mother Courage. As a long-time admirer of the confrontingly surreal Canadian film director David Cronenberg and a childhood devourer of B-grade creature features, Nowra could have made an interesting intervention into mainstream popular culture. It is inferrable, however, that the discarded 'Alien' material's ambivalant thematics concerning motherhood and monstrosity bore some relation to the still-developing 'Boofhead' project, gestating during this period.

Meanwhile the script of *Map of the Human Heart* was in progress; and from the perspective of a cold, grey and financially depressed Melbourne, Sydney was appearing increasingly attractive. While the Collingwood victory was a bonus, the gregarious and extrovert Nowra, sceptical of literary incestuousness, did not easily fit back into the literate, courteous but sometimes clannish world of literary Melbourne with its tenacious loyalties and blokey feuds. Melbourne seemed somehow enclosed and bourgeois, and the tribal tone altogether too Irish. Nor was Nowra one to back away from a stoush. Dinny O'Hearn, reviewer of *Palu*, had been punched in the nose by Nowra in Stewart's Pub in 1987 over remarks involving black women. Subsequently, after allegedly assaulting some cops at a street festival, Nowra, like his mother before him, had his day in court.[89] Amidst these dissatisfactions he began to write a novel as a homage to the lost paradise of Sydney: sunny, brash, polluted, corrupt, fashion-driven and full of amoral energy, but above all physically glorious. Thus was born the 1997 novel *Red Nights* and its companion text the radio 'screenplay' *Sydney*, wherein, as a trace of its Melbourne genesis, rain falls throughout its twenty-four hours of fictional time. Nowra departed for London at the end of 1990 to work on the *Map of the Human Heart* screenplay and inspect locations with the production company Working Title, producers of *Sammy and Rosie Get Laid* and *My Beautiful Laundrette*. Filming commenced in early 1991. This meant four months in Montreal and a stay in Barcelona, two cities with which Nowra fell in love, plus visits back to Munich to confer with the director Doris Dorrie on a screenplay for a 'Palu' film which never reached production. A Nowra film treatment of New Zealand's notorious Parker-Hulme murder case of the 1950s had also been in play for some time, but this incident was a hot international property and Peter Jackson's 1995 film *Heavenly Creatures* eventually pre-empted the rest.[90] Yet again the 'Boofhead' final draft became sidelined since Aubrey Mellor, its prospective director, wanted the part of the mother filled out. This excellent advice could not be acted upon in time to make the 1991 QTC season; however, when 'Boofhead' surfaced in 1994 in Adelaide under the title *Crow*, the now fully-developed black Mother Courage became a virtuoso role for Lydia Miller.

By the end of 1991 Nowra was back in Australia doing post-production on *Map of the Human Heart*. He was still keeping to his conviction that a writer must be a hands-on professional who understood all elements of production, just as his father had been in working his way up in the trucking business. *Summer of the Aliens* was scheduled by the Melbourne Theatre Company for early in the new year, to be directed by Nadia Tass, while its sequel *Così*, the second of the planned autobiographical trilogy, was already written. Pre-production location research was undertaken in a now-respectable Fawkner with Tass and designer Trina Parker, who produced marvels in suggesting expanses of sunburnt grass and doll's-house dwellings on the cramped stage of the Russell Street Theatre. *Summer of the Aliens* also marked Nowra's debut as an actor. When the scheduled Narrator dropped out through illness Tass persuaded Nowra to take over the role of the older Lewis.

This period was saddened by the long decline of Rex Cramphorn through an AIDS-related illness, and his death at the age of fifty in a Sydney nursing home on 22 November. In his obituary notice for this friend and colleague, Nowra described the characteristics of Cramphorn's ensemble productions of the classical European repertoire in terms that could be applied to his own writing.

> At the core of his productions, beyond the clarity of his interpretations and the subtle ebb and flow of emotions, there was a great calmness; a sense that even in the most terrible bloody Jacobean deeds he was not reacting blindly and emotionally to the horror on stage, but contemplating it, as if trying to discover the essence of humanity even in a heart of darkness.[91]

The tax muse

Nowra's burst of theatrical creativity in the early 1990s was driven by rigorous financial imperatives. His prolific output in the late eighties had earned him the customary reward of the enterprising self-employed: a colossal provisional tax bill. He determined to work his way out of his financial hole and, if possible, out of Melbourne as well. His usual workaholic temperament went into overdrive: 'It's amazing how the tax department makes you a driven man.'[92] Driven or not, the growing-up plays spilled out as if something important was at last being released. *Così* took only four weeks to commit to

A discount Tristan and Isolde. Margaret Schindler and Gregory Massingham in *Love Burns*, Lyric Opera of Queensland, 1992. (Photo: Daniel McGovern. Photo courtesy of Opera Queensland)

paper. Moving around overseas and staying in hotels, Nowra found, made one fall back more on oneself. About one thing he remained adamant: the plays 'are not angst-ridden'. He believed that both his style and emotional content had loosened up. 'When you are younger you want to separate yourself a bit from society, you want to see dissimilarities. When you get older you want to find familiarities, you want to find connections with people and relationships and societies.' A trilogy was planned, with a *Così* sequel 'Cythera' envisioned as centring on Lewis as himself 'two years ago', on the move 'and understanding as little as he always did.'[93]

The 'opera about sex' surfaced at the 1992 Adelaide Festival on 28 February. It took the form of a chamber piece by the composer Graeme Koehne, directed by Neil Armfield and performed by the Seymour Group conducted by Warwick Stengards. The principal singers were Christine Douglas, Stephen Ibbotson and Margaret Haggart.[94] The libretto of *Love Burns*, originally titled 'Love Kills', is redolent of the higher kitsch and probably found its genesis in the 'Cheated' tabloid scrapbooks. Koehne's wittily melodious score uses popular dance rhythms: waltzes, tangos and rhumbas. The program notes declare the creative team's intentions: 'No room is given here to the simplistic equation of seriousness with aesthetic ugliness. From music that entertains and seduces, true artistic experience is just as attainable as from music which ignores the possibility of enjoyment.'[95] The libretto's inspiration is the fifties tabloid case of the 'honeymoon killers', a deranged but mutually infatuated pair of petty-bourgeois social aspirants (Angela is an asylum nurse, Jack a conman posing as a dance teacher) who ended on the gallows for murdering 'superfluous' old women for their money. Love, sex and murder, Nowra explained, were after all staple opera topics, but he wanted to explore how love could be at once an intensely felt emotion and a bundle of clichés: both high opera and soap opera.[96] In a violent and sordid story of a 'discount Tristan and Isolde', humour and post-modern irony were intrinsic to the collaborators' balance of aesthetic and moral responses.

Summer of the Aliens opened in the small Russell Street Theatre on 17 March—an apt date given its 'autobiographical' positioning—with Tamblyn Lord as the younger Lewis, and including in the cast Kylie Belling, Geneviève Picot, Robert Grubb and Vince Colosimo. Nowra found his acting role as Narrator a steep learning curve. He found himself unable to remember his own lines: 'They are endless', he decided, 'they lack rhythm, they lack focus and I've put actors through this for years and years and years.'[97] 'I realised just how incredibly vulnerable [actors] are... I never realised how many sibilants I write—it's a revelation.'[98] Typically, he seized upon the opportunity offered for renovating his craft. While performing the older Lewis he would try to work out the shifting dynamics of the live theatre compact; why, for example, a scene which had fired the previous night was now falling flat despite the actors' best efforts. Why were some audiences lively and appreciative and others thick and slow, causing the performance to drag? Why the disconcerting solitary laugh in the unexpected spot? Why did the carefully-planned focus shift arbitrarily? 'I'd find myself mentally stepping back, trying to find some answer. In the process of mentally rewriting the scene I would invariably miss my cue.'[99] All parties concerned agreed he should stick to writing. *Summer of the Aliens* found a huge and unexpected audience of secondary students, since the play was speedily placed on Victoria's new Australian Studies syllabus. It was later as swiftly removed due to a complaint about the depiction of child abuse in the performance.

At Belvoir Street *Così* premièred on 21 April directed by Adam Cook. This genial comedy is loosely based on his youthful *Trial by Jury* production in the Plenty Mental Home but is in essence a fantasia of Nowra's experience of the various cast 'families' of professional theatre. The première was hilarious if lengthy; cuts soon followed. Barry Otto's Roy, maniacal Mozartian and oblivious mythomaniac, stood out even in a vigorous team of eight actors playing eleven characters. Along with Ben Mendelsohn's bemused Lewis and David Wenham's volatile pyromaniac Doug, Otto recreated his Belvoir Street role in the *Così* film of 1996. Of the Melbourne Theatre Company production opening on 29 April 1994, with Christopher Gabardi as Lewis and the lanky comic Kym Gyngell as a ravaged-faced Doug, Pamela Rabe's poignant characterisation of the repressed obsessive Ruth made it to the film. This pared-down MTC version, on a single set with the domestic scenes cut or relocated, was directed by Nadia Tass with designs by Trina Parker. *Così*, with its surefire rehearsal play device and Jonsonian-humour characters, was to receive numerous Australian productions; its theatrical jokes and rich roles making it a favourite with performers, directors and audiences.[100] But with commercial success came critical doubt: was the uncompromising author of disturbingly dark visions now softening up?

In a 1992 overview, the *Australian*'s theatre critic John McCallum saw Nowra as rivalling David Williamson as the major writer surviving from the 1970s; but at the price of his 'sentimentally backward-looking' autobiographical scripts being eagerly seized by companies while so many of his earlier plays had received no major production after their première.[101] McCallum was certain that 'even in rosy-hued, reflective middle age [Nowra's] plays will be surprising', but saw the profession as less supportive of daring than hitherto.[102] Nowra, while agreeing with the perception that the cultural climate had changed, read the early nineties mood as part of a cultural swing which he was determined to ride out. Nor was he going to become the prisoner of his admirers. 'I'm frightened of building up audience expectations because it puts you in a *cul de sac*. People expect things from a David Williamson play, which is fine, because part of his charm is his ability to confirm those expectations. But I don't like that for myself. It doesn't work for me.'[103] Live theatre he saw as the creature *par excellence* of 'the mores, manners and even politics of the time', a form for good or ill 'at the mercy of society, economics, audiences, reviewers and the haphazardness of human relationships.' The feedback in live theatre is immediate and unmistakable. Whereas a novel or film can wait decades or centuries to find its appreciators, here-and-now livelihoods depended on full houses. 'The change in audience tastes can happen with bewildering suddenness', he considered; look for instance at Shakespeare's late-career move into trendy romantic material to accommodate new theatre spaces and technologies:

> If a playwright is to survive as a creator, he or she has to acknowledge the impermanence of the bond with the audience, a bond that can be altered and changed by many factors... and if a playwright is not willing to change with them then the works are not performed. It's as simple as that.'

Equally in play is Nowra's determination to retain his own vision. In 1987 he stated: 'I always write for myself. To write for anyone else is dangerous, because there is no such thing as "the audience"'.[104] Epic plays and fierce questioning of comforting certainties found fewer industrial champions in the 'post-historical' early 1990s. Nowra believed that young directors, once the champions of new drama, now wanted to direct deconstructive versions of the classics or else films.[105]

But typically, when questioned in connection with what by 1993 was seen as the preponderance of hastily-prepared and sudden-death productions by major companies of untried new scripts, Nowra insisted on the preparation period between author and director as the most precious and productive resource in new script development. He'd prefer to have companies budget for an extra week's rehearsal and organise regional tryouts, than to avail himself of workshopping or dramaturgy.[106] For him the director-writer relationship remained the creative keystone, and furthermore new directors were now moving into play. Gone were the days when the Cramphorns, Bells, Armfields and Sharmans would seize upon a new Australian script to display their art. Cramphorn was dead, Wherrett and Sharman had largely retired from the fray, Bell was now running his ensemble Shakespeare company, and Armfield, much in demand for opera production, was increasingly committed to establishing his own ensemble at Belvoir Street.

In May *Map of the Human Heart* was released at the Cannes Film Festival, and next month *The Golden Age* was produced by the Druid Theatre at the Galway Arts Festival, in Ireland, with the participation of Mark Pegler who had performed in the Nimrod productions of that play and *Capricornia*.[107] The movie garnered awards at the 1993 Tokyo Film Festival, and at home at the AFI and Film Critics' Circle awards. The Lyric Opera of Queensland produced a stylish *Love Burns* in August 1992, directed by David Bell and performed, appropriately but to the bemusement of some opera patrons, in the intimate space of La Boite which had so quickly scooped up the 'difficult' *Inner Voices* fifteen years ago. By the years' end, with *Così* winning the New South Wales Premier's Award for Best Play, Nowra's taxing problem had begun to recede. The charming but financially draining South Melbourne house was sold, and Nowra and Gerri Williams moved to Elizabeth Bay in Sydney.

Re-inventing oneself

Two new theatrical projects were on the boil; *The Temple* for Playbox and *Radiance* for Belvoir Street, and the ABC were producing the radio play *Sydney* with authentic locations recorded around that city's inner-urban milieu. Seeing the point of supplying training institutions with large-cast material and predominantly female roles, he reworked *The Widows* for Wollongong students with the action placed back in Hungary. In Brisbane, Metaluna Theatre combined with the

Queensland Performing Arts Trust to produce a fine *Summer of the Aliens* at the Cremorne Theatre directed by Peter Barclay, with Eugene Gilfedder as the older Lewis, Andrew Buchanan as his younger counterpart, Errol O'Neill as a charmingly feckless father and the talented Deborah Mailman as the abused but feisty Dulcie.

Research for speculative films floated on even more speculative international finance took Nowra to Sulawesi, where he was able to seek out the sources of childhood memories originating from his mother's first marriage and his Australian Indonesian cousins.[108] The bulging-eyed wooden 'demon' statue that rested on his mother's mantlepiece had already found a place in his dramatisation of *Capricornia.* Upon his return he launched himself, with a vigour worthy of Patrick White, into a simmering cultural debate by giving a widely-reported speech at the National Press Club luncheon in Canberra on 6 April 1993. (The occasion was the opening of a production of *The Golden Age* by Canberra Repertory Club.) He made two perhaps unrelated criticisms of the Australia Council, the federal funding body for the arts: one about the problems of peer assessment, a process he believed had been hijacked by 'arts bureaucrats'; and another about how dictates of 'political correctness' were forcing writers to accept women directors willy-nilly. This latter point was a difficult one to handle without offending personalities, but Nowra's just target was not so much institutionalised cultural *diktats* as a commercially-driven caution about risky new scripts: assignments which tended to be given to less experienced—hence largely women—directors. This policy pressure Nowra saw as indirect, 'cowardly and snide', coming from bureaucrats interfering in the artistic negotiations between author and company.

Though Nowra offered few concrete suggestions as to who or what might replace either peer assessment or indeed the Australia Council, he was voicing the unease of many while releasing a head of resentment of his own. If artists must continually re-invent themselves, he considered, so too could the Australia Council. As one who, practically alone of mainstream playwrights, had conspicuously and consistently written roles for black and multicultural performers, perhaps he felt emboldened to speak out. The talk became a media event and was picked up by ABC television's *Lateline* program.[109] In August 1996 Nowra was himself appointed to the Literature Fund of the Australia Council, gaining more hands-on experience.

The Press Club talk was less notable for its intervention into national arts policy debate than for signalling Nowra's perception of the writer's altering relation to social agendas, theatre structures and audiences. His toughest assault was reserved for his own generation—characterised as a managerial élite creeping from under the dank rocks of seventies tertiary courses wherein they imbibed psychobabble and lifestyle feminism, believing 'the individual was the most important person on this earth'.[110] These 'baby boomers', of whom he himself ambivalently was and was not one, appear in fact to be that same middle class whom in the early seventies he had believed to be imprisoning the Australian theatrical renaissance within their specific class and aesthetic concerns: 'boozing men, wife-swapping, the problems of being stuck in the middle echelon of the bureaucracy and the crucial problems of a second mortgage.'[111] Now they were accused of promoting patronising or ghetto versions of multiculturalism and feminism. Australian society was indeed experiencing increased economic and social polarisation under the deregulating and privatising policies of Paul Keating's federal Labor government, and the anti-authoritarian Nowra remained no admirer of politicians, as the characters of Richard in *Sunrise* and Nick in *Così*, or the Ion of *The Incorruptible* indicate. But more relevantly for his concerns, the ossified aesthetic tastes of the boomers (and their policy-making instruments) masked the theatrical interests of a media-wise younger generation; interests which could—and predictably would—be affronting to the established *bien-pensant*: 'sexy', 'violent', 'scary', 'full of the stupidity and energy of youth'.[112] The STC's Tarantino-esque production of *The Jungle*, Nowra's Menippean satire of metropolitan high and lowlife, would seek to address this new audience. Re-invention was again on the agenda.

Back in Sydney, crisis loomed. Howard Gelman, the American radio producer who had collaborated on *The Widows*, abruptly left the production of *Sydney* in mid-stream. Nowra stepped in as producer and did the complicated stereo sound-mix for this two-part 'screenplay for radio' recorded live in such venues as the Manly Aquarium, a harbour ferry, Chinatown, Pier Three, Oxford Street bars, restaurants and clubs, the Opera House foyer and at a performance of *Voss*.[113] An almost hyper-real aural verisimilitude was important in this 'love letter to Sydney' in which the desperate *nouveau riche* Nelson (born Steve) Taylor has twenty-four hours to raise illegal money, put bankruptcy and disgrace behind him, and reclaim his position as king of the social set. Nowra insists he walked Nelson's last route in order to time it exactly. By its thriller genre and multi-layering of environmental sound, *Sydney* was pitched at non-traditional radio audiences: 'I was kind of hoping that maybe some young people would accidentally turn it on and go, "Hey, this sounds like something I would listen to on my CD, or a film soundtrack, or Clint Eastwood in *A Line of Duty* [sic] with all those noises coming at me."'[114] The radio format enabled him to try out a large-scale project beyond the capacity of a theatre company. As for the prospect of obtaining auteurial unity, 'everyone has an opinion, from the grip to the producer's girlfriend. Everyone goes to the movies, so everyone thinks they know the formula to make it work.'[115] In the event, the *Sydney* 'screenplay' once trialled on radio mutated into the 1997 novel *Red Nights*.

On 17 July 1993 the Red Shed Company in Adelaide opened their *Così* production, directed by Simon Phillips with Luciano Martucci as Lewis. Workshops were under way at Belvoir Street for the forthcoming première of *Radiance*. The next première was to take place in Melbourne, and was the result of Nowra's 1987 personal research on business entrepreneurs and corporate takeovers for the abortive mid-eighties Film Australia 'Takeover' mini-series, which brought him into personal contact with the financial giants of those days: Robert Holmes à Court, Christopher Skase, John Elliot and Alan Bond. Nowra found it hard to take quite as seriously as the politicians and media had done these magnates' claims of showing Australia the path to prosperity through asset-stripping and international money-laundering. The putative descendant of Ned Kelly, Victoria's famous colonial bank-robber and primitive social bandit, believed he knew crooks when he saw them. The takeover kings were to him shady confidence men and economic clowns, albeit with plenty of culpable allies in trusted public positions. They were adulated as national heroes until the 1987 stock market crash—and some subsequent criminal trials—bankrupted the worst of them along with thousands of ordinary Australians. As with Vietnam, Maralinga, Anzac, Aboriginal dispossession and other national traumas pushed out of sight, Nowra considered it a historical necessity for a playwright to bear witness to those greedy times of public folly.

It is extraordinary how many people forget just how admired, how famous and how influential these entrepreneurs were. It is as if collective amnesia has gripped us. All we are prepared to acknowledge is that there are governments, banks and some entrepreneurs to blame for the mess we are in. But we forget that we, too, were a part of that era of greed.

But money has no memory, he concludes, and if the economy ever picks up again the business entrepreneur, like the Terminator, will be back.[116]

Melbourne, capital of the economically ravaged state of Victoria, was the appropriate site for Bruce Myles' production of *The Temple* on 27 July 1993. It premièred in the beautifully restored CUB Malthouse Theatre, Playbox's new home and one of the beer baron John Elliot's former assets which he generously, if strategically, donated to the company as his own financial sun was sinking. The stand-up comedian Mark Little headed a brilliantly comic cast: Geneviève Picot, Anthony Wong, Joseph Spano, Nikki Coghill, Tony Hawkins and the mime Neill Gladwin, half of the comic act Los Trios Ringbarkus. In 1989 Nowra had pondered whether an 'intimate epic' was an oxymoron, now his cast of seven impersonated twenty named characters in what Little described as a 'comedy of bad manners'. The style was slapstick, the tone cartoonish and pugnacious rather than soberly denunciatory, as might befit the modes of dystopic tragedy or documentary exposé. 'I realised I'd been taking the wrong attitude to these guys', Nowra considered, 'I'd been treating them too seriously... I decided I'd be a bit more comic and savage, like *Dr Strangelove*.'[117] No sight gag was left unexplored in Laurie Blake's parade of grand machinations, with Little's driving energy—a 'Ned Kelly on speed'—genially seducing and affronting his audience.

The Playbox *Temple* was appropriately Melbourne in style and content, with its cartoonish characters, satirical disrespect, blokey humour and knockabout physicality displaying Melbourne's comic talent and reminiscent of the 1970s radical theatre tradition. As this vaudevillian show toured eastern Victoria its language became spontaneously fouler.[118] At the point of initial reception its contact was immediate, feeding the hunger of audiences to see their tormentors satirised and the eighties financial ethos cut down to size. But behind the comic absurdity was visible a serious and actually well-researched play about public deeds, private passions and moral seduction; a political satire with a savage and anarchic edge. 'You're attempting to write like Stephen Sewell', his agent told Nowra, somewhat to his surprise. He considered: 'But it's supposed to be a comedy!'[119] The Sydney Theatre Company production at the end of the year sought to readjust the play's tone towards a bleaker and more brutal reading.

Not long after this Melbourne première the STC launched its own *Summer of the Aliens* directed by Angela Chaplin with ten actors, including Nicholas Eadie as a snakeskin-booted older Lewis. (Nowra's beloved snakeskin boots, which he had worn in Melbourne, were by now a signature.)

Nowra's plays were now hot properties. The next month saw yet more visibility when the stereo play *Sydney* was broadcast on ABC-FM radio on 21 and 28 September 1993, while Rosalba Clemente's dynamic production of *Radiance* also opened at Belvoir Street on 21 September. *Radiance* had developed through a prolonged creative maturation and goes deeply and painfully into Nowra's imagination. While Laurie Blake is a grotesquely comic and hyper-real fantasia on the father figure, *Radiance* centres its dynamic around the powerful but enigmatically absent image of a mother who retains her essential secrets beyond the grave.

Its immediate spur towards production had been a request from Lydia Miller in 1992 for a play for Kylie Belling, Rhoda Roberts and herself. The long-pondered *Radiance* project, initially inspired during the 1987 Rockhampton sojourn, became a priority. In the event, Rachael Maza, daughter of the actor and playwright Bob Maza, created the part of Mae. The most dramaturgically concentrated and naturalistic-seeming of Nowra's works, *Radiance*'s poetic compression and theatricality suggest invisible forces and histories. As a retrospective family drama it uses mainstream stylistic structures in what can be seen as a dark personal poem, as well as a timely exposure of the Australian 'secret history' of black and white sexual relationships and the trauma of the stolen generations of black children. The actors insisted that the word 'Aboriginal' be expunged from the script—why labour what is implicit in the casting?[120] *Radiance* inspired the Australian Literature Society to award Nowra its Gold Medal in 1994, proclaiming him 'Australia's most outstanding contemporary playwright and, quite probably, the most outstanding playwright in Australia's cultural history.'[121]

Sydney's version of *The Temple* opened at the Wharf Theatre on 31 December directed by Richard Wherrett and with Colin Friels as Laurie. Sydney critical reaction to a portrait of the eighties was mixed; the ebullient optimism of past public greed seemed irrelevant in a constrained and privatised nineties. Ross Wallace's set went for cold corporate elegance rather than the temple/slaughterhouse image of the Playbox première, with 'metal, perspex, surfaces that glint.'[122] The casting of Friels, a dramatic actor of commanding presence, changed the perception of the central character, and observers recorded their ambivalence.[123] The stylistic excesses of this corporate predator had worked so well in socially-responsible Melbourne, but, performed in a more realistic and documentary mode, the comic effrontery was alienating. In theatre one thing can be depended upon: when difficulties are perceived, the writer will be blamed.[124] Nowra judged the problem as one of style. In the Playbox première Mark Little and Geneviève Picot had remained endearing despite their characters' outrages; in Sydney audiences found the more ruthless and sinister Laurie and his crass wife Brenda ultimately unforgivable.[125] Nonetheless, and despite critical reservations, the STC's *The Temple* ran to capacity houses and was twice extended. Nowra resolved to write for Friels a new role to exploit his candid, frank-eyed physical presence with its hint of sinister command.

The years of *Così*

1994 saw *Così* become something of a national phenomenon. Zootango in Hobart led off with David Bell's production at the Peacock Theatre commencing 29 April, and the MTC production, scheduled to tour nationally, opened at Russell Street on the same day. Next month it won the New South Wales Premier's Award for Best Play and the script of the movie version was well in hand, while Terry Kenwrick directed it for the Darwin Theatre Company at Brown's Mart. Meanwhile in Adelaide workshops with Bob Maza were under way for *Crow*, the former 'Boofhead' script with its augmented central female role, taken by Lydia Miller. It opened at the State Theatre Company of South Australia on 14 May directed by Adam Cook, with eight actors playing fifteen named characters. *Crow* in a sense takes up Territorian history at the point where *Capricornia* leaves off; showing the civilian and military chaos of the bombing of Darwin and the titular heroine's long-running battle of wits and will with the white authorities to have her claim to her family's land recognised in law. Despite its clear applicability to the High Court's historic Mabo decision of June 1992, which abolished the concept of *terra nullius* in Australia and established, if precariously, the principle of native title, *Crow* is comic in tone, with carnivalesque larrikinism, magic realism, and surreal scenes of dreams and ghosts. Nowra wanted his characters to 'live a little bit more, breathe a little bit more' rather than '[slap] them around'... you have to go halfway to an audience rather than saying... you have to come a hundred per cent my way.'[126]

In Toowoomba he inspected the students of the University of Southern Queensland's acting course, for whom he was devising a graduation play, later to be called *Miss Bosnia*. *The Incorruptible*, the Colin Friels vehicle with its strong Queensland-inspired historical undertow, was also in preparation. On 21 July, the same day the Melbourne Theatre Company's *Così* opened in Sydney as part of its national Northern Australia Regional Performing Arts Complexes Association tour, David Fenton's sparkling rendition commenced at La Boite. It had Andrew Buchanan as a decently bemused Lewis, Paul Bishop as a forceful Doug, a zesty Cherry from Karen Crone and Kevin Hides in an award-winning performance as Roy, a fruity old rep survivor. In May 1995 the play was directed by Andrew Ross of the Black Swan Theatre Company at the Subiaco Theatre Centre, with Peta Toppano as Ruth, George Shevtsov as Roy and Kelton Pell as Doug. Abroad, the Canadian première of *Summer of the Aliens* was directed in November by Richard Rose for the Great Canadian Theatre Company in Ottawa, while *The Golden Age* was produced in Berkeley, California.

When in July 1994 the Australian Literature Society awarded Louis Nowra its Gold Medal, he joined a distinguished list of winners including Henry Handel Richardson, Patrick White, Elizabeth Jolley, and his former Australia Council adversary Rodney Hall. Nowra was particularly pleased to learn that the first ALS award in 1928 had been won by his favourite Australian novelist, Martin Boyd. *The Temple* received the Louis Esson Prize for Drama in the 1994 Victorian Premier's Literary Awards. These honours showed that the tax muse had done her work well.

Having in addition won the 1993 Canada-Australia Award, Nowra soon left for Canada to revisit his beloved Montreal. An exchange deal had been completed between the ABC and CBC by

A comedy of bad manners. Mark Little, Genevieve Picot and
Anthony Wong in *The Temple*, Playbox Theatre Centre,
Melbourne, 1993. (Photo: Jeff Busby.)

which a Canadian producer would direct an Australian radio play and vice versa. David Britten directed Judith Thompson's *Stop Talking Like That*, while James Roy directed Nowra's *Moon of the Exploding Trees* with music by Sarah de Jong.[127] While Thompson's play was broadcast in both countries, *Moon*, dealing with a female serial killer, fell victim to managerial timidity within both organisations and to date has not been broadcast.[128] From Montreal Nowra returned to Toowoomba and the USQ residency, where *Miss Bosnia* was premièred on 28 October directed by Graham Byrne, with a one-night stint at La Boite in Brisbane. The play was tailored for the graduating class: a vehicle for diverse characterisations and comic rehearsal/audition acts, for six women and one man, plus a 1991 graduate who returned to play the other male role of General Jez. La Boite's Artistic Director Sue Rider scheduled the play for the 1995 season.

In that year a vignette of sexual and multicultural politics, *The Price of Prayer*, played at the STC's Wharf Theatre as part of a program of one-act plays called 'Sydney Stories'. This acerbic playlet on the topic of sexual power in a socially unequal gay relationship can stand alone, as it did in the program 'Subi Shorts' performed by Black Swan, but it also forms Scene Nine of the full-length work *The Jungle*, a chronicle of twenty-four hours of Sydney life, which had its première in STC's New Stages program the following year.

Shooting now began on the *Così* movie, directed by Mark Joffe with finance by the Film Finance Corporation and the American company Miramax; and the action set in the present to avoid the expenses of a 1970s 'period' production. The Vietnam War context of the play was thus expunged. Overseas finance meant concessions to American taste had to be continually negotiated (which Nowra thought a bit rich coming from the producers of the resolutely bad-taste *Pulp Fiction*). Julie emerged as no longer lesbian and her heroin addiction (and eventual doom) are played down, while much argument with Miramax ensued about the fate of the relationship between Lewis and Lucy. In the Australian print they separate, as in the play; in the American one they stay together. The published screenplay documents these battles.[129] But Nowra never lost control of the rewrites and the final cast was wholly made up of distinguished Australian theatre actors. Sadly, before the shoot had progressed a few weeks the accomplished New Zealand actor Bruno Lawrence, whose role as the wily TV producer in the satiric ABC comedy series *Frontline* was endearing him anew to television audiences, was suddenly diagnosed with cancer. Lawrence died shortly afterwards, and Colin Friels was brought in to take the part of the pragmatic asylum nurse Errol.

In July of 1995 occurred two premières: *The Incorruptible* at Playbox directed by Aubrey Mellor and Sue Rider's *Miss Bosnia* in Brisbane. The former borrows topical details as generously from the political career of Johannes Bjelke-Petersen as *The Temple* had from that of Alan Bond or Christopher Skase, but *The Incorruptible* is a political fantasy of larger relevance. What if Petersen's 1987 push for the Prime Ministership had been successful? What if he had been not clownish in presentation but an articulate person of considerable charisma offering quick-fix emotional solace to an electorate damaged by economic restructuring? Based on the career of the American Huey Long, *The Incorruptible* suggests that populist politics are no regional peculiarity of limited archival interest, but endemic within Australian public life, as the rise since 1996 of the One Nation Party and its leader Pauline Hanson has demonstrated. Playbox used five actors, three of whom did not double, to portray fourteen named characters. Yet again, the oxymoron of the 'intimate epic' was being challenged. Good dialogue ideas arising from rehearsals were now fearlessly pirated by the playwright. 'I have become much more interested in actors and their own input. I'm stealing every good line they come up with.'[130] They came up with some very funny ones. But instead of the outrageous comic seductions of Laurie Blake, *The Incorruptible*'s Ion Stafford mesmerises through the purity and clarity of his moral convictions, at once attractively simplistic and appalling in their social implementation. Friels' candid blue gaze and body language of slight naivety projected the charisma of the doubt-free true believer, suggesting the rural background which makes him initially appear an easy puppet of sophisticated power-mongers.

The immediately arresting character is the foul-mouthed and cynical Gabo, dynamically created by Denis Moore in an award-winning performance. This compound of Australian politicians' grossest style is described by the *Age* reviewer Tim Robertson as 'a Richo out of Rabelais, a Jonsonian creature of over-the-top repulsiveness, firing on sex, booze, the perks of power, with comic rhetoric so energetic that it perversely draws sympathy.'[131] Gabo's volubility and dependable outrageousness threaten to position the play as a comic satire on public life like *The Temple*, but in fact Nowra's anatomising of the authoritarian populist is being carried out with some seriousness. Jack Hibberd's perceptive response in the *Australian* picked up Ion's iconic status exemplifying long-held Australian dreams of mastering nature by, for example, making all the rivers run—backwards.[132] When the Playbox production was restaged by the STC in September 1996 on a regional tour including Canberra and the Gold Coast, the heroically powerful actor John Howard with his 'farmer's body'[133] played a convincingly rural Ion, with Rachel Szalay as an elegant and desperate Louise.

For *Miss Bosnia*, co-produced by La Boite and Sydney's Teatar di Migma, some observers found the treatment affrontingly frivolous. Nowra was sparked by the well-publicised account of the beauty pageant held in 1993 during the siege of Sarajevo, but reports that he originally intended writing on the fall of Constantinople in 1453 and instead hit on the contemporary siege where 'the descendants of those Ottoman victors were besieged by the descendants of the vanquished Byzantines.'[134] Multiracial Sarajevo 'prided itself on its beauty, its culture, its liberalism' and if communally-based civil war could happen there 'it could happen in Sydney or Perth', he considered, alluding to the Hansonite racial purism then astir within Australian public discourses.[135] Also, he liked to present the unpredictable and avoid the obvious response. 'There is so much angst-ridden matter on the conflict over there [the former Yugoslavia], I wanted to rediscover and flesh out the human element that exists underneath the numbing, desensitising tragedy.'[136] A characteristic explorer of the resilience and unpredictability, as well as the bastardry, of people surviving under stress, Nowra relished the irony of a beauty contest, deemed politically incorrect in the west, being used in these extraordinary circumstances as a proudly sanity-saving measure.[137]

For a play which had ambitions to echo the high-comedy tone of Thornton Wilder's anti-fascist film *To Be or Not to Be*, its La Boite première in the week of the fall of Srebenica struck immediate problems of response. The original Toowoomba script had grown from eight to nine characters, with the central drag role remaining intact. The driving character emerges as Mira (Khristina Totos), the pageant organiser and an avatar of *Visions*' *demi-mondaine* Eliza Lynch redone as a super-bitch from a television soap. The *Miss Bosnia* characters are all survivors, but this is survival in its dark aspect, an imperative which overrides political convictions or communal loyalty. Underneath its farcical showbiz gags and *Così*-like theatricality the play has potentially much to say about the madness of war, and costs of constructed femininity and the misery of beauty: an imperative now bearing on men as savagely as it has always done on women, Nowra believes.[138] Black Swan's Perth production in February 1996 proved controversial,[139] while in Melbourne shortly afterwards feelings ran high amongst people with an interest in all sides of the Bosnian conflict, and the theatre received bomb threats. The MTC production directed by Nadia Tass which toured interstate had Geneviève Picot as Mira and Frank Gallacher as the macho General who falls for a transvestite.

In October 1995 *The Jungle* directed by David Berthold opened at the Wharf Two theatre as part of STC's New Stages program. In 1985, speaking of his *Lulu* adaptation, Nowra had declared himself unable to place characters in bars and nightclubs;[140] now it is precisely this nocturnal milieu which forms the social texture of *The Jungle*, representing the tropically fecund and frightening landscape of the human mind. With its drugs, violence, sex, hard language and criminal scams, the play was scarcely mainstream fare: it was intended instead to bring in a younger, media-habituated audience. The positioning of a play by an established writer amidst a season of experimental work by new playwrights may seem odd, but once again Nowra was re-inventing himself. 'There's something fascinating going on with young playwrights in Northern Ireland and England. It's a liberating thing. The plays are Tarantino-influenced—witty and violent. Theatre isn't precious any more. The attraction is—you can do anything.' As for his foes the baby boomers, 'I despise the anger of middle-class reviewers towards the grunge writers. They are still fighting the causes of the 70s.'[141] It is as though Nowra was writing the plays that might have been expected of him much earlier in his career.

The Jungle consists of fifteen self-contained scenes of interconnected vignettes of love, hatred, survival, obsession and misapplied ingenuity in contemporary underworld, suburban, *haut-bourgeois* and show-business Sydney. It was played by five actors, who among them doubled twenty-nine characters. Seven years earlier *Capricornia* had created the same number of characters with eleven actors. This was 'intimate epic' with a vengeance. Lightning doubling gave the production a speed-fuelled youthful energy which

Above: 'Vietnam!' Deborah Kennedy, Colin Friels and Paul Goddard in the Sydney Theatre Company production of *The Temple*, 1994. (Photo: Stuart Campbell) Below: The misery of beauty. Kaarin Fairfax, Nicki Wendt and Deborah Robertson in *Miss Bosnia*, Melbourne Theatre Company, 1996. (Photo: Jeff Busby)

made a virtue out of these restraints; less recession-scaled casting might eventually be able to re-explore this architectually structured and tonally varied scene-sequence. Louche and picaresque in construction and tone, the subject does not elude its author's characteristic detachment. It is Nowra's Sydney *Satyricon*, an updated Menippean satire of a haunted and vividly fragmented metropolis complete with slapstick violence and magical, mystical elements, with satirical vignettes of *déclassé* debauchery and *arriviste* Harbour City Trimalchios. The shifty partnership of Vince and Jason, like Petronius' Encolpius and Ascyltus, encounter a pungent parade of courtesans, lowlifes, charlatans and bullies while surviving as enterprisingly as they may, somewhat as the teenage Gloria Herbert had done years ago in wartime Sydney. Within the riotous mosaic of violent excess and calculated outrage are incisively crafted realistic episodes.[142] 'In the Name of the Son' (Scene 3), in which a dying gay man taunts his repressed and agonised father with the details of his sexual encounters, contains writing on gay sexuality more confronting than most encountered in subsidised theatres.

On 19 March 1996 the *Così* movie was released in Sydney. Response was good, and in a year dominated by *Shine* and Geoffrey Rush's fine and much-awarded performance as the mentally unstable but resilient survivor David Helfgott, *Così* at least earned Nowra the AFI Award for Best Adapted Screenplay. Filming commenced on the Nowra-scripted movie 'You Don't Know What Love Is' (later titled *Heaven's Burning*) directed by Craig Lahiff with the male lead played by Russell Crowe. Upon this movie's eventual release in late 1997, controversy arose when the producers decided to cut from the Australian print a speech they feared would be considered anti-Japanese. Nowra and the actor Ray Barrett publicly defended the speech on the grounds of dramatic context, but the deciding factor in restoring it for Australian release was probably the success of the uncut version with overseas audiences and critics.[143] Work on a movie with Mark Joffe titled 'The Crack' took Nowra back to Ireland, with which he remained as unimpressed as ever. The film version of *Radiance*, directed by Rachel Perkins, commenced shooting around Queensland locations in early 1997.

There was a return to television writing, this time with commercial production companies, with a half-hour drama *Directly from My Heart to You* screening on the Nine Network on 30 December 1996 as part of Bryan Brown's series 'Twisted Tales'. Directed by

Catherine Millar and with Tim Ferrier's gleaming primary-colour high-key postmodern design, the screenplay exploits the irony of discrepant vision. Betty, the android creature who sets out to destroy her various Frankensteins, can see only in black and white: at times the image blurs into that grainy monocoloured world she is determined to escape. Betty the automaton assassin is the ultimate survivor: Ivan the Czar reborn as a *Miss Bosnia* plastic beauty queen who gropes towards a fuller experience forever out of her reach. Kimberley Davies creates a sinister doll in dominatrix costumes inside whom lurks a limited but pitiable consciousness. The film-noir playgirl Betty is a conventional male sexual fantasy, and indeed she turns out to be the creation of another android whose dreams are as derivative as the Mickey Spillane 'memories' which Albert teaches to Edward.

Nowra's most recent theatre play *Deceit* opened in Hobart in August 1996, directed by Louise Permezel for Zootango with five actors playing eleven characters. In this searing examination of the destructive double life of a gay Australian public servant, in which sexual and political lies become interchangeable, art ambiguously conceals and testifies to the emotional contours of 'autobiography'. *Deceit* received favourable notices praising its 'satisfying complexity' and 'ironic twists and turns',[144] but is to date a script that the playwright has not developed further. Nowra's aims as a writer were summarised by him in 1980 as 'somehow to do everything with passion but with detachment',[145] and while the detachment persists the passions have if anything become bolder, more inclusive and generous. As Nowra continues to earn his distinguished career in the Australian theatre, his innovation and renovation of both national themes and their dramatic treatment continually surprises, delights, affronts and moves his critics and audiences.

Sydney Satyricon: throwing Cynthia out the window.
Joshua Rosenthal, Kate Fitzpatrick and Simon Bossell in
The Jungle, Sydney Theatre Company, 1995, designed by
Peter England. (Photo: Tracey Schramm)

The lesson. Rebecca Smee as Betsheb and Max Donati as Stef in *The Golden Age*, Theatre North, Queensland, 1994. (Photo courtesy of Peter Derrett)

Chapter 2

Learning, power and seduction

A theatre of powerful visions

The woman wipes [the boy's] face, then her own. She then blows loudly and theatrically on his face, pretending to be the wind. The boy pathetically tries to mimic her. She stands up and spins around in her beloved dress for him. He takes no notice, his eyes looking past her. Abruptly she drops to her knees and slaps him on the face. He yelps in pain. She kisses him where she has hit him and then moves away so he can see her properly. She smiles broadly and stiffly, trying to teach him. She pushes at his mouth until it turns into a smile, but when she lets go his face returns to its expressionless mask. She is frustrated. She hums. He follows suit, but his gaze is distant. She bites his leg and he yelps in pain. As he cries out she mimics him. He looks at her for a brief moment, then beyond her. The routine is over.[1]

At the heart of Nowra's theatre lies a power struggle manifested through the process of teaching. Characters who hold individual and compelling visions of the world attempt to impose supremacy through forcibly co-opting or seducing their fellows to their own visions. These 'pupils' may respond with forced submission, with ironical acquiescence or enthusiastic collaboration. Transmission of cultural visions thus becomes a highly theatricalised process, as in the mimed lesson quoted above where Betsheb of *The Golden Age* tries to teach her autistic brother Stef the rudiments of human interaction. As well as producing verbal narratives of their peculiar validating myth, the authoritative transmitters of vision employ various emotional and physical strategies: willpower, gesture, demonstration, costuming. Moreover, like Betsheb, they are obliged themselves to enact those states of being which they wish to impress on their fellows. They will, in short, stage self-performances and theatrical spectacles; rehearsing their own dreams of culture and co-opting their pupils as players in the spectacle.

Under the force of this epistemological incursion, the intended victims (where they are not, like Stef, simply unteachable), may be variously dazzled, seduced, crushed, or sceptical. Since they are relatively powerless in a social sense, the 'pupils' may either endure heroically or else exploit every trick in the survivor's book: passive compliance, naughty subversions, serious and contestatory parody. Resistance and the will to survival may be displayed through violent reaction, opportunism or through the exploitation of sexual magnetism. As an extreme reaction, the pupil characters may adopt that ardent and wholehearted discipleship which disguises competition as emulation: the pupil surpasses the teacher. Whatever their response to this incursion, the pupils are now performers in a script initiated by, though not perhaps resolved by, a world outside. The relative success or failure of the imposition of strong dreams is legible within the theatrical interplay; where music, dance, language, silence and gesture indicate to the audience the progress of the battle of visions. While in Nowra's apocalyptic struggle there are some absolute winners or losers, the outcomes are mostly ambiguous and unpredictable. The pupils may, for example, prove ungovernable, like *The Incorruptible*'s Ion Stafford who absorbs the teaching of his political mentors in order to discard them; this 'Frankenstein's creature' model of cultural interaction is dealt with in Chapter 3.

Where whole countries or communities undergo this imposition of outside visions the result can be devastating. But it may also be productive of new cultural syntheses that will necessarily contain and hybridise elements of the imposed fables or performances.

All Nowra's plays 'remember' by allusion and by revisionary re-enactment. It is as though the survivors of historical cataclysms are enforced to replay, as an eternal consequence, fragmented versions of the repressed originary trauma until these can be incorporated into some new kind of future—a future containing the potential of creative reassembly and appropriation of the inherited imperial codes into enabling rather than disabling metaphors.[2]

Engaging in strong acts of cultural coercion or seduction necessarily exposes the visionary initiators themselves to unstable processes of metamorphosis and transformation, which may affect them as profoundly as the turmoil inflicted on their victims. In teaching and enacting their world views, the mentors are locked into a demanding and collaborative performative process which will transform both parties; the seducers may themselves be seduced, their victories may sow the seeds of their own defeat. The pupils may alter the original import of the vision through wilful creativity, selective emphases, or simply through limited understanding. What typically emerges is a powerful hybrid dream more or less adapted to serving, for good or ill, as a new cultural script.

Typically the pupils will the more tenaciously maintain their own hybrid interpretations of the received message because of the very forcefulness with which this 'learning' was experienced. Thus in *Inner Voices* the boy Ivan, upon assuming power, cruelly tortures his tutoring voices, demanding that they 'correctly' recite 'his' poem 'Nightingale the Robber'. The mentally destroyed but still charismatic Juana of *Visions* finally proclaims to her devastated country the cargo-cult high culture which through torment she has learnt from Lynch. After the early plays, however, from *Albert Names Edward* to *Inside the Island*, where the visions of such characters as Edward, Ivan, Juana or the maddened soldiers are largely obliterated, these theatrical contests become more evenly matched. Eventually, in the character Betsheb of *The Golden Age*, we encounter a figure who, while having been brought close to destruction, is able to survive with something of her vision intact.

But even in Nowra's early tragic parables, where the consequences of these contests are pushed to extremes, cultural power remains a two-way street. Even the most socially powerless may resist with tenacious, if tunnel-visioned, spirit. Or, through their very abjection they may seduce, subvert, captivate or parasitise the socially powerful, as Juana the inarticulate visionary fascinates and invades the imagination of Lopez. Like performers, these hapless learners will inform their subordinate roles with their own meanings and energies; the mute or ecstatic body resists the imposed texts.[3] All players in the theatrical conflict are locked into a sometimes catastrophic, frequently funny, symbiotic exchange of self-performances: an exchange which will decisively alter their cultural field and produce dynamic hybridised outcomes—hybrid people, hybrid cultures.

In these strongly involving dramatic situations nothing less than absolute survival is at stake. The audience, like spectators at a football game, are engaged emotionally while remaining able to assess intellectually the complexities of the contest. 'Detachment', as we have seen, is the phrase Nowra uses for his cool encoding of hot and dangerous cultural and political struggles;[4] and this 'detachment' manifests itself theatrically through tragic or comic irony. The audience is in the position to see that the sometimes grandiose visions of the teachers are not all they are cracked up to be, and that behind these mentors' confident facades lie a fair bit of wilful self-delusion and desperate self-coercion. Nowra's visionary teachers can turn out to be tricksters, like *The Temple*'s Laurie Blake who tutors his disciple Nick in the art of wheeling and dealing, making it up as he goes along. Or they may be honest madmen like *Cosi*'s Roy; or, like *The Incorruptible*'s Ion Stafford, a moral monster who imagines himself the sole originator of pure and immutable meanings. Despite the desperate violence with which his characters maintain them, there are no pure, immutable or 'authentic' origins or meanings in Nowra's theatre. Authenticity is itself a dream, the ultimate vision of a lost Eden of transparent certainties. In the place of 'authenticity' they are only revised narrations of other people's memories, themselves a pastiche of inherited memories cathected around traumatic emotions. Culture is a product of mind.[5]

Identity and empire

The Guyanese writer Wilson Harris, in his novel *The Infinite Rehearsal*, outlines a dynamic post-colonial process in which constructions of personal and national selves will be perpetually rehearsed[6]— or perhaps one might rather say workshopped, since these rehearsals can result in no final or definitive performance. Nowra's dramatic contests show not so much the clash of real and false visions, or even of the indigenous and the colonial in a polarised sense. They suggest rather that those cultural narratives, which we must all necessarily learn and use to think with, exist in unstable and relative states; being eternally 'workshopped' in a process which for its participants is frequently funny, frequently painful. No matter how powerfully these narratives are experienced, they remain essentially works of fiction possessing no guarantee of either immutable truth or even of their own ultimate origins. This is in itself a tough and blackly comic vision, rendering provisional and ironic the strong emotional investments of Nowra's teachers and pupils alike. His theatre accords with the postmodern moment of de-centred authority, with its scepticism towards 'grand narratives' and inherited meanings. Contemporary culture finds itself uncomfortably positioned between two views of reality. On the one hand, there is disenchantment with the truth-claims of such traditional authoritative discourses as science (or of theatrical realism); and, on the other, the conviction that cultures and individuals alike require articulated meanings and coherent narratives to ensure their emotional survival.[7]

However, Nowra's theatrical creations do not live purely discursively, locked within their minds. They must in addition negotiate the historical pressures exercised by various imperialisms, political or cultural. Imperial dreams, fantasmatic as all visions are, deploy awesome material power and can inflict bloody scars on the real bodies and minds of their subjects. The collective fate of teachers and pupils, colonised and colonisers alike, assumes the form of immersion in a kind of black hole of history: my name for that historical 'void' which Nowra sees at the centre of white Australian experience. Rather than being effects of unstable postmodern shadow-play or mere brute fate, historical memory and 'rehearsal' in Nowra's theatre possess strong moral and social force. Speaking in 1983 of Australia's involvement in the Vietnam War, he said:

If a writer has value, it is to remind us of our past, because if a nation practises forgetfulness then that nation is in trouble and unfortunately Australians have a tendency towards amnesia. We are at an age now when we should be able to have the courage to remember and question.[8]

Besides Vietnam, Nowra's theatre 'remembers' and re-visions other national dramas: the convict era, the horror of total warfare, the rapacity inflicted upon an ancient but vulnerable landscape, the greedy monetarist eighties, and above all that dispossession of indigenous peoples which remains Australia's foundational trauma. The processes and results of capture by, or resistance to, various cultural visions is most evident in *The Golden Age*. The inbred tribe's fragmented but ecstatic bodies, and their hybridised compacted speech, 'remember' the now-deformed sacredness of sexuality and the body.[9] *The Golden Age*, while using Australian history as its immediate paradigm, is making a larger statement about transformed and occulted energies within western culture generally, but does it within a peculiarly post-colonial moment and mode of theatrical expression. In a significant chapter 'Body Politics', Helen Gilbert and Joanne Tompkins explain how international post-colonial performance in general 'offers opportunities to recuperate the colonised subject's body'—especially when it has been 'violated, degraded, maimed imprisoned, viewed with disgust' or otherwise rendered 'incomplete'—and to 'transform its significance and its subjectivity.'[10]

Nowra's world of competing visions and objective power relations may be readily recognised as post-colonial Australia, where the impact of empire must continually be renegotiated by indigenous and migrant peoples alike. As for non-Aboriginal Australians, Nowra's opinion is that 'we have no identity', just:

> ... a skein of skin and bones that covers a void. The void at our centre, where our soul should be, is our refusal to comes to terms with the fact that we conquered a race of people and confiscated their land, without understanding the enormity of what we had done... unless you understand the land you live in, then you have no soul.'[11]

This version of the white post-colonial condition as eternal exile is clearly dramatised in *Inside the Island*, his 1980 play for Nimrod Theatre, proclaimed, incorrectly, as his first one set in Australia. In this play the dark moral energies of the 'void' of historical denial suck in and destroy the fragile achievements of white settlement. The action conflates theatrical images of Aboriginal massacre and cultural displacement with allusions to the mass-mechanised devastation of the Western Front. The land, granted a semblance of sentience, appears to reject its parasites: images of bushfire and floods are used as theatrical agents of this rejection and destruction. Those characters in Nowra's theatre striving to lay some renewed claim to the land, like Roma of *Byzantine Flowers* or the stubborn matriarch Crow, tend to be Aboriginal people who must overcome immense and apparently insurmountable historical obstacles. White male dreams of national supremacy, pursued with tenacious energy, tend to collapse in comic or gothic failure, damaging the fabric of Australian society as they fall.

Nowra has been seen as the Australian writer *par excellence* of tragic historical parables, particularly of the post-colonial predicament in which the dispossession of the original peoples has left much unfinished business for black and white society alike. Without over-coding Aboriginal experience as the sole master-key to our cultural identity, Nowra's theatre frequently returns to this theme, whether overtly or through parable and suggestion. He examines more profoundly than any other white Australian playwright the impact of Aboriginal claims on white self-imaginings since the 1970s resurgence of land rights demands. *Inner Voices, Visions, Inside the Island* and *The Golden Age* show the appalling costs of blind but well-meaning policies brutally imposed on entire cultures: cultures which are clearly readable as metaphors for post-invasion black societies. *Capricornia, Byzantine Flowers* and the opera *Whitsunday* are explicit theatrical responses to the questionings raised by Australia's Bicentenary in 1988; while the Aboriginal theme of homecoming recurs in the post-Mabo 1990s plays *Crow* and *Radiance*. However, Nowra's theatre is not unremittedly tragic: the ironies and jokes of the battle of visions are rich indeed and frequently presented through slapstick and grotesque farce. Neither is it consolatory or triumphalist; the oppressed don't necessarily win or retain pristine innocence, the powerful are allowed their own compelling stories, victims can themselves be agents of oppression, and the moral and cultural consequences of survival can be lasting and severe.

The outcomes of Nowra's theatrical 'lessons' are thus ambiguous, and the plays explore a variety of alternatives. In the best option, the ongoing processes of historical rehearsal and performance may be deployed as agents of moral choice. The imposed mythologies may be transformed into a fertile resource for reworking old or creating new empowering narratives which are more than self-perpetuating exchanges of nationalist for imperial stories. The experience of interaction with strong visionaries may, of course, simply imprint upon the pupils of history new and fiercely-maintained charismatic visions which in turn will require re-assembly. These complex dynamic processes may be summarised by the motif of 'empire', the subject of Nowra's abandoned five-play sequence of which *Byzantine Flowers* is the sole remnant (see Chapter 1). Yet in a deep sense, all of his plays explore the imaginative possibilities of various responses to empire. According to Wilson Harris, 'cultures must be liberated from the destructive dialectic of history, and imagination is the key to this.'[12]

An anti-naturalist theatre

For a theatre audience, surveying these demonstrations of the ragbag nature and deep emotional underpinnings of authoritative cultural narratives, wherein the hidden agenda is more powerful than the overt, can be an intellectually intriguing and richly comic experience. Nowra's theatre explores the huge existential and historical black jokes of which we are all the victims, but which we nevertheless recognise: in his own phrase, we can remain 'detached'. Yet even at their most farcical these theatrical contests remain basically serious, since integrity and survival are at stake. Where there exists no ultimate 'reality' to either envision or revision, Nowra's characters possess the opportunity to unmask both their tutors' and their own obsessions. They may endeavour to take charge of their history by devising new scripts—a dynamic process which brings into play further comic or tragic possibilities. The new cultural or historical scripts now entering the workshopping process may possess immediate value as liberating departures from rigid old formulae, but they in turn remain necessarily relative and strategic, and possess as little guarantee of absolute truth or finality as those they have displaced. There can be no absolute beginnings; the newer visions remain creative hybridisations of those imposed narratives they have absorbed and transformed. The audience is invited to take up an ironic stance to the plots and outcomes that carry these processes, but without abandoning empathy with both history's teachers and its hapless, or resilient, pupils.

The performative nature of history, and the shifts in perspective brought about by the imperative to perform, create a volatile dramatic world in which characters must strive with both real historical conditions and powerful ideological phantasms. For all their dubious origins, these visions, as we have seen, are necessary conditions of the characters' existence as cultural subjects: representation is as necessary to human survival as eating. But the visions remain an ambiguous heritage which may pose obstacles to spiritual integrity or prove capable of mobilising powerful energies, providing a new lexicon of resistance and creativity. Hence, while teaching, performance and rehearsal are characteristic devices within the structure of his individual plays, the canon of work progressively and self-consciously rehearses and retells its own fables.

For these reasons Nowra finds the conventions of naturalism, with its psychologically coherent subjects, its structure of crisis and resolution and its narrative closure, an inadequate form for theatricalising these complex dynamics of 'empire'. His theatrical vision is better served through parody, playfulness, music and dance, metatheatre, quotation of cultural myths (from both high and popular locations), and structuring through formalised parables rather than mimetic plots. Realism as a dramatic style is limited by its origins in the narratives of late nineteenth-century European high bourgeois culture, and its efficacy as a theatrical vehicle for postmodern or post-colonial drama is widely considered as compromised. Nowra's non-naturalistic styles are a deliberate choice on political as well as aesthetic grounds, and he has often voiced his opposition to dramatic naturalism. Life is a combination of details and an accumulation of unsaid and said things, Nowra believes, whereas the well-made play, with its 'deliberate positioning of exposition, confrontation and resolution', seems to him strange and unnatural. Even Ibsen doesn't impress him:

> [Naturalism] basically says that it's easy for an individual to change his or her life. All a wife has got to do is walk out the door. I think that life is tied up with so many other forces, economic, power, political, and social, so that the individual's decisions and actions are a product of more complex issues and forces than what's happening in a cosy living room.[13]

In theatrical terms, Nowra's plays operate on the level of subtext: not the psychologised subtext of Stanislavskian naturalism but the detached comic subtext of intellectual demonstration. The theatrical transactions are informed by powerful emotional interactions which performers and audiences must decode, while noting the comic or sinister import of the 'lessons'. On the page, the early plays with their strong scenic construction seem contained and precise; production, however, brings out their vital emotional subcurrent. (Detailed examination of his use of non-verbal theatrical devices forms the subject of Chapter 4.) Increased experience in working with casts and directors eventually allowed Nowra to loosen the carefully non-naturalistic dramatic structures of his early plays, to let his characters breathe a little.[14] He later understood that naturalism and psychology were not synonymous; one could create strong psychologically-driven characters without using a politically compromised style he despised. However, this 'psychology' is not to be understood as isolated and static individuality but as a hybrid and dynamic historical product.

'Everyone has their reasons'

Teaching in the early plays is more akin to indoctrination. Entire societies, like *Inner Voices'* Russia, *Visions'* Paraguay or the wheat property of *Inside the Island*, are devastated by visions imposed with all the certainty of superiors acting as cultural missionaries to inferior or non-existent cultures. It is the arrogance, blindness and brutality of the lessons which wreak destruction, more perhaps than their content as such, flimsy or irrelevant as it can be. Albert (of *Albert Names Edward*) paternally scolds Edward, dictating which sandwiches Edward should eat: 'It's for your own good' (95). Parental characters, like parental cultures, 'teach' through more effective messages than verbal instruction; it is their perceived motivations and acts of both commission and omission that provide the compelling scripts. Just as Albert 'decides' Edward is his long-lost brother, so many of the tutorial relationships in Nowra's theatre gain their dramatic power by drawing on the close dynamics of family relationships. This is a complex dynamic wherein the vital tutorial interactions are mystified and confused by unequal power: there may be pride and love, brutal coercion and the desire to foster, ignorant methods and deep inarticulate emotions. Here the male autodidact who assumes of role of teacher shades into the symbolically powerful figure of the 'king', suggesting the father's psychic importance and his various but ambiguous powers over his children/pupils. King Lear is the model used in *The Golden Age*, a powerful magic symbol of a character with at least as much to learn about himself as to teach his children.

The tutorial relationships of Nowra's theatre clearly contain strong familial undercurrents. Childhood is the time when we are most vulnerable to the imposition of other people's visions, yet without some kind of given script or map, no matter how flimsy or provisional, we would be unable to understand, create, alter or resist our culture at all. The most tragically devastated character in Nowra's theatre is Ivan the boy Czar of *Inner Voices* who is raised sequestered from language and community. With a severely imperfect model of human interaction and no enabling script, not even *El Cid* or Zane Gray, Ivan is utterly unable to make sense of his world when the

long-delayed time of his release comes. His father/liberator/
tormentor Mirovich tries to teach him certain lessons—the Universal
Catechism, his coronation speech, and hilariously mimed sex
instruction—but only the erratically rhythmic epic poem 'Nightingale
the Robber' compels Ivan's attention. Ivan does, in fact, learn severe
and profound lessons, not through the content of his pedagogic
projects, but through the way in which they are imparted to him:
through isolation, terror and coercion. These are the lessons he will
in turn impose when his kingship is achieved. At the play's end Ivan
becomes like Nightingale, 'half man, half bird', a hybrid Ovidian
metamorphic being suspended between culture and nature.

This then is the unstable 'metamorphic' dramatic world within
which the process of learning and the battle of visions takes place.
This chapter will now examine in greater detail, through the analysis
of several plays, the dramatic agency and didactic energies of the
tutor characters, both male and female. In Nowra's early theatre that
agency is limited by the typical expatriate or colonists' desire to
exploit the colonies in order to remedy their social abjection at 'home'.
Thus they typically impose on the new society an imported discursive
system, selectively modelled, in which their dubious class and
cultural supremacy will be validated. In *Visions* Madame Eliza Lynch,
wife of the militaristic President Lopez of Paraguay, explains her
determination to return to Paris, 'the centre of the world' and use
her triumph as cultural missionary to her adopted country to gain
revenge for past social humiliations (19).

> I had some famous people visit me. I had a well known—not a
> great—salon. I'm the first to recognise that. To have a great salon
> you have to be old and ugly, but some famous people went out
> of their way to come and speak to me. Baudelaire and his nigger.
> They came once. (9-10)[15]

Lynch's *petit-bourgeois* social-climbing and abrasive snobbery are
evident in her own words. As in high comedy, which depends for its
impact on shared social values, the audience can see further than
most of Nowra's self-incriminating tutor characters, but not far
enough to patronise them. No matter how deluded, culturally limited
or malevolent these may be, as dramatic characters they are treated
with an essential respect. As Neil Armfield writes of Lillian Dawson,
'the play aches with the pain of her suffering, but leads us away
from it... ultimately we cannot afford to share her pain because it is

confused, self-obsessed and greedy.'[16] Nowra cites the revelatory impact of a line in Jean Renoir's 1939 comic film *La Règle du Jeu* (*The Rules of the Game*): 'everyone has their reasons.'[17] From a theatrical point of view his 'detachment' from overt moral comment creates obsessive characters who are immensely vital and playable: even tyrants like Bao (*The Precious Woman*) and Lopez (*Visions*) have their reasons.

The male autodidact

Nowra's male tutor characters are relatively easy to see through, since to signify their cultural pretensions and aspirations the playwright uses mass popular culture of a particularly class-specific lowbrow stamp. These aspirations, gauche and lightweight as they may appear, are treated seriously as dramatic engines, and their cultural references send recognisible signals to Australian audiences that the dreamers' visions are our common property. The early tutor characters are firmly set in the historical world of those working-class men who survived depression and war service, were deprived of educational resources yet still aspired to the self-employed class. While they wish to participate in the post-war Australian dream of relative affluence, it is post-war American popular culture that is rifled to articulate these characters' driving aspirations. Albert devours Mickey Spillane gangster fiction, Ion Stafford has 'read every single Zane Grey novel',[18] while Nelson Taylor of *Sydney* and *Red Nights* is inspired by Charlton Heston in the 1961 movie *El Cid*, leading his army by riding dead along the beach strapped to his horse. *Così*'s Roy clings obsessively to a fantasy of an aristocratic childhood which Lewis and his madhouse opera production are compelled to realise for him, but which clearly derives from seeing too many Greer Garson movies. 'Tea parties, dances in our ballroom, circus performers coming to perform just for me. My mother in Parisian gowns—she flirting with the men, waving her fan so fast, it was a blur...' (64). These male tutor characters are in fact autodidacts, who set out to transmit their hybrid patchwork of kitsch culture and hard-won personal insights with the moral fervour and dogmatic literalism typical of the species.

The simultaneously phantasmatic and compelling nature of cultural narrative is brilliantly exploited in *Albert Names Edward*, originally devised for the stage but premièred on radio. It is an insidiously comic short script with a premise that makes it ideal for radio. The derelict recluse Albert 'rescues' Edward, a homeless amnesiac, and instals him as prisoner-pupil in his tiny room. Since radio listeners must rely solely on the resources of language and imagination it is easy for them, like Edward, to share Albert's world while observing the underlying desperation of his drive to 'teach' the amnesiac and evidently cultured Edward. Though he presents himself as a hardboiled denizen of the post-war mean streets, Albert's cultural references and wish-fulfilling 'memories' clearly come from Mickey Spillane, and he claims he knows how to deal with Edward's amnesia since in a movie he once saw Rock Hudson had it, or was it Clark Gable?[19] Albert relishes this opportunity to play teacher; he himself, he tells us, 'left' school early since he was 'too intelligent' for his teachers and earned the title 'monster brain' (88). When Edward decides that his only chance of recreating a personality is to remember what Albert tells him, he unwittingly creates in Albert the role of sole transmitter of culture; one who will fashion Edward into a facsimile stuffed with his own pulp fiction dreams. These narratives are no less than Albert's bid for immortality: 'If I die, what will happen? You'll be left alone without any memories if you don't remember mine. If you remember my memories, then I won't die. You'll be me' (104). While on the narrative surface it is Albert who plays the omnipotent Frankenstein to Edward's patched-together creature, it is Edward's vulnerability which has truly created a didactic monster of Albert.

The dramatic working-out of the tutorial process is funny, menacing and pathetic, since Albert's own personal limitations, loneliness and needs are readily on display. Edward is 'named' by Albert after his brother killed in the war (92), and eventually the opportunity to realise his wish-scripts through identity-imposition becomes too powerful for Albert to resist: 'After all these months you still don't know who you are—brother... Yes... you are my long lost brother' (100-101). Albert is quick to appropriate Edward's fragmentary memories as his own yarns, and protects his ward from contaminating contact with an evil outside world by instilling fear. Peanut butter sandwiches are full of 'invisible fungus'; better Edward sticks to Vegemite (95). The windows are blacked out to spare Edward painful memories while the Spillane books, which give the game away, will be removed since they are a 'great temptation' from which Edward must be protected (97-100).[20]

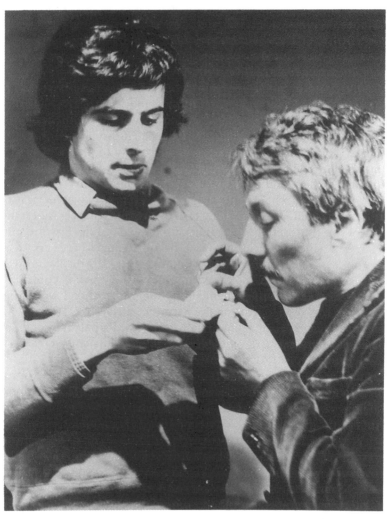

Reciting a life. Peter Dahlsen as Edward and Bruce Kerr as Albert in *Albert Names Edward*, La Mama, Melbourne, 1976. (Photo courtesy of Louis Nowra)

The narrative of this early play pushes Edward into total incarceration, reversing the plot movement of *Inner Voices* where the self-made opportunist Mirovich releases his pupil Ivan from prison before formal lessons commence. In both plays mentor and pupil are locked into a symbiotic exchange in which the pupil gains power through the mentor's ultimate dependence. At the end of the radio play, when Albert tutors Edward in the fluent recitation of 'his' post-war hardboiled adventures, accosting hourglass redheads on the Brisbane train, it is difficult to tell who is the prisoner of whom. Like the childish Ivan, Albert demands his story in correct and unvarying fashion, being now both creator and prisoner of his own visions. *Inner Voices* takes the process further. The paternal mentor Mirovich likewise wants life's comforts—money, food, warmth, sex, respect—and ruthlessly does what he sees as necessary to procure them. This involves administering a sequence of lessons to his pupil. When dying, Mirovich attempts to teach Ivan his last—but first genuine—lesson: 'Listen... they'll overthrow you...' only to receive a furious kicking from his liberated pupil (57). While *Albert Names Edward* leaves Albert incarcerated with his creature in ambiguous supremacy, Ivan enjoys a period of revolt and ascendency before his final immurement with those voices upon which he is now become as dependent as Albert is on Edward.

The male autodidact, while parasitising the archive of popular culture, does have his creative, even charismatic, aspect. The narrator of the 1985 short story 'Instructions to a Painter' is Laurie Blake, 'self-made man and proud of it': essentially the exuberant Laurie of *The Temple* in more introspective mood. Deformed by a stroke and contemplating death, he commissions a painter to 'write his autobiography' by creating twelve iconic images of his life, painted 'with the precise clarity of a dream and yet real'. This project is inspired by the *Très Riches Heures du Duc de Berry*. It is typical of the playful processes of cultural transmission in Nowra's writing that the story's Laurie knows of these late-mediaeval aristocratic illuminations from a childhood book of reproductions. Laurie's descriptions of his visions reveal a reserve of surreal insight into his life and his wishful self-creation: he would have been *Sir* Laurie, he believes, but for the election of a Labor government.[21] *The Temple*'s Laurie Blake amazes his patrician art instructor Miranda, more his lackey than his tutor, by absorbing the high points of Australian art from a slide lecture while apparently occupied by wheeling and dealing. Ion of *The Incorruptible* tells his disciple Louise that his great strength, as he sees it, is that he needs 'only to be told something once' in order to learn its lesson (64). The limitations of the autodidact are clearly exposed, as is his self-delusion masked as self-confidence. Directly after Laurie impresses Miranda with his quick study of high art, he goes on to seduce her, more carnally but just as destructively as Ion seduces Louise.

The father as King Lear

At the heart of *The Golden Age*, when the young men from 1930s civilised Hobart encounter the lost tribe of forest people, lies a moment of self-performance in which a strong vision of group history and cultural tradition is re-enacted. With naïve gusto Betsheb's family perform their version of a 'King Lear' playlet. Melorne, the failing but authoritative patriarch, plays a king exiled in a terrifying waste: 'Bleak street o' fen 'n' bellies. Dark trees 'n' no trees betide bleak sand.' Nowra often proffers his Platonic precept that 'when the ruler is mad, the state is mad', and this mimic ruler's madness has devastated his land. Melorne as Lear curses the Fool character, played by the impotent Mac, but his moment of 'profoundest outcastin'' is reserved for his daughter, mimed by the mute Angel with dialogue spoken by Ayre. When she begs for comfort and reconcilation, he rejects her: 'Ye child, dry quim.' He then, as king, blinds her: 'Now, forsooth, ye can eye me pain o' outcastin'. Ye pain goldy sow o' me tarse!' A different welcome is given to the second daughter, played by Betsheb, 'true treasure o' quim 'n' tarse', when father and daughter rush ecstatically into each others' arms proclaiming 'Nowt more outcastin'!' (15-16) The lost people have hybridised and adapted various versions of the Lear story. They use the pre-Shakespearean redactions of this traditional folk-tale, wherein the king's misfortunes teach him finally to discern what love (and language) really mean. Their language, however, is recognisably a reduction of Shakespeare's original, in which neither the king nor his three daughters survive his long-delayed learning experience. In its immediate dramatic context, that of performance before visitors from the world beyond the forests, the lost people's play enacts the history of their own ancestors' 'outcastin'' in the convict Tasmania of 'rack 'n' cat'; and contains the utopian vision of their eventual return from exile and hopes for survival. In the latter aspect the 'King Lear' playlet functions as an oblique condensation of the larger plot of *The Golden Age*, in which only Betsheb/Cordelia will survive their renewed 'outcastin'' of imprisonment in Hobart.

Significance for the present argument is the way the 'King Lear' playlet interprets the family dynamics of the lost people and the symbolic power of the father as both progenitor and articulator of cultural messages. Sterility and inbreeding are the tribe's real curse, and the processes of cultural transmission through language and performance are complicated and refuted by biological entropy. Betsheb performs a fertility dance to instruct and entice Mac, who to his shame is unable to respond because of his genital deformities (19-20). The forest people are now so reduced and compacted that actual blood relationships are obscurely intricated, but family dynamics remain in operation. Melorne's player King curses his children as well as blesses, and like his Shakespearean model he is magically powerful; both his blessings and curses take effect. Whereas in *King Lear* (I, iv) the king curses Goneril with sterility, in *The Golden Age*'s playlet Angel's character is cursed because of it. Since Angel is mute, it is typical of the strong reliance on physical interplay in Nowra's theatre that the unfolding of her small tragedy of filial dependence is created solely through mime; after Melorne's death her own decline is rapid.[22] Later in Nowra's theatre there emerge patterns of violent and 'magically' potent paternal rejection of sterility, particularly of sons unable to carry on the line. *The Temple*'s silvertail brewery patriarch Macarthur rejects his gay son Terry with homophobic and dynastic loathing, but although the loathing is mutual Terry eventually compromises his sexuality for the sake of regaining the family fortune. As his father has told him, 'Great families are not about love, they're about the past connecting to the future.'[23] In *The Jungle* Mark kills his AIDS-infected gay son Owen because he cannot bear that 'your own flesh and blood will not give birth to their flesh and blood, that they're a dead end.'[24]

The strongest and bleakest versions of father-son cultural transmission in Nowra's theatre are those which are, in patriarchal terms, the most successful; where the brutalised son fashions himself as a replica of the tyrant father, rendering him the sincerest form of homage. Lopez of *Visions* loathes his father, the too-long-lived El

King Lear: Marilynne Hanigan as Angel and Robin Cuming as Melorne in *The Golden Age*, Playbox Theatre Centre, Melbourne, 1985. (Photo: D.B. Simmonds/Sterio Stills)

Presidente, and triumphs over his corpse: 'El Supremo, dead? Immortal, El Supremo? Not so immortal now, are you?' (16) Yet in a sense the father is immortal, since Lopez has learnt from this mute figure only the deathly lesson of replication. His inherited vision of history is a nightmare of eternal repetition in which there can be only victims or persecutors, powerless and powerful, haplessly exchanging places inside a sealed ahistorical world. Lopez tells his sisters that the Triple Alliance will treat their own corpses like effigies in a Mardi Gras:

> Our father did it to some revolutionaries during the 1830s. I remember. I was only little and he held me up so I could look over the balcony down at them. They were tied to posts and had been dead for days (67).

For him the war is an infernal process which nobody can stop, where the slaughtered dead keep charging, to be hacked to pieces 'like roosters just beheaded' (70).

Bao, the deformed son of *The Precious Woman*, is equally his warlord father's eager pupil and strives to outdo him in governing the province through atrocity and the 'logic' of terror. The club-footed Bao despises his own body and hence all compassion as 'weak'; he rejects his mother and femininity with hysterical violence, and scorns those without what he believes is his principal strength: emotionless will.

> They were incapable of pursuing anything to its logical conclusion... but I can see, with a sharpness and clarity that is crystalline and as pure as a diamond, what is the right action. I know my father didn't go far enough' (178).

Terry Macarthur of *The Temple*, despite his initial filial revenge of selling the family shares to an upstart, finally steps into his hated father's dynastic shoes: 'Australia comes first', he says. 'I discovered I valued my name and I'm going to restore it. I'm even marrying' (89). This cyclic mimicry of paternal scripts in Nowra's theatre counters the more improvisatory historical process of rehearsal and carnivalisation by which tutored characters and groups can re-assemble the elements of their scripts or lessons until a way can be found out of historical *impasse*. Here the pupils surpass their teachers. These filial lessons result in a tutored culture imprisoned inside the imperial phantasm in a semblance of death in life. Like the corpse battle of Lopez's nightmare, 'everything and everybody is dead, but they keep on going through the motions' (70).

In these early plays the father figure's teaching through action is likelier to be benevolent in intent, although not always in result, when the child is female and the father figure is attempting to protect her from a cruel outside world. The first emergence of the father-daughter bond appears in 'Dreamhouses', Nowra's important unperformed 1974 script. A bush autodidact called George has built dozens of 'dreamhouses' to fulfil the exacting emotional needs of his disturbed daughter Lillian, who has multiple personalities and hence many competing and impassioned scripts and dreams. George's protectiveness in keeping Lillian out of an institution has resulted in their isolation from society, and he is as much the overworked prisoner of her imperious imagination as she is the typical imprisoned 'cheated' feral child protected by fearful love from a terrifying world. George takes on as handyman 'apprentice', the shady Arch who is hiding from justice, and oversees his work with the same dictatorial fussiness with which Albert controls Edward. Arch, however, revolts from his apprenticeship and commandeers Lillian and the dreamhouses just as the Melbourne authorities arrive to reclaim George's land. Nor can the George of *Inside the Island* ultimately protect his alienated daughter Susan from her mother Lillian's imperious visions. When disaster falls George becomes an impotent King Lear cradling his dead daughter, 'the only thing in this whole world I ever loved,' and like his Shakespearean counterpart hurls curses of universal destruction amidst the firestorm (87).

The emperor of darkness

More sinister and seductive patterns of historical violence and sexuality can also form the underlying texture of the tutorial relationships between 'father' and 'daughter' figures in Nowra's theatre. In *The Temple*, Miranda's seduction by Laurie Blake's grand visions and sexual 'electricity', and his subsequent abandonment of her, result in her despairing suicide. But this symbolically incestuous dramatic pattern may also be a strongly reciprocal relationship, where overt or submerged sexual attraction and dependency complicate the clear lines of parental authority and cultural imposition. While the male authority figure can seem almost godlike in his social power—a gothic tyrant with a captive maiden—his bond with the woman (or women) whom he attracts or forces into his orbit can weaken or destroy him. Frequently the woman is of a subordinate group, a racial Other, as the half-caste Roma is to the aging and lonely sugar king Tom Harris in *Byzantine Flowers*; or else in her enigmatic separateness she functions as a theatrical metaphor for cultural otherness. Juana in *Visions* fascinates Lopez with her helplessness and captivatingly chaotic visions. Similarly, Betsheb in *The Golden Age*, with her vulnerability, compellingly exotic physicality and intense inner life, seduces the imagination of Dr William Archer; and destroys him in a dramatic counter-movement of the destruction of her people by Australian authorities. Such partially erased figures of the indigene haunt Nowra's theatre and resist through their own strong visions.

While indubitably a tyrant committed to the brutality of imperial deeds, the father/captor can appear a pitiable monster in the gothic mode, desperately seeking through his semi-coerced relationship with his 'daughter' redemption for the historical wrongs he has inflicted on her group. Sometimes she can use this dependence to destroy him; as the young Englishwoman Patricia destroys her powerful lover in *The Precious Woman*. The ruthless Governor Teng has taken her as his lover, in flat contradiction to his official policy of hostility to westerners; but when he threatens to leave her she shoots him, transforming him into a deathly grinning grotesque. By this uncompromising action Patricia in a sense liberates Su-ling from her blindness and starts her on her own path to resistance. The suffering and madness of many of these captive heroines, like the narrator of the novel *Palu*, gives them witch-like powers with which they can destroy their opponent by the intensity of their will and imagination: a magical overthrow in which the passionate vision of the oppressed burns out the mind of the oppressing power.

> Sometimes our only defence is the imagination. Perhaps that's why I like Nabokov's work, because he stresses the power of the imagination and is saying that even in the most hideous circumstances you can defeat a brute or a tyrant by the power of your imagination. I wouldn't go as far as that but I think our imagination gives us profound pleasure and can create the most terrible and beautiful things.[25]

This imaginative power is most clearly demonstrated in Nowra's libretto for the 1988 opera *Whitsunday*. This is set on a magical tropical island in 1913, an island full of the voices of exiled 'spirits and demons' who can no longer live in what has become the white man's world. The cultivated family of a sugar magnate arrives by boat for a picnic, rather as the passionate pilgrims of Watteau's painting embark for a day of enchantment on the island of Cythera. Their half-Kanaka maid Clara is shyly loved by their son Lawrence. With them also is the ex-blackbirder Johnson, in whose eyes the Pacific islanders were and will remain nothing but children, to be taught painful lessons but never to achieve autonomy. He sings of his dark past:

> We gave them trinkets
> Things to amuse
> Things you'd give children
> They wanted to come
> to the sugar cane plantations
> so they could get
> more children's things
> ...
> you couldn't talk reason to them
> only a whip
> would calm them down
> Like children
> they understood only pain
> ...
> Sometimes the deck
> ran with their blood
> bits of their flesh
> scattered about
> but still they'd shout
> for their island home[26]

Once on the island, an eclipse of the sun turns the daylight world of the picnic into a nocturnal dream, where the night aspect of the characters emerges and Lawrence and Clara are tested. Johnson is now the Emperor, who 'likes all things black' and begins to seduce Clara into his world of darkness, offering her wealth, power and sex so that she can no longer tell whether he is an evil spirit. The strongest seduction he offers is the pain of his own exile and evil:

'I am not a monster'. John Shaw as Johnson and Miriam
Gormley as Clara in *Whitsunday*, Australian Opera, 1988.
(Photo: Branco Gaica. Photo courtesy of Opera Australia)

You must understand my pain
and my love for you.
You and Lawrence are children
just children.
I am not a monster.
I was famous once
in a time when fame
was as rare as gold.
I was in love
but a crazy dance
exploded in my head
...
My lover and I argued
and I killed her
with my bare hands.
I would never hurt you.
...
Filled with guilt
I roamed the country
mad and naked
under a blue sky
wanting to die
but no one would kill me
...
My soul howled like a dingo
lost in a desert.

He needs Clara's love, her tells her, to make him 'human again'; she is offered a future in his palace singing for him forever like a 'little blackbird'. Clara is able to resist his sinister seduction by reminding herself that 'evil spirits want you to forget your past'. She must overcome her trial through remembering who she is; and Lawrence must pass through his own test by acknowledging his love for her. The Emperor is defeated by his former lover, the witch-like Madwoman, just when he reveals his evil side to the lovers: 'I am master of this ship... I am the Emperor of this darkness. And I will make the night run with your blood.' The Madwoman's discarded love has turned to rage and madness, and now dying, she has become the stronger. In a blaze of light she is able to destroy the Emperor in a deathgrip:

> I am burning from the inside
> burning a hole into you
> a hole as bright as a thousand suns.

So too the imprisoned and dying Palu in her cell is able to will her tyrant husband's death by using a dreamstone, destroying him by the force of her will and imagination:

> ... you Emo will die in your cave in a world of lonely darkness and if you are not dead by the time I am then I will hunt you down through the afterlife I know you can hear me because look your dreamstone is splitting cracking open... you were weak enough to have allowed yourself to become the emperor of darkness.[27]

The unpublished *Byzantine Flowers*, the condensed version of the planned five-play cycle 'Empire', pursues the theme of the fall of empire and the accession of the oppressed in a clear but dramatically compressed dialectical pattern. Tom Harris is the nineteenth-century empire-builder who carved a sugar plantation out of the rainforest brutally exploiting Kanaka labour. By the time his son dies fighting in the Western Front he is lonely and vulnerable, and has learnt, as *The Incorruptible*'s Ion Stafford never does, the consequences of land conquest and displacement.

> You take it from the earth, it goes back to the earth. Will there be anything left? There'll be nothing, empty holes where the gold was, where the water was, the coal. Nothing. It's all coming home. Like something circling, waiting to pounce.[28]

Tom is drawn to the sexual dynamism and untutored vulnerability of the indigent half-caste Roma, who is determined to find herself a home by whatever means necessary. Roma works her way from being a millhand disguised as a boy to being the mistress of Tom Harris, ruthlessly displacing the incumbent black housekeeper Meg in so doing. Her quick intelligence, urgent innocence and survivor cunning soon make her ruler of the empire which once enslaved her people. Finally the 'uppity black trash' with her charismatic sexuality becomes wife of the failing Harris.

Her lover Eddie, however, is embittered by his nightmare experiences in the war and more so by the contemptuous treatment he received on his return:

I get back to Australia and I'm getting demobbed. I asked the Sergeant for a suit. 'What you need a suit for, Jacky? You don't need one out in the mulga. Just wear your birthday suit.' I was just a piece of shit. A half-caste. Trash. (67)

Eddie sees Roma's emotionally ambivalent survival strategies as a betrayal, and discounts the real affection she feels for the man who has taught her white culture and made her more than 'trash' in her own eyes. He urges her to rob Tom and run away with him, reminding her of the brutal past:

Your kind old white man, how do you think he made this plantation into one of the biggest in Queensland? Blackbirding, that's how he did it. Stealing Kanaks from the islands. Years ago he would have whipped your back until it was like a butcher's shop. And you fuck him. (66)

Eddie dies violently and Roma accedes as 'princess' of her kingdom, wearing as her wedding wreath the golden Byzantine flowers of the title. Her first cares as inheritor are to honour the dead emperor, guilty as he may have been, and to restore the lost landscape displaced by the sugarcane. As mistress of the house she orders the burial of Mr Harris, new parts for the mill from Brisbane, '[a]nd birds. I want you to bring back as many parrots and lorikeets as possible. The sort that used to live here' (84).

Byzantine Flowers shows the clearest narrative pattern in Nowra's theatre of the colonised subject subverting the incursions of white history and coming into her own. In its narrative completeness it provides a dramatically satisfying fable of the fall of empire, but the ongoing public events of the early-nineties Mabo debate rendered suspect such historical closures. This legal judgement about the persistence of native title signalled the commencement, rather than the achievement, of the homecoming journey. Nowra's later plays *Crow* and *Radiance* return to the unfinished post-colonial moment, where the Aboriginal characters still strive for the heritage which is theirs by right of origin and long occupation; but which remains unattainable, blocked by legal machinery and by obscure or disavowed white paternity. *Radiance* is a complex working of the female-male dyadic pattern. It is now the ghost of the witch-like mother, both victim and agent of racist oppression, who must be burnt out by razing her powerful white lover's house in order to exorcise the old order of rape, lies, mysteries and abjection. Mae tells her dead mother: 'Ghosts burn, did you know that? And you'll burn... even ghosts can't live in a place that doesn't exist any more' (1). As for their own ancestral island across the tidal flats, the sisters can return there only as paying tourists since it is now a luxury resort.

The immediate object of the sisters' fiery revenge is their mother's perfidious and secretive white lover Harry Wells, the owner of the house from which he is now summarily ejecting her—and possibly his—daughters. He functions in this play as their own Emperor of Darkness, whose imposed regime of secrecy, lies and denial will be dispersed through the beacon of his burning house. Painful mysteries surround the paternity of all of the women and particularly of Nona, born of the rape of the child Cressy by one of her mother's unnamed lovers. Nona has elaborated a dream of her unknown father as a rodeo star, a 'Black Prince', even advancing the incestuous fantasies typical of such situations (51). Yet whoever the rapist is (Cressy unconvincingly says she wouldn't even recognise him), Nona's fantasy points to a deeper truth about black-white relationships in Australia. The names of all fathers, like that of the sisters' dead mother, have in this script become unsayable; a black hole of pain around which language dies, just as the 'secret history' of sexual exploitation of black women remains largely unnamed. *Radiance* is Nowra's most complex dramatisation yet of the quasi-familial entanglement of seduction, power and love that comprise the Australian hybridisation of peoples and dreams. As the play ends, the sisters must continue learning the hard lessons of survival, reconstructing from its hybrid heritage of pain, guilt, enigmas and competing visions a post-imperial history which can be just and fair. In a sense the 'Black Prince'—whether identifiable as Harry Wells or nameless others—is indeed a member of this black family, whether he will acknowledge it or not. But all too often such an enigmatic paternal figure is revealed, not as a glamorous prince, but as a brutal emperor of darkness.[29]

The female autodidact as the imperial mother

Imperial discourse typically imposes filial or tutelary roles on its Others, seeking to co-opt them into colonial subjection through use of such organic metaphors as trees and saplings, parents and children. These seduce the colonised to view their supplementary position as

The princess. Kylie Belling as Roma in *Byzantine Flowers*,
Sydney Theatre Company, 1989. (Photo: Branco Gaica)

inevitable, harmless, natural; more insidiously, they beguile the colonised to see it as ahistorical and eternal. Parents can never be supplanted in their function as biological originators; and in Nowra's theatre attempts to do so lead to the Frankenstein situation (see Chapter 3). In the same way subject cultures in the post-colonial relationship are offered the abject script of perpetual tutelage.[30] As Australia engages yet again in a 'republican debate' and seeks to regularise its dealings with the 'mother country', Aboriginal land claims which contest the fantasy of *terra nullius* maintain constructs of origin and authenticity at the centre of public controversy. The image of motherhood—of origin, belonging and authenticity—is a strong metaphor through which post-colonial cultures, and individuals, define their identity. Motherhood functions as a symbol of ambivalent and troubling force in Nowra's theatre. The mother's authority is a principal engine of dramatic action with the power to impose crippling historical stasis or impel regeneration.

Nowra has frequently expressed his preference for women characters as dramatic catalysts, and he is far from being the first male writer in the European theatre tradition to encode through feminine personae the potential for historical change and the emergence of repressed energies. Ibsen's Nora Helmer of *A Doll's House*, for example, encodes utopian desires for personal freedom which perhaps only co-incidentally chime with the social programs of contemporary feminist activism. His Hedda Gabler, too, embodies his self-contempt as one of those lacking courage to break out of the stifling but supportive conventions erected as their refuge and prison by the triumphant middle classes. In Nowra's theatre the culturally marginal but symbolically potent role of the feminine is a rich site for on which to register both the deep impact of history's harsh lessons and the will to transformation.

> [Women] are more interesting from a playwright's perspective, because they are always serving two purposes—what other people expect of them and what's actually inside of them. I am drawn towards that because men only have one purpose and are directed to that one purpose, whereas women are serving two consciences all the time.[31]

The mother appears as both redeemer and monster; sometimes achingly absent, sometimes too insistently present. In *Inner Voices* the power of the Empress Catherine is felt through her absence. It is she, fearful of usurpation, who has consigned the infant Ivan to the mental half-life of the prison cell, and her death is the factor which ensures his succession as Czar. Later, her Francophile pedagogical literature is used by Mirovich in a vain attempt to inculcate in Ivan some socially-acceptable intellectual accomplishments.

VLADIMIR'S VOICE: Saint-Lambert. *Catéchisme universel.*
    Pause.
What is man?
    Pause.
IVAN: Feel. Under... feel...
VLADIMIR'S VOICE: [*quietly*] Understanding.
IVAN: Understanding.
VLADIMIR'S VOICE: Correct. That being so, what should he do?
IVAN: Race... follow.
VLADIMIR'S VOICE: Follow what?
IVAN: Run.
VLADIMIR'S VOICE: After pleasure?
IVAN: After pleasure.
VLADIMIR'S VOICE: Correct. What next?
    Silence.
MIROVICH: [*irritated*] Come on.
VLADIMIR'S VOICE: What about pain?
IVAN: [*upset*] No. No. No pain. (39)

Nowra calls this *sorites* (or chain-reasoning) the eighteenth-century 'equivalent of psychobabble'. Knowledge cannot be reduced to an 'objective mass'; the march of universal enlightenment as envisioned by Diderot and the Encyclopaedists he finds 'ridiculous' since it rules out the 'power of the irrational' from historical process. However, despite the historically compromised nature of their content, Nowra finds philosophical systems do provide the benefit of method; of some provisional structuring for individual perception of the world.[32] In this sense, Saint-Lambert as a pedagogic tool is no more or less useful than Zane Grey—both can provide a framework wherein individual or group visions may be workshopped. But while Ion Stafford transforms Australia via didactic use of Zane Grey—'I liked the way he wrote about the Indians. I admired their stealth and patience' (14)—Ivan's autistic personality renders him incapable of using his culture's most exalted official wisdom. Though she can teach him nothing through language, the Empress Catherine's sentence of exile creates the conditions for Ivan's profoundest lesson about the world; one which is ironically echoed in her *Catéchisme*: to avoid pain and pursue pleasure.

Juana, the damaged *idiot savant* representing her violated country, is the 'child' struggled over by Lynch and Lopez in *Visions*. Juana maintains her own powerful visions of alien abduction which prove ambiguously sympathetic to the imperial project. Her abjection and charisma equally attract Lopez, who tries to see in her disturbed visions vindication of his doomed war against the Triple Alliance. Lynch, who should know, suspects Juana of being a 'fake' (73-74) out to capitalise on Lopez's credulity. Lynch's own manoeuvre is to use high culture to compete with her consort's imposition of militarism on his country; these lessons are complementary versions of the imperial project. The *bal masqué* scene (I, 7) dramatises the rulers' own conflict of visions. Lynch, characteristically using intermediaries to ventriloquise her visions, has a singer perform a gentle parlour song taken from Baudelaire about the erotic union of twin spirits.[33] The soft eroticism of this text is countered by Lopez's brutal demonstration of the masculine and military prowess expected of Paraguayan troops in the incipient war: two men are inescapably bound together and must fight with rocks until one surrenders. He theatricalises for Lynch his understanding of his nation, and indeed of the power dynamics of their own relationship.[34]

In the retreat from Asunçion Lynch stages in the swamps with a ragged cast of soldiers her ultimate performance of the future of Paraguay: a naïve carnival which co-opts Juana's starmen visions into a prophecy of 'a future of beauty, games and love' presided over by the imperial couple (64).[35] Lynch's appropriation of Juana's voice (she holds Juana like a baby, or a ventriloquist's doll) reworks the blind girl's visions, already translated by Juana's cousin Valera whose renderings are self-interested and probably inaccurate. Juana speaks in tongues and, since her voice is subject to a series of translations and co-optations, the audience never truly knows what she is seeing. She is the most opaque—and the most theatrically intriguing—of Nowra's visionary characters. However, Nowra insists that Juana's inner agony destroys her; at the play's end she is again being ventriloquised by her 'mother' Lynch: 'There is a library as big as a city. Soirées every evening. Dinner parties with orchestras and beautifully dressed women... The world has changed' (81). The manic-depressive Roy in *Così*, who has been institutionalised all his life, also clings to a compensatory vision involving a gracious and cultivated mother: where truth is too painful, a fantasy of lost aristocratic maternal origins becomes the refuge of a damaged spirit. Juana survives her torment but at the cost of going mad, metamorphosing into the medium who will introduce the *demi-mondaine* Lynch's hybrid of European salon culture, into her country's dreaming.

Inside the Island's Lillian and George Dawson likewise fight over whose vision will prevail for their daughter Susan, and by metaphoric extension Australia, just as Lynch and Lopez struggle with each other over their vision of Paraguay. Lillian wants Susan to escape what she sees as provincial abjection: 'She's going to be a great lady. She can't spend the rest of her life in this backwater with riff-raff. She has to learn, and experience what the world has to offer'. On the face of it, this may appear an appropriate, if snobbishly expressed, parental ambition: to escape Lillian's own fate as a clever woman condemned to rural isolation. Yet her vicarious ambition for her daughter has the effect of imbuing in Susan the cruel legacy of colonial self-contempt and shame. 'She'll come back from England like you', is George's summation (33). He is, however, equally implicated in her revolt, since Susan is also driven away by shame at her father's alcoholism. Susan is the victim of the love of both her parents: of Lillian through her inflexible ambition and of George through his example of defeat and impotent love. Since Lillian has a forceful personality, it is her brilliant vision of imperial femininity that draws and consumes Susan, just as the young soldiers maddened by the poisoned wheat are dazzled and consumed by bushfire. All the child-figures of *Inside the Island* die, the most tragic being the idiot Andy who functions as eternal 'child' to everyone. George rescues him from the cruel pranks of his disaffected workforce; Susan reads him his favourite story, 'Little Black Sambo', from which he derives a lesson: when the tiger threatens, climb a tree. This proves fatal in the bushfire when the tree blazes with the rest of the landscape.

While Andy cannot interpret from his lessons how to preserve himself from the fire, another figure of acute partial vision, *Così*'s Doug, the unstable pyromaniac, has evolved cunning survival strategies by co-opting and mimicking the 'psychobabble' narratives of modern therapy. Within the populist discourses of 'psychobabble', the lasting effects of the maternal role conventionally credits the mother with almost witch-like powers, and Doug is astute enough to realise that 'learning' these lessons will endow him with some authority. Far smarter than Andy, Doug has learnt that assiduous ventriloquising of his mentors' authoritative narratives gives the appearance of acquiescence and buys him immunity to pursue his fire-setting obsessions. He is the master of the carnivalising of what Baudrillard calls the 'violence of interpretation' with which psychoanalysis seeks to hold at bay 'the shiny surface of non-sense and all the games that renders possible.'[36] Doug's discursive strategies mutate so fast that he is himself dangerously seductive in his unpredictability. The psychiatrist was to blame for his burning of cats, he tells Lewis, since he told Doug that he had 'an unresolved problem with my mother [and] I had better resolve it, stop her treating me like I was still a child. It made some sort of cosmic sense.' In order to land the first punch Doug sets fire to his mother's cats, which in turn set the house alight 'and within half an hour there was no bloody front door to knock on'. 'If it wasn't for that damn cat, I wouldn't be here', he concludes (19-20). Doug the autodidact, who proves himself a quick study at 'psychobabble' discourses, adds the luckless cat to the psychiatrist and his mother as conventional authors of his gratifying pyromaniac urges.[37]

Doug is a disturbingly comic version of the monster son Bao in *The Precious Woman*, where the battle between mother and son is played out on the tortured body, not of a cat, but of their entire country. Here it is the son whose actions succeed in teaching his mother hard and insoluble lessons. Are her wilful blindness and over-protective love the sources of his rage and evil, Su-ling questions, or is he himself responsible for choosing to follow his father on the mad path of domination? She must try to remember the moral function of love while leading the rebel army to defeat him. The play's finale, where she first kicks her son's body and then cradles it, is a sharply dialectic doubled conclusion to what, with its dance idiom and choral rendering of conflict, is the most theatrically formal and dialectically structured of Nowra's plays.

'We're nearly home, Mum' [38]

In the post-Mabo plays *Crow* and *Radiance* the figure of the mother
takes on the main role of transmitter of culture, like the matriarch
Queenie Ayre of *The Golden Age*, but now it is specifically Aboriginal
perspectives which she must foster. Teaching is here bound up with
questions of survival and social justice. Hard lessons have taught
Crow to be a hard teacher, and while she wheedles, seduces, bullies
and cheats white authority into assisting her long-running claim to
her land, her family can be the immediate victims of her necessary
toughness. Says Nowra, 'I became fascinated with the idea of devising
a character who was so mercurial and stubborn and wilful that, at
the same time as she was trying to get back the tin mine for her sons,
she almost destroyed them.' [39] In order to protect her good character
as a plaintiff in a white law court Crow must let her son Boofhead go
to prison for her own blackmarket chicanery. Prison is Boofhead's
worst nightmare, since he remembers being imprisoned as a child in
the Darwin compound 'sweatbox' when he and his brother Vince
were taken by the authorities after their white father's death. The
desperate Crow uses her every resource to release Boofhead,
including blackmail. 'You're a bloody monster', the lawyer Thompson
tells her, with mixed admiration and apprehension (37-38).

The responsibilities of motherhood in a racist society place Crow
in impossible situations where whatever she does for her children
must in some way hurt them; as with Su-ling, motherhood tears Crow
apart. Her son the innocent Boofhead, however, accepts his mother
as she must be. Ruth in exasperation exclaims that the obdurate Crow
is a 'monster'. 'Yeh, she is sometimes' is his cheerful response (70).
Crow's example of resource and determination, artful chicanery and
forceful bloody-mindedness teaches her children the sometimes bitter
lessons of survival. It is her actions which principally seduce, control
or instruct them, and these in turn are outcomes of her predicament
as an Aborigine in a society where 'blackfellas can't own land' or
marry whites. Crow teaches her children resistance to oppression
while also being the involuntary transmitter of its rigors; cruelties
for which at moments she almost appears to be the originator.

The nameless dead mother in *Radiance* is also powerful, but now
not for tenacious dreams of justice, but for her painful absence and
perceived compliance with imposed power. Freely chosen or not,

her acts of passivity and collaboration taught her daughters the bitter lessons of evasion, alienation and abjection. This mother is both victim and transmitter of the brutalities of white invasion; two of her daughters were taken from her as children by white authorities, and this betrayal, as they see it, is bitterly resented. Her pathetic romantic dreams of gaining a home through sexual services to white men availed her little. She was regarded as the town's black slut and eventually its uncanny madwoman and outcast 'witch'. Now even the home for which all was risked is being taken back. Worst of all, her daughter Cressy has become cruelly sacrificed to her own emotional survival, and in order to secure them that 'home' whose possession has proved delusive. This enigmatic mother figure, an emotional forcefield around which her daughters revolve and from whose deathly lure they must somehow free themselves, is as powerful through her death as is that of the Empress Catherine of *Inner Voices* through her absence. In dramatic terms her silences function as metaphor for that historical 'void' which Nowra sees at the centre of white Australian history: a kind of black hole of mystified good and evil meanings which her daughters must now decode if they are to find some sort of enabling script for their own survival.

> CRESSY: [*motioning to box of ashes*] That stranger. That selfish
> woman. Look at us, we're strangers because of her. We
> have hardly been together. She had us without any con-
> cern for our future. No concern for me and Mae.
> NONA: She was kind to me. When officials came, she always
> hid me.
> CRESSY: You were special. When they came for Mae, she just
> handed her over. Easy as pie; like she did with me. And
> then forgot us.[40]

Typically, each of her pupils has learnt a different lesson and holds to different narratives of her life story. The lessons are ambiguous and the good and evil legacies are inextricably mixed. Mae has learnt her mother's repressed fury and also her endurance; the talented Cressy duplicates her internal exile but has developed a professional discipline and determination; and Nona inherits her mother's obdurate romantic fantasies but also her comic emotional buoyancy and sexual charm. It is the dialectic of the sisters' visions of their 'scattered' common history which structures *Radiance*, where the mother is a teacher-figure of magical occluded powers, encoding traces of a repressed history of Aboriginal dispossession and sexual exploitation, and pointing the difficult path of survival.

Chapter 3

The fall of empire and its survivors

Frankenstein's creatures

Performing bodies in many of Nowra's plays undergo a process of metamorphosis through the impact of strong visions from within or without. The physicalisation of this process provides performers with rich physical metaphors and powerful mime roles. Images from carnival and masque are characteristic of his theatrical method, and his characters living within the imperial process can also be physically presented as grotesque, deformed, diseased or quasi-human. Ivan the child king of *Inner Voices*, like the half-man half-bird Nightingale the Robber of his favourite story, is a non-acculturated hybrid. Ivan's court appropriately contains the grotesquely fat Mirovich, the dwarf Peter, a shadow eagle, a man in a bear costume, and a dancing doll-woman. In *Visions* a seven-foot rabbit dances in a *bal masqué* with a seven-foot carrot (they turn out to be secret police disguised for duty).[1] Fusion of physical actions from various species suggests the rich creative turmoil of the hybrid cultural state, as when Stef in *The Golden Age* savages the Minister's ankle like the family dog. Disguises, masking and cross-class costuming characteristically reveal the emergence of hidden or potential selves, as with Betsheb's 'princess' frock, or else flaunt comic images of social roles in larger-than-life camp parody. Many Nowra plays contain internal performances and costume balls where social roles are displayed through comic overcoding: in *The Temple* Laurie Blake disports himself as Ned Kelly, his English nemesis Freddie Arrow appropriately impersonates a pirate complete with stuffed parrot, and Terry cross-dresses as a glamorous and tricky Cleopatra. In a kind of double-bluff manoeuvre, these characters boldly masquerade to display their actual purposes (61-65).

Besides such colourful masquerades and hybrid images, the more sombre themes of Nowra's theatre are indicated through graphic images of incarceration, disease and mutilation. *Inside the Island*'s hallucinating soldiers, poisoned by ergotic flour, blind themselves with cricket stumps. In the television script *Displaced Persons* with its group of European refugees marooned in the North Head Quarantine Station, metaphors of disease and isolation are used, as in *The Golden Age*, to suggest the pressure of intense cultural and emotional transformations. *The Watchtower*, with its grotesquely bandaged and surgically mutilated patients, is set during World War Two in a Blue Mountains tuberculosis sanitorium. In the 'morally legible' mode of melodrama,[2] social or moral deformities are impressed on the body. The club-footed Bao of *The Precious Woman* shows the deformity of his understanding through his bodily presentation. Bao is a Hamlet-like son who, unlike his Shakespearean counterpart, enthusiastically assumes those brutal duties of state to which his mother has been blind. The blind Su-ling and her rebel night army, who in a parallel path are also obliged to cleanse the state, display their own driven automatism through dance-like military manoeuvres.

Excessive somatic states and phenomena are enacted in these plays and telescripts as means of revealing repressed processes inscribing themselves on the body. The theatrical nature of this device is essential to understanding the vitality of the plays in performance, since these eruptions of the repressed surpass language and instead explore the extra-verbal languages of performance. This theatrical metalanguage uses the actors' physical energies to indicate that which can find no other legitimate means of expression. Nowra refers with admiration to the gothic horror movies of the Canadian director David Cronenberg where 'the body is a weapon that can be used against self'.[3] This is a motif which Nowra shares with Cronenberg, deriving from the gothic modes of excess and monstrosity. As critics have discerned, the gothic is not incidental but intrinsic to Nowra's project.[4] The actual theatrical devices by which his theatre explores the categories of the monstrous and the metamorphic form the subject of Chapter 4; but first the cultural underpinnings of this monster theme must be more closely investigated, in order to approach an understanding of the thematic implications of plays which so insistently require physical manifestations of the monstrous body.

In her study of the traditions of fantastic and gothic literature in the post-romantic world, Rosemary Jackson writes that:

> Plato expelled from his ideal Republic all the transgressive energies, all those energies which are expressed through the literary modes of the fantastic: eroticism, violence, madness, laughter, nightmares, dreams, blasphemy, lamentation, uncertainty, female energy, excess.[5]

She sees it as a basic feature of the fantastic and gothic modes that these energies will merge promiscuously together through shape-changing metamorphic imagery. Typically they are embodied in hybrid and deformed projections of lost selves who are at once rejected, feared and desired. Jackson explains such 'monster' characters as 'deconstructed, demolished or divided identities [with] disintegrated bodies [which] oppose traditional categories of unitary selves' (178). This gothic aspect of Nowra's theatre is evident in the instances cited above, and in the mixed tonal range of the plays which may encompass the comic, the camp, the folkloric, the eerie, the violent and the culturally eclectic.

One insistent gothic theme in particular, which typifies Nowra's dramatic explorations of the Australian post-colonial condition, is that of Frankenstein and his Creature, or Monster, first created by Mary Shelley in her 1818 novel and recycled throughout modern popular culture in countless retellings. Jackson writes, 'The monster confronts Frankenstein as his own body in pieces, re-presenting his existence preceding "the mirror stage", before he acquired a cultural identity' (100). The Frankenstein myth configures the desire, and more frequently the act, of expulsion and abjection of parts of the self.

Implicit in this image, then, are the incompleteness and monstrosity of the creator figure (Frankenstein) no less than of his patched-up creatures. The creator must discard parts of his own self as well as—or indeed instead of—appropriating spare bits of corpses from in a lifeless external nature removed from the self. Dramatic interest in Nowra's theatre is typically focussed on the Creature characters, the embodiments of potential or 'lost selves' of Australian history. But the would-be creators, as we have seen in Chapter 2, are drawn into an intense mutual exchange wherein their own dominance and the eventual consequences remain alike uncertain. Also essential to the Frankenstein myth is its narrative counter-movement to the impulse of rejection: a quasi-incestuous drive towards reunion and fusion with these rejected parts of the self. This may prove a tragic quest or a comic one, but it remains an ultimately impossible outcome, since 'separation [remains] the condition of having a "human" identity' (100).

In the various retellings of Mary Shelley's story of *Frankenstein* the doctor's Other, to whom Shelley gave the ontologically relative but morally neutral appellation of 'creature', was rapidly elided with the abjected category 'monster'.[6] And in the popular mind there lingers also a fertile and perceptive confusion between Baron Frankenstein, the scientific hybridiser of paternal and maternal biological functions, and his deformed and botched Creature; the latter being sometimes miscalled 'a Frankenstein'.[7] As we have seen, Nowra's imperial Frankenstein figures, whether autodidact bush carpenters or kitsch-addicted *bourgeoisie*, are no grandly heroic Prosperos. Nor are they in perfect control of their creatures. The creators' strong incursions and self-interested narratives unleash powers in their hybrid creations beyond the control of the originating bricoleur-authors.[8] But while he will typically present himself to his Others—and perhaps himself—as a self-created source of monologic truths, the Nowra version of the Frankenstein character resembles his creatures in being a hybrid mishmash. A bricoleur himself, he (or she) is typically the product of outrageously eclectic and provisional cultural bricolage appropriated from a range of high art and popular sources. In the cases of Albert, Eliza Lynch or Ion Stafford, the Australian Frankenstein as theatrical agent is a compound of pulp narratives and urgent emotional demands, communicated through authoritarian pedagogic methods. As discussed in Chapter 2, the teacher/creator's own provisionality is clearly discernible. Hence, no matter how dire their deeds or urgent their emotional drives, such discrepit awareness subjects these characters to the critical view of an audience, rendering them essentially comic creations.

Being a creature of powerful historical forces is a mixed destiny, producing survivor figures patched together from imperial and colonial discourses who will typically destabilise the authority of all of them. For the Creatures, this ontological relativity need by no means result in a uniquely tragic or over-determined fate. Nor does it continue the discourses of existential Absurdity prevalent in the theatre of the late 1960s when Nowra commenced writing: the colonised Creature is not static, dependent or trapped, like Beckett's Vladimir and Estragon. He or she operates in a highly performative and transformative historical condition, wherein states of being are assumed like a series of sometimes rapid costume changes (see Chapter 4). The Creature, herself the bearer and deployer of a ragbag of narratives, can prove capable of recognising a story when she hears one, and indeed of spinning one as well since—as Crow discerns—'sometimes bullshit is the pathway to truth' (11). But the Creature's first imperative is sheer survival, through whatever means are immediately to hand. Rats and cockroaches don't die for love, sings the condemned murderer Jack in *Love Burns*, they survive.

Survival, an amoral drive, bears the potential for achieving moral autonomy if the implications of Creature status are recognised and accepted. Such characters as Laurie Blake, who denies the consequences of his own agency, or Ion Stafford who refuses to understand that he is not a creator-god of meanings but a contingent Creature, produce immense social and spiritual damage within their societies. Typical Nowra survivors, unlike their autodidact mentors, can understand themselves as provisional, a bit of a fake; carnivalesque constructs in endless process—and this is not necessarily a tragic or hopeless perception. While the abjected origins of the survivors and their resistant ambitions may drive them towards what they see as the top of the heap, the 'creatures' of the colonial experiment develop in the later plays into morally tough survivors like Crow, or carnivalesque self-creators like the madhouse cast of *Così*.

Nowra's historical agents—his 'Frankensteins'—initiate processes which usually produce grotesquely defective results, at least by their creator's standards: creations infuriatingly mutinous and comically unteachable. Having set out to create a clone—an identical or perhaps even improved version of himself—the inventor-teacher finds himself locked into an eerie symbiotic relationship with an Other who both is and is not himself. For their part, the Creatures experience abjection and sometimes intense spiritual darkness, but prove hard to destroy and harder to control as they pursue their own eccentric evolution. Some, like Ivan, Juana and presumably Edward, are irremediably deformed, but many of Nowra's later characters demonstrate the Creatures' evolutionary process from historical victim to ambiguous agent. Chapter 2 has examined the teacher/creator figure; in this Chapter Nowra's dismembering of the Frankenstein myth itself will figure the post-colonial predicament in its tragic, ironic and comic aspects. It will in particular investigate the various implications of those historically deformed and re-formed survivor 'Creatures' who populate Nowra's theatre and provide its peculiar resonance and vitality.

The translator as transgressor

The Frankenstein parable has been explicitly used by Nowra to image the act of dramatic creation, and he sees the writer in the role of the bricoleur resurrectionist. Of *Summer of the Aliens* he writes: 'Like the doctor I have raided the graveyard of my memory and have created a monster out of the various limbs and appendages I could dig up.'[9] The transformatively open-ended agency of Frankenstein in unleashing his motley creations is economically demonstrated through an account of Nowra's comic short story 'The Translator'. Its narrator is Laurie Dunne, an undistinguished academic specialising in Kleist and Fontane who turns a dishonest penny translating into English the pulp fiction of a minor German crime writer. Reuchtsnichts' naïve outpourings of 'American gangster movies, pornographic magazines and gutter life' appeal to the gay Laurie's sense of camp even as he is appalled by their brutish heterosexism and airport-novel mundanity. While Reuchtsnichts' texts appear to him pure kitsch, Laurie himself is definitely camp in both the sexual and the aesthetic senses.

> While kitsch functions fundamentally as the external, negative judgement of the critic on the margins of popular culture, camp directly engages with popular tastes by trying to aesthetise them... camp still maintains a distance between its own selective appropriation and the wider, everyday movement of popular culture.'[10]

Like many Nowra 'translator' characters, Laurie, by directly engaging with the aesthetising of kitsch—by 'translating'—subverts the original texts by making over their inarticulate thug hero into a tragic but heroic gay. This metamorphosed hero is in his own fashion a detective, an Oedipal seeker-out of the source of traumatic crimes.

So in Laurie's English 'translation', the uneducated 'peasant' writer Reuchtsnichts becomes a high culture *succès d'éstime* fêted as a species of authentic feral talent: the Ern Malley of the crime fiction world. Laurie's scam is however sleuthed out by the inquisitorial doctoral student Hanna Goode, now the author's mistress and literary hatchet-woman, who accuses him of 'poisoning' Reuchtsnichts' 'updating of the eternal male ethos'. Laurie protests that he has made masterpieces out of the originals' 'crap', but he is exposed as a fake and publicly disgraced. 'Like Frankenstein I had raided the cemetery of Reuchtsnichts' talent and out of assorted limbs and organs I had constructed a marvellous monster which was now destroying me.' His consolation, apart from his succession of black lovers, is that he comes to see his translations as 'supreme creations' which will in the future vindicate him:

> Just as Shakespeare's *King Lear* vanquished its source, so Reuchtsnichts' work will vanish and my versions remain. And Hans, the gay gangster, with his copy of Proust in one pocket and a pistol in the other, will be seen as Laurie Dunne's greatest creation.[11]

Between the actual origin, or indeed content, of translation and creation, kitsch and camp, high and low art, there is little to choose: social intention, textual context and aesthetic perspective are what matter. A cultural creator is always in a sense necessarily a betrayer of somebody's vision, since in cultural production mere identical duplication is impossible; re-told stories will be inevitably refashioned in new contexts. In *Capricornia*, the didactic Bible lessons read to the disaffected compound girls are 'translated' by Tocky into an enthusiastic polyglot performance wherein the triumph of David over Goliath becomes a comic fable of the girls' own repressed situation and possible release (30-31). Rather than mongrelising some sort of original purity of vision—in Reuchtsnichts' case his earnest 'originals' are themselves autodidactic textual purées—the colonised pupil or the camp translator reconstitutes culture into new hybrids which may yet prevail in some imagined future.

History's survivors

In Nowra's early plays the impact of the incursion of would-be creators into the minds and bodies of Others is theatricalised as chaotic, agonising and traumatic, earning him the joke title

'Apocalypse Nowra'. He is insistent that such Creature characters as Ivan in *Inner Voices* or Juana in *Visions* end up mentally and spiritually devastated. However in performance these enigmatic and theatrically powerful characters, with their intriguing physical intensity, tend to imply the possession of extra-linguistic resources which escape the capture of the spoken text. The actors' energies and exclusion from authorised verbal discourse keep alive the image of the resistent body and spirit. Text and performance here can be in implicit contradiction. Even Ivan, puppet king of a horror-comic kingdom, produces words or reactions which suggest he is gaining the ability to link language to action and emotion. As a feral child raised ignorant of language and without humanising social interactions, a 'real' Ivan would have lost the ability to speak once past the age of eight or ten, but Nowra is adapting clinical data to the needs of his own fable. Dramatic interest is focussed by Ivan's small learning victories, which counterpoint the tragic irony of his major learning curve: learning not what he is taught, but how he is taught. Such a breakthrough moment occurs in Scene 4, as Ivan is being prompted through his coronation scene:

> VLADIMIR'S VOICE: To govern with the best interests...
> IVAN: To govern with the best interests...
> VLADIMIR'S VOICE: Of the people at heart...
> IVAN: Of the people... of the people... [*Pointing triumphantly to his own heart*] Heart... heart... heart! (32)

Ivan here appears for the first time to associate language with his own alienated body, that body which has been treated by the medical guards as an inanimate thing. In a subsequent scene he may begin to suspect how he appears to others:

> FYODOROVICH: They have to be signed.
>
> > *He holds out the papers.* IVAN *knocks them from his hand.* FYODOROVICH *turns to voice.*
>
> Where's Mirovich?
> VLADIMIR'S VOICE: How should I know? I've had my hands full with the idiot.
>
> > IVAN *looks up as if in shock. He tries to say something and looks in direction of voice. He reaches out his hand in direction of voice.*

The feral child. Tony Sheldon as Ivan and Robert Faggetter as Mirovich in *Inner Voices*, Nimrod Theatre, Sydney, 1977.
(Photo: Paul Melchert)

IVAN: Vlad? [*Quietly*] Vlad?
VLADIMIR'S VOICE: [*nervous*] Yes, Your Majesty.
IVAN: A... Again. [*Pointing to himself, meaning: 'Tell me again'.*]
(36-37)

In performance a spectator is likely to find Ivan's reaction as ambiguous as Vladimir does. Does Ivan understand the meaning of the word 'idiot' or merely respond to the change in Vladimir's tone of voice? In his final soliloquies, Ivan in his solitude runs through the catalogue of insults which have been directed at him, playing out alternative scenarios:

Talk. This is how you do it. You come in. Say: 'Good morning, Your Majesty. How are you? Are you well? You look beautiful.' 'Sing me a song,' I say, 'Dance me a dance.' [*Shaking his head*] So simple. So easy and yet... you cannot do that right. You forget words, add steps... change it. (69)

Although Ivan is still trying to rehearse his inverted world of childish comfort and validation rather than envisioning scenarios of free human interaction, the fact that he can imagine and theatricalise alternative social responses suggests that he has gained some sense of the cruel arbitrariness of his own shaping experiences. He has learned enough to propel him into painful consciousness of his irrevocable human uniqueness, but not enough to allow him to escape his imprisoned fate. At the play's end 'He tilts his head like a bird and listens to some unknown, far off voice. He almost whispers: "I'm listening"' (71). All that the audience hears, however, is silence. Ivan is compelled to script and direct his inner performances from his limited repertoire of interiorised lines and characters. As a metaphor of personal or cultural survival, the bricoleur Ivan's story is an entropic one, with an outcome simultaneously more appalling yet more human than his initial condition of blank solitude.

Juana too ends by reproducing the voice of her coloniser; in the 1985 Melbourne Theatre Company production of *Visions* this point was underlined by her speaking in Lynch's acquired French accent. Unlike Ivan, whose learning of all the wrong lessons structures his play, Juana has no developing path through the action; she has been destroyed by some alien force before the play commences. When she is first seen in her bloodied and muddied white dress, incursion and invasion have evidently already occurred. Her private language or glossolalia ensures that as a theatrical figure requiring maximum decoding she will intrigue and dominate audience response. Hence the audience view is partially aligned with that of Lopez who is intrigued by Juana's essential otherness, imagining it as a repository of arcane spiritual wisdom which he may be able to harness to his nationalist and military dreams. Within Australian discourses, Aboriginality occupies much the same cultural space as Juana the dispossessed victim does in Lopez's Paraguay.

The concluding scene of *Visions* shows an interesting playing off of diegetic versus theatrical space, and demonstrates too the unauthorised instability of meaning within the multi-layered theatrical image. Within the fiction, Juana's final speech about 'magnificent buildings', 'dinner parties with orchestras and beautifully dressed women', and 'a magnificent opera house with golden stairs and marble floors' (81) resounds through a devastated swamp. But in the immediate performance moment an actor on a bare stage is commanding the audience's imagination through largely uncontested language (Valera's counter-movement of contradiction and protection lacks dialectic force by comparison) with the added impact of it being a curtain speech and Juana's first and long-awaited comprehensible one. Besides, talk of patrician luxury and aristocratic performance modes in fine buildings presents a utopia, the class-bound nature of which many audience members may choose to overlook. Such local details as the 'magnificent opera house' (p. 81) refer the parable of *Visions* to the specific dreamings of white Australian culture. Socially or historically specific performance contexts, however, can further frame (or subvert) the text. John Milsom's 1977 production of *Visions* at Brisbane's La Boite occurred at the height of the Bjelke-Petersen regime of organised corruption and police repression. This production became a vehicle of protest and utopian prophecy for its left-liberal audiences, implying that spiritual resistance was possible in the face of overwhelming state power and that a just society might in the future prevail. The utopian content of Juana's final speech was legitimated and its irony diminished by taped operatic music: the audience could experience a healing visionary moment as the production was itself repositioned as a image of political survival.

History's survivors toughen up in Nowra's later drama, which becomes more interested in such characters' own political agency and resistant strategies as well as in their violated and richly unpredictable ragbag inner worlds. The innocent proletarian Sergeant Collins, alone of the lost soldiers, appears to escape the full catastrophe of the ergot outbreak of *Inside the Island*.[12] Many layers of historical metaphor are folded into these scenes of violent ecstasy, combining music, euphoric dancing, class insubordination, rape, fire, mutilation and intense hallucinations. Raw young soldiers at a country cricket match run riot in a private hell, which, however, has many resonances within the Australian public consciousness. The flour-poisoned and flour-whitened soldiers, streaked with blood, seem ghosts from the land, as the violent history of Aboriginal dispossession is replayed in a phantasmagoric pageant before its onstage audience of squattocracy and military. Thematically, these soldier characters seem doubly over-determined and doomed; possessed vehicles compelled to bear witness to suppressed history when the horrors of a traumatic invasive past burn out their bodies as paper curls in a fire. Moreover, the ergot scenes prophesy the next stage of the imperial legacy, since the theatricalising of the young soldiers' nightmare picks up details of apocalyptic mechanised warfare on the Western Front: an event which in the play's fictional moment of 1912 lies in Australia's immediate future.[13] Within the play's original moment of reception in 1980, the images were also readable as those of traumatised and poisoned Vietnam troops. The Captain attempts to understand what this Dionysiac performance is trying to tell him:

> What was going on inside of them... it would be a mistake to believe that what they experienced—the hallucinations, the horror—wasn't a part of them. What they saw... the things that went on in their heads... Can they ever see the world the same way they saw it before? (90)

The play's final image is an enigma. Sergeant Collins, with blackened hands bound in the same socks with which he had previously attempted to amuse Susan in a sock-puppet performance, is 'staring blankly into the distance, immersed in his own thoughts—a shell of his former self' (91). An audience may read the silence of this stoic survivor, a character they have come to enjoy and trust, as inner devastation or as contemplation and resolve to understand and learn.

The Golden Age is Nowra's most culturally complex and searching dramatisation of the damaged but resilient colonised. In its lost tribe of Tasmanian 'ghosts' he presents a theatrically rich and rewarding spectacle of the ambivalences of survival. The lost people, and Betsheb in particular, embody all the 'transgressive energies' of the gothic mentioned above: 'eroticism, violence, madness, laughter, nightmares, dreams, blasphemy, lamentation, uncertainty, female energy, excess.' Their physical style, like their hybrid language, is not naïvely carnivalesque[14] but confrontingly sexual and excretory – the Bakhtinian 'carnival body *par excellence*'[15] producing piss, menstrual blood, spit, farting, masturbation, convulsions. This pre-modern cultural archive of lost somatic energies may serve to satirise class pretensions, as when Betsheb does her party piece imitating the great lady patronising the flogged convicts (29, 38-39). But since it is imbricated in genetic degeneration, this somatic vocabulary also complicates a reading of the lost people's culture as an unproblematic way forward. When the forest people are incarcerated in the same prison/asylums from which their forebears fled to the wilderness, their time of testing commences and only Betsheb survives, but in a shattered and almost destroyed state. She and Francis have little ability to form the nucleus of a new community: Betsheb's fertility is rendered suspect since when she and Francis attempt love-making her body convulses and betrays her (30). As Nowra says of Cronenberg's films, 'the body is a weapon that can be used against self.' Betsheb's physicality and immense spiritual strength define occulted energies suppressed within white Australian civilisation; of which the powers of Aboriginality are the most obvious. However these energies, manifested by means of her sexuality, tenacious metaphysical visions and ability to destroy her captors through her very abjection, also ambiguously link Betsheb to the meretricious 'Baby Face' survivors discussed below.

In dramatic terms Betsheb is not only demonstrating the contours of her own torment, but doubling the more externalised trial of the working-class soldier Francis who is abroad participating in the horrors of a genocidal war. They are parallel characters who seek re-integration, scattered fragments surviving from the catastrophic impact of empire. Like Orestes and Iphigenia, they are as much separated brother and sister as they are lovers. Here the parable connects with the 'Frankenstein' incest theme outlined previously, figuring the impossible but urgently desired union of divided selves. Francis endures his own social abjection as a struggling working-class boy, one of the damaged survivors of empire. The short powerful scene in his dead mother's stripped rented room (Act 2 scene 1) shows that his own survivor determination has bred its dark and uncompromising side: 'One should forget the past. Do you know why I never invited you [Peter] here?... Because I was too ashamed' (45). Here Francis is tempted by the option taken by the survivor Lillian Dawson of *Inside the Island*, who walks out of another devastated room declaring: 'We must forget all of this. It's too terrible. The strong forget, the weak remember' (91). While in the forest Francis and the lost people are drawn into the exchange of their validating performances (Peter's own performance site lies in Hobart where after his father's death he takes his place impersonating Orestes to his mother's Iphigenia). Francis most forcefully performs his own desperation through his violent wrestling with the forest patriarch Melorne for ritual top male position, where he thrashes the old man with unnecessary force: 'He just seems to be asking for it. It's the only thing he understands.' Peter's retort is apt: 'The same would apply to you, it would seem' (22).

Francis returns from the war, and from his own Berlin imprisonment with the neo-convict class of the abject, criminal and mad, with his 'Emperor of Darkness' potential about to take over (see Chapter 2). But when he holds the gun to Betsheb's head to release her, he realises 'I should have been holding it against mine' (74). The return of the mutilated or traumatised Australian soldier from various cataclysmic conflicts is a frequent motif in Nowra's writing (*The Song Room, Spellbound, Royal Show, The Watchtower, Byzantine Flowers, Map of the Human Heart* and by metaphoric extension *Inside the Island*). In both *The Golden Age* and its companion play *The Watchtower*, the soldier's ordeal abroad is echoed in intensity by his lover's trial where she must survive illness, incarceration and despair. The narrative option of the concluding ghostly union of lovers is worked out more fully in *The Watchtower* when the soldier Andrew and his tubercular lover Beatrice reunite after death in the snow-covered garden of a Blue Mountains sanitorium. Francis and Betsheb survive with the chance to recombine their energies and visions after the brutalities of their history, but it's a solution which heals Betsheb while remaining ambiguous for Francis. Peter, his loyal Pylades, tells him: 'She lives in a world of her own... She destroyed my father just as she'll destroy you. You have done the wrong thing.' Francis replies: ' Maybe I have; I don't know. But she's all I've got to believe in.' (70).

The interest of *The Golden Age* within recent Australian theatre lies in its metaphoric folding-in of Aboriginal history into this Tasmanian fable. In Queenie Ayre, matriarch of her tribe and transmitter of their culture, it is easy to read photographic images of incarcerated nineteenth-century Aboriginal Tasmanians in their stiff dresses, and to understand in the lost people's spiritual tenacity, and their cultural transmission through performance and hybridised language, the outlines of a displaced oral culture. When Ayre dies, Betsheb in the asylum inherits her roles as her people's chief survival and cultural agent. As in the later *Radiance*, the survivors of various historical traumas sustain parallel but interconnected fates as the impact of history is shared across several characters. Most evidently of her family, Betsheb principally embodies the charismatic enigma of survival—its emphatic abjected physicalised dimensions, its spiritual richness and vision, its desperate intransigence, its rigors and cruelties. When the survivor character in Nowra's theatre becomes overtly Aboriginal these themes are pursued by less metaphorical methods, through narratives analysing in detail the ambiguous moral agency of the survivor. These black survivor characters have to use a lot of performative powers, disguises and seduction in order to further their survival projects within an unstable and ambiguous dramatic world still reeling from the impact of white cultures' incursions into their territory, and into their very physical and mental beings.

Mongrels and hybrids

In order to dull his grief about his son killed at the Western Front, Tom Harris, the elderly and lonely owner of the sugar plantation in *Byzantine Flowers*, begins to take an speculative tutorial interest in his part-Aboriginal housemaid Roma:

> TOM: ... You must learn to read—to find out what's going on. He learnt to read when he was four years old. [*Looking directly at her*] Pure white. Mixed up blood, like you—your type can't do that.
> ROMA: [*stung*] I'll go back to the hut.
> TOM: It's raining.
> ROMA: Doesn't matter.
> TOM: Stay here for a while. I need my monkey.

ROMA: I am not a monkey. I'm a dog! I'm like those dogs with mixed up blood. The mongrels. The best dogs. They're smarter and they hunt better.

TOM: So you're a mongrel. Not so smart—you can't read, can you? (31)

Roma keenly feels the social shame of her racial abjection, since it has consigned her to a makeshift life rolling drunks and generally living on her wits, and she finds her illiteracy and ignorance humiliating. But she is a quick learner who loves her role as maid inside the big house and her access to Tom's attention. When she grasps the rudiments of literacy she is overjoyed, while Tom's attitude is also changing:

ROMA: ... I'm not a stupid coloured, am I?

TOM: No.

ROMA: I'm a mongrel.

She barks and suddenly almost at the same time, he lashes out and hits her. She drops the flowers and almost falls.

TOM: Don't ever say that.

Horrified at what he's done he looks away. (36)

The ambivalence surrounding the categories of 'mongrel' and the hybrid are pinpointed in these exchanges. Roma wants to claim the category of mongrelisation to validate the superior survival ability of hybrid vigour in both racial and cultural senses. By contrast Tom, as he plays Frankenstein tutoring his rapidly metamorphosing Creature recoils violently from the shame implicit in his own racist understanding of the term. As Mirovich in *Inner Voices* tells Leo who has called him 'a tub of lard', 'names can hurt' (24)—he then murders Leo to prove it, just as Robert Herbert once reaped the consequences of abject labelling (see Chapter 1). For Tom, Roma is no longer Other but is disturbingly transforming into a lost and desired aspect of Self; lost son and lover magically fused. It is Roma's celebratory counter-hegemonic use of the term 'mongrel' which recurs in Nowra's theatre. This appears a deliberate manoeuvre of discursive reclamation and decontamination of a still-current and hurtful racist insult, directed at Aboriginal and migrant Australians by those who imagine themselves, like Ion Stafford, to be 'the real thing' (see below).

'Don't ever say that'. Simon Chilvers as Tom and Kylie Belling as Roma in *Byzantine Flowers*, Sydney Theatre Company, 1989. (Photo: Branco Gaica)

Some characters are not slow to hurl this insult. *Crow*'s Administrator throws puppies to feed the sharks, since his bitch 'got off with a mongrel' and the pups are thus 'useless to sell' (30). He is an unreconstructed polygeneticist who terms Crow's family 'mongrels' and whose callous action symbolises official treatment of the mixed-race children under government care, some of whom who 'looked as white as [he]' (31).

In Nowra's reclamatory reading of the term, to proclaim oneself a mongrel is to be fully aware of what it is to be human: a dynamic and necessarily heterogeneous confluence of ethnicities and cultural influences propelling growth, change and history.[16] Tribal or pseudo-scientific fantasies of racial purity or cultural superiority are displaced in this figuring of the relational operations of cultural exchange. It is in this sense that Salman Rushdie reclaims the term 'mongrelisation' in defence of his novel *The Satanic Verses*. '[It] celebrates hybridity, impurity, intermingling, the transformation that comes of new and unexpected combinations of human beings, cultures, ideas, politics, movies, songs. It rejoices in mongrelization and fears the absolutism of the Pure.'[17] Mongrels, being hungrier, have also their sinister potential. In Australian parlance, a 'mongrel' can be a forcefully unscrupulous person: when disdained for his lack of 'good breeding', Laurie Blake of *The Temple* informs the blueblood dynast Macarthur that 'humans are mongrels' and that good breeding is strictly for the birds (23).[18]

'Hybridity' is a more involved term, trailing a long history of imperial and scientific usage. As Robert Young explains, the terms 'hybrid' and 'mongrel' are both deeply implicated, as abjected categories, in the history of imperial race relations and its discursive self-explanations. Are all human groups related and sprung from a common stock (monogeneticism), or do they have distinct origins and hence different and relative claims to the status of 'humanity' (polygeneticism)? As a term deriving from agricultural practices, 'hybridity' appears at first the less pejorative ascription than 'mongrelisation', yet when used to describe products of mixed-race relations it retains the ghostly echo of nineteenth-century debates. 'The use of the term "hybridity" to describe the offspring of humans of different races implied, by contrast, that the different races were different species.' 'By contrast' with the term 'amalgamation' (or to the mid-century 'miscegenation' suggesting fertile fusion), human 'hybridity' was believed by polygeneticists to result only in sterile 'mulattos'. But the evident fertility of such people confounded attempts to read them as genetic dead-ends: monogeneticists were proved right by empirical experience.[19] Sexual reproduction, all too often a result of unequal and violent colonial power, is precisely the agency which can destroy the very conditions of racial supremacy. Mixed-race people proliferate in the wake of empire—they are its earliest and most lasting products, who will survive its fall. 'Paradoxically it was the very desire of the white for the non-white, and the proliferating products of their unions... that undid the claim for permanent difference between the races while at the same time causing the boundary territories of the racial frontier to be policed ever more possessively'. So the 'proofs' of a humanity consisting of separate and inviolate species undid themselves through sex.[20] Betsheb and her tribe are examples in Nowra's theatre of technical 'hybrids', or infertile genetic inbreds, and are so seen by the authorities who read their biological abjection as confirming, rather than challenging, fascist doctrines of racial purity. Their characteristic miming of animal behaviour (Betsheb as bird or Tasmanian devil, Stef as dog) theatricalises their hybrid state, since in cultural terms they are more properly mongrels, having hybridised and evolved a spiritual understanding of their place in the world from their inherited ragbag of European culture.

'Hybridisation' as an image in Nowra's theatre encompasses less the scientific-racial signification (alive though this may remain in Australian discourse), but alludes more to the poetic sense suggested by Ovid in his *Metamorphoses*.[21] In this epic-length poem of mythical origins, metamorphosis is a violent but transfiguring process of incursion and invasion, usually figured by an erotic interaction between divine and human beings. As Mikhail Bakhtin explains the ancient use of this folklore trope, 'metamorphosis or transformation is a mythological sheath for the idea of development—but one that unfolds not so much in a straight line as spasmodically, a line with "knots' in it.' It encodes individual (and by extension historical) processes as moments of crisis: 'there is no evolution in the strict sense of the word; what we get, rather, is crisis and rebirth.'[22] In Ovid's poem the outcome for his ravished or seduced characters is crisis transformation through organic fusion between categories of being now seen as distinct—the human and the natural.

Ovid's sometimes violent and usually erotic encounters may be invasory, traumatic, deforming, seductive, transfiguring, comic or sacred. Metamorphosis may occur as divine punishment, through the sheer pressure of emotion, or even as compassionate rescue from violation; physical abjection and divine ecstasy are conflated. The Birdman in the eclipse sequence of the opera *Whitsunday* is such an evolving Ovidian hybrid: 'part bone, part strut, part muscle, part wire, part metal, part gristle'. Dramatic images of fused beings are thematically and poetically suggestive, like Ivan transforming into Nightingale the Robber; a hybrid of tsar, prisoner, child, bird, idiot, necromancer and cunning ruthless bandit.[23] As we have seen in Chapter 1, Nowra's theatrical metamorphoses are not teleologically over-determined or narratively closed, but symptoms of on-going Bakhtinian crisis and rebirth.

The Aboriginal plays

By the casting of Aboriginal actors in *Capricornia, Byzantine Flowers, Crow* and *Radiance*[24] questions of racial hybridity and sexual 'amalgamation' are theatrically foregrounded in explicit way which in some senses makes dramatically redundant the richly complicated metaphors for indigeneity and hybridity explored in *Inner Voices* or *The Golden Age*. Nowra's early parable plots lose some of their metaphoric density, and what appears as more conventional dramatic structures take its place. As we shall see however, in the next Chapter dealing with *Radiance*, the naturalist impulses of the later dramaturgy are more apparent than real. In these Aboriginal plays hybridity retains much of its poetic as well as its historical resonances. The most evident products of black-white Australian relations, after all, are people; real, present-day and self-determining subjects who are both Ovidian spiritual 'hybrids' bearing the traces of originary trauma and agents in charge of their identities and destinies. Nowra's Aboriginal characters, while dealing with the unfinished business of empire in a less occulted and more narratively explicit way, bear the right and the capacity to inherit and create a new order. They are also survivor characters, with access to the repertoire of carnivalesque self-performances and survival strategies of the 'real fake' discussed in the next section.

The black Australian characters appear poised between Bakhtin's related categories of 'organic' and 'intentional' linguistic hybridity.

The first, organic, hybridity is where a mixture of systems is fused into a new world view which remains 'mute and opaque' but which '[has] at the same time been profoundly productive historically: [it is] pregnant with potential for new world views'. Intentional hybridity, a more dynamic and politicised construct, is more internally dialogic, conscious and intentional. It sets different viewpoints against each other in a conflictual structure which retains 'a certain elemental, organic energy and open-endedness':[25] a hybridity Ovidian in its poetic intensity but transcending historical stasis. These two potentials of cultural hybridity exist simultaneously within the Aboriginal characters and may be in conflict. Young understands Homi Bhabha's reading of Bakhtin's 'intentional hybrid' as a site of 'challenge and resistance against a dominant cultural power' which displaces colonial authority without simply creating a new 'organic' fusion, antithetic and playing Other to an originative purity. Hybridisation, by this reading, is metamorphic; 'the permanent revolution of forms'.[26] Within the post-colonial situation, sexual and reproductive power places black women in a position at once abject and central, and Nowra's theatricalisations of Aboriginal historical agency are dominated by female characters. No mere muted womb-bearers for white masters, such articulate and forceful characters as Crow set out to transform their social environment and to make history.

Capricornia, set in Port Zodiac (Darwin), creates a world wherein, as in *Crow*, the 'boundary territories of the racial frontier' are being frantically but futilely policed. In this play 'the thematic and theatrical focus on miscegenation fortifies the disruptive potential of the body as an unstable signifier.'[27] Mrs Hollower's 'island' of the prison-like Compound, full of mixed-race children whom she sees as 'the products of men unable to restrain themselves' (24), is a desperate attempt to stop their further reproduction by restraining the girls' sexuality. Otherwise, 'in a year's time you'll have more half-castes because of them' (26). Dr Aintee, by contrast, sees such further breeding as a reasonable idea, voicing contemporary eugenic views and government policy: 'The good thing about the Aborigine is that all signs of him will disappear in three generations of white marriages' (24). This interbreeding project is furtively being carried on apace by Port Zodiac's white men and, if Dr Aintee's theory is correct, it would shortly solve the 'Aboriginal problem'. But white society; far from applauding and validating this process, violently disavows, labels and rejects both the practice and its human products. The internalised abjection possible within the lived experience of 'organic' hybridity is accepted by the 'mission Christian' Christobel (34) but contested by the intransigence of the defiant Tocky and the cheerful Fat Anna. Fat Anna is able to place Norman's torment into context:

> NORMAN: I'm white, I'm black. I don't know what I am.
> FAT ANNA: So what? Look at me, I'm half black, half Jap. Is this part Jap, is this part black? I don't like raw fish, does that mean my mouth isn't Jap? (94)

Abjection is internalised and abjected in turn by Norman's shadow-double Charlie Ket, Red Ochre's part-Chinese overseer. Ket is brutal and contemptuous towards Sally, the Aboriginal stock worker who he despises and desires, and particularly detests the Chinese with all the force of projected self-hatred: 'I know you people. I got you inside of me. I got your blood', he tells the Chinese shopkeeper whom he murders (50). Hybridity is experienced by Ket as an 'opaque' state of intense anguish; his advances to Marigold and his denunciation of Norman as 'the jumped-up son of a murderer and a gin' (44f) demonstrate that while he hates being a 'yella fella' within racist society he refuses identification with other half-breeds. 'Do you reckon me a coloured man, Miss?' (40), he demands of Marigold in a sinister courting gambit. After Norman's trial, Mrs Grey ponders 'Coloureds should not mix with us.' When Norman's father Jack Ramble protests about this exclusion of his own 'flesh and blood', Mrs Grey rejoins, 'The coloureds are right for this country. We whites are wrong' (98).

Both Tocky the 'white quadroon' (90) and Norman are racial and cultural hybrids. Norman's cultural hybridity and multi-layered identities are suggested through his various names and costumes (see Chapter 4). For all her tough buoyancy and performative energy, Tocky partakes of the tragic vulnerability of the survivor whose cruel lessons cannot be unlearnt or evaded. Hiding from the police, she drowns in the water tank while pregnant with a 'half-caste' child whom she dreads will be taken from her just as she was taken. Norman's courtroom speech articulates himself as pre-eminently Australia's cultural Creature; despised, disavowed but indestructible:

I am like a scientific experiment that has gone wrong. Like the monster in Doctor Frankenstein. Instead of being made out of bits of corpses from here and there, I have been made up out of black and white blood, taught to act and think like a white and then told to be black. Now you want to get rid of me because you can't bear to see what you've created. Well I'm here and you'll have to hang me. (91)

The three fatherless sisters of *Radiance* are also 'fragments', indicating the shattering and hybridising impact of white social and sexual inroads into black culture and black women's bodies. The 'scattering' is theatrically emphasised through their carnivalising self-performances and costumes (see Chapter 4) and thematically through the play's characterisation and construction. Each sister manifests aspects of their mother's compartmentalised reactions to her own abjection and oppression. Cressy, most obviously physically marked by invasory and violent sexual experience, has inherited her singing voice, her iron determination, her dread, and something of her 'witch-like' magic powers.[28] Mae is shamed by her own replication of her mother's practice of buying love in an unequal social compact, except instead of using sexual favours Mae has become a 'criminal' by stealing money to buy presents for her own love object. Now Mae functions dramatically as the double of that demented and witch-like mother with whom she was imprisoned '[doing her] time' (39). The bitterness and rage Mae must orgiastically discharge through self-exorcism visibly theatricalise both her mother's repressed inner life as well as her own emotional inheritance. A third aspect of the hybrid knowledge of the mother is embodied in Nona, who inherits her warm sexuality, romantic optimism and spirited refusal of moral abjection. Nona too has been beaten up and imprisoned by her lovers, which replays Cressy's trauma and hints at what might have been her grandmother's experience. Nona has adopted a resolutely romantic myth of her own origins and maintains it in the face of tough experience and her sisters' pain. As a compensatory utopian narrative by which abjection is denied and rendered bearable, fantasy becomes a poor person's version of hope. Between the lived history of alienation, humiliation and anger carried by the older sisters, plus their attempts to find within themselves the love that was averted and denied, and Nona's stubborn insistence on a coherent optimistic narrative, no choice can properly be made. All are lived and valid

'See what you've created'. Bradley Byquar as Norman in *Capricornia*, Queensland University of Technology/ Queensland Performing Arts Trust, 1995. (Photo courtesy of Jamie Maclean)

responses by survivors of a painfully fragmented hybrid history. Mae says of Nona 'She's a born survivor. All us three are.' 'Sort of', Cressy equivocally replies (54). As the threat of the extinguishment of native title remains on the late-nineties Australian political agenda, this play picks up the seemingly unending and provisional nature of the 'home-coming' of Aboriginal Australians.

The relatively integrated accretionary Creature which Norman in *Capricornia* embodies is in *Radiance* torn apart anew, with the three sisters sharing diverse shreds of the hybrid experience of sexual colonisation. In their very 'scattering' or fragmentation lies their fragility and their potential strength. The context of Crow's survivalist toughness towards her own children is displayed in the narrative and can be understood as hard choices in a circumscribed situation; the elimination of the mother as a character from *Radiance* makes her the pre-eminent muted image of the colonised survivor. One may infer that this mother, like all Nowra's characters, had 'her reasons'; but an audience must deduce what they might have been through their own knowledge of the long-running Australian policy of separating mixed-blood Aboriginal children from their mothers. Clearly the over-riding imperative to gain a 'home' has driven this black mother to desperate actions. Survival is ambiguous—a harsh and morally hybrid state—and the emotional heritage of the racial, social and sexual abjection of indigenous women is a legacy agonisingly borne by their children. The dead mother of *Radiance* poses a moral and historical enigma which is her daughters' task to decipher: herself the hybridised creation of white racism and sexual exploitation, she functions to them as their own immediate Frankenstein.

Baby Face

Nowra's 'fake' characters—his 'translated' Frankenstein creatures—can be transparently artificial to an audience, but are placed in dramatic situations where they must strive amidst brutally real historical forces. Their hybrid origins and lack of ontological validity is their necessary torment, but it impels also their resistent versatility, comic acts of boundary violation, and their creative survival potential. They can be, paradoxically, real fakes. Their moral and social agency increases the more they assume responsibility for their ragbag state of becoming; the necessary condition of their being. The theatricalisation of fakery structures *Inner Voices*. For all its un-illusioned dramatising of a betrayed and destroyed consciousness, the play's lucid theatricality could have originated in the camp sensibility of Laurie Dunne, that hybridising 'translator' of high and low discourses. This early play demonstrates that aesthetic manoeuvres of relativising and intertextual framing are by no means incompatible with social insight, nor of the creation of characters able to project real emotions and suffering. Indeed, to infuse an essentially parodic and camp perspective with deep passions and moral critique can be seen as Nowra's distinctive achievement within Australian theatre.

Inner Voices plays out, with unmistakably Australian proletariat verbal idiom and social relationships, the ancient fables of the moral testing of the ruler and the king-for-a-day motif.[29] It is an ironic Australian post-colonial fairytale recalling our haunted convict past; whose nursery-prison is filled with dark shadows and nameless horrors, where colourful trinkets distract while oppressive power guarantees that real throats and tongues will be cut. Fakery and relativity pervade the play; in its construction, characterisation, its perversely parodic range of cultural reference and through its performance modes. The play merely masquerades as historical drama, while its 'fakery' borrows and subverts the naturalistic obsessions of 1970s New Wave Australian theatre. The comic interactions of Mirovich and Leo, the 'mates' indulging in gamesmanship, name-calling and sniping about stolen food, resemble grumbling students forced to share squalid accommodation: Stork's flatmates on frontier guard duty.[30] Despite his pronouncements about rejecting 1970s Australian Performing Group blokey obsessions, Nowra proves an acute anatomiser of the egalitarian bonhomie which masks the competitive style of Australian male social interactions.

John Bell's Nimrod Theatre production supported its dark comic tone by using self-consciously theatrical make-up and Ruritanian comic-opera costumes to distance the action from the 'real' world of Russian history upon which the plot is a speculative fantasia. As 'true progeny of Princess Anne of Mecklenburg and Prince Anthony-Ulrich of Brunswick' (20) Ivan is himself something of an ethnic fake as the 'true Russian king' (32) which Mirovich forces him to become—a 'pretender' like his replacement 'Pretend Paul'. Ivan the quasi-human dynastic hybrid responds with intuitive fear to the 'whispering death' hand-shadow eagle, and with delight to artifice and metamorphic images: the dancing bear-man, the spinning top. Equally he toys with the romping colourful goodtime girl Baby Face, a 'cheap little music-hall singer'(60) 'pinched from Toulouse Lautrec'[31] who is his last playmate. 'I like song, noise and dancing', Ivan tells her (60). He can make little distinction between people whose physical otherness is innate, like the dwarf Peter, and those who, like the singing and dancing gold-digger, are different through studied self-presentation.

> BABY FACE: [*in a lower class accent*] I never though I'd dance with a king, Your Majesty. A real king.
>
> > *Pause.*
>
> Just to be inside this palace.
> VLADIMIR'S VOICE: Thank you. You're very kind.
> IVAN: Thank you. You're very kind.
> BABY FACE: [*in an upper class accent that soon returns to normal*] It is I who should say thanks. I mean, wait until I tell my parents.
> VLADIMIR'S VOICE: I will send you home in my gold coach.
> IVAN: I will send you home in my gold coach...
> BABY FACE: When I saw the coach... I pushed my way through the crowd ... People said I was rude... but I wanted to see my king and there you were... and [*giggling*] there I was. I bet you all my friends will be jealous. They'll like you a lot... make sure the coach stops right outside my front door. (59)

The play's other 'fake', Princess Ali, an adventuress with a badly-assumed French accent, is never comprehended as a human by Ivan, since he cannot understand distinctions between the categories of human, animal and the inanimate; categories which in his court metamorphose weirdly together. After her wedding Ali is 'broken' like an inanimate doll. (60)

Baby Face however survives the counter-coup which re-imprisons Ivan, changing sides and using that golden coach to decamp with stolen loot. It is this 'Baby Face' character who will grow in theatrical and thematic significance in Nowra's later plays. In *Inner Voices* she is required only to be a colourful performing cartoon—dancing, singing and using tarty sexual wiles—accompanied by her parasitic brother Pavlov who capitalises on her attractions, as *Visions'* Valera does with his cousin Juana. Nowra grew increasingly interested in developing the minor and marginal characters of his early plays—the Baby Faces, Maids and Valeras—giving them their own 'reasons' and mapping their drives through the plays' narratives.[32] However sketchy she may be in this first play, Baby Face is a survivor, and the first such in Nowra's performed theatre.[33] 'Baby Face' characters recur as vehicles of increased dramatic agency in such plays as *Crow*, in which the heroine must stage every performance she can to ensure her family's survival; and *Radiance*, whose Nona is a fully-realised version of the vibrantly alive if flakey showgirl, surviving by her wits and determination on the edge of an oppressive society. Where the plays concentrate on Aboriginal stories, Baby Face's survival strategies become confronting experiences for a white audience, as has been discussed in the preceding section.

The real fake

Survival in Nowra's theatre tends to be, in cultural rather than biological gender terms, a Feminine-ascribed potential, and one which grows in moral complexity and theatrical meaning as the plays develop. Imposter, performer, parasite, sexual adventurer and self-made social 'fake', the Baby Face persona recurs in the courtesan Lynch of *Visions*. This fake-Parisian Irish adventuress instructs her Maid in the art of survival during their retreat across the swamps, unsqueamishly looting the corpses of their own soldiers of 'anything that's valuable and can be sold or used' and taking it to her own escape coach (53). In *Sunrise*, the Czech Eva pretends not to know the meaning of the bawdy song she sings in English (many 'fake' characters, including Laurie Blake, are singers or performers) upsetting Tristan who jealously imagines a sensational past for his mysterious lover. The camp family annalist David is, however, quickly on to Eva's performance: 'We Australians are putty in the hands of a European lover' (43).

Frequently one fake will strive to evict another in a battle for control of territory, or at the very least of the few rags and scraps they may be able to scavenge. Tocky the compound girl in *Capricornia* survives through attaching herself to Norman, unceremoniously ousting his present housekeeper and concubine Opal: 'I'm going to take over both your jobs. If you don't go back to the camp, I'm going to smash your face in.' To Norman she fluently explains: 'She's gone back to the camp. She said I could have the job... in the kitchen' (64).

A fake destroyed. Barbara Sambell as Baby Face
(foreground), with Ian Cousins as Vladimir, Mark
Columbani as Peter, John Fulford as Mirovich, and Pauline
Ashleigh as Anna, in the opera *Inner Voices*, Victoria State
Opera, 1979. (Photo: David Parker)

Low origins, self-creation and desperate parasitism on the delusions and needs of the powerful likewise drive Roma of *Byzantine Flowers*, a survivor figure who like Tocky is theatrical in self-presentation but not an actual professional performer. Being black, Roma's social abjection, unlike Baby Face's class masquerade, is not capable of even token concealment, but her precarious life has given her resources as an accomplished liar, seducer and fantasist. Her grieving employer's delusion that she can see the spirits of the dead induces him to promote her as substitute for his wife and son simultaneously. Roma's mingled opportunism and desperation eventually excludes even her lover Eddie; when he begs her flee with him and to bash and rob Harris like any feeble drunk she recoils—Tom is no longer just another mark for her. In her rise to 'empire' Roma usurps the place in Tom Harris's home of the Aboriginal housekeeper Meg, a potentially tragic figure whose own parallel survivor story critics found underdeveloped.[34] Only at the play's end when Meg begs Roma to let her stay ('I ain't got another home. This is all I've got') does Roma understand that her supposed rival's pain is the same as her own.[35] In *Crow* and *Radiance* survival and attainment of a home become not exclusive individualistic prizes, but communal responsibilities.

The Jungle, full of desperate gambits of bloody-minded and slapstick survival, contains many female characters, notably the pethidine-addicted former rock star Cynthia, desperately and with foul-mouthed tenacity trying for an Antipodean come-back success. Structurally, the play's scene sequence balances two such survivors who are not in immediate competition: an apparently ultimately 'cheated' victim and a resolute and mendacious tart.[36] Olive begins and ends the play. In Scene 1 she is an Ivan figure, a retarded hybrid dog-girl imprisoned without language, filthy and incontinent. The death of her gaoler (and presumably mother) allows her emergence into the light of Sydney where she finds shelter, tuition and acceptance with the motherly dressmaker Gloria; and in the final scene she ecstatically levitates into the light of the rising sun. Of even tougher material is the young prostitute Nikki, who in Scenes 5 and 12 is being bashed and menaced by the murderous cop Metzger who believes she has stolen his ill-gotten drug loot. In a desperate twelve-hour game of seduction and wits Metzger, fuelled on booze and speed, tries every intimidation trick he knows to break Nikki, who, he reasons, is guilty because she hasn't confessed in order to take the

Rivalry for a home. Kylie Belling, Justine Saunders and
Simon Chilvers in *Byzantine Flowers*, Sydney Theatre
Company, 1989. (Photo: Branco Gaica)

heat off, as an innocent person would. 'The guilty survive a lot of punishment.' In an intense psychological duel the battered Nikki defiantly maintains her innocence until the arrival of the undercover cops, then gleefully admits that 'of course' she stole the money: 'I've been fucked by experts. You were easy.'[37] Nikki's sustained performance has won her the survival game; she is a real fake.

In *The Jungle* too is Scene 9, titled 'The Price of Prayer', which has been performed separately. This incisive and ambiguous playlet is set in a bourgeois Sydney penthouse before a visit to the opera. It anatomises the emotional and social interdependence of a parasite and his host without judging which is which. Here the self-creating survivor, though male, is culturally femininised through his relative social powerlessness. The wealthy but insecure businessman Sean is lover and also immigration sponsor of the Romanian Nicolae, who while awaiting his permanent residency in Australia feels like Sean's houseboy or 'kept woman'. In order to overcome this abjection, he demands that his wife and son join them from a cold and desperate Romania, and moreover that his relationship with Sean be concealed from the boy who must see his father as a manly provider. Sean, after a moment of appalled shock in which he understands that Nicolae may have been using him right from the inception of their affair in Romania, fights back. His terms are that, since he will be paying for it all as usual, Nicolae must continue to sleep with Sean during the visit, so that his wife at least is under no illusion as to the state of things. Sean ends by warning Nicolae to be on 'his best behaviour' when mixing with his friends at the post-opera party. 'The Price of Prayer' is a finely tuned emotional duel where at any moment it is difficult to assess where the real power lies; who is being used or blackmailed.[38] The misogynistic and homophobic Nicolae whose sexual involvement with Sean, instrumental to the requirements of survival, appears simultaneously genuine and 'fake', remains a moral enigma impossible to decipher. He may be an opportunistic tart, or an extension of the desperate hunger striker Michael of the teleplay *Hunger*, who pushes himself and his Australian supporters to the moral and physical limit in order to rescue his wife from Romania at the cost of his own death. Michael, like the socially dependent and hence feminised Nicolae, instrumentally and ruthlessly exploits his lovers, his sexuality and his own emotions and body alike as mediums for his family's survival.

A fake survives. Tony Phelan and Susan Prior in *The Jungle*,
Sydney Theatre Company, 1995. (Designer: Peter England.
Photo: Tracey Schramm)

Survival is what drives the motley contestants in *Miss Bosnia*'s beauty contest, for which the first prize is a place, not quite in the golden escape coach, but on the United Nations truck out of Sarajevo. Again, survival means moral compromise and exploitation and transformation of the body, since the women must create a conventional mask of femininity in a life-and-death situation in which such concerns appear at best incongruous, at worst frivolously irrelevant. Each woman must transform herself into glamour-puss Baby Face and perform a short entertainment routine, outwitting her fellows in the best soap-bitch tradition. The reward for the most enthusiastic, skilled and heartfelt performance of gendered masquerade is a chance of survival, though at the cost of deserting their besieged community. For all the play's performative élan and farcical comedy, this rigid imposition of the conventionally Feminine dramatises in miniature the madness of the savage political conflicts outside this small room, waged under the pretext of racial purity. But since one of the beauty contestants is a desperate deserting soldier in drag, it is easy to guess whom the macho General Jez will select as winner. Boris's hybrid impersonation of the Feminine is necessarily the most convincing, since he produces the masquerade as camp artifice rather than as nature. Besides, the contest is rigged for other reasons: Boris has been performing sexual services for the infatuated General in the lavatory. Although all the *Miss Bosnia* women are temperamental survivors, Boris the self-created 'woman' most successfully combines the elements of the type: dubious origins, driving desperation, engaging performance skills, kitsch glamour and sexual opportunism.

As a clear example of a real fake 'feminised' survivor, Boris is comparable to the android Betty in the 1996 teleplay *Directly From My Heart to You*, a hybrid character who is only apparently human. As played by Kimberley Davies and costumed by Annie Marshall, Betty is high camp incarnate in a leather bustier: a technological Frankenstein's Monster of the Feminine; a punter's wet dream of the conventional playmate in towering heels and designer red leather bondage costumes. She is also lethal, determined to survive and to become self-authored, eliminating not only all those with a hand in her creation but also the 'younger model' Rita Dove, her supplanter equipped with superior colour-vision technology. The character of Betty suggests that the ideal of feminine glamour, even when

Parasite and host? Yves Stening and Russell Kiefel in *The Price of Prayer*, Sydney Theatre Company, 1995. (Photo: Tracey Schramm)

constructed as product of her culture's most technologically potent visions, is, when viewed from within, a spiritually dead and desperate state which reduces the moral dimensions of survival to a mere computerised drive. The hybrid Betty, like Ivan in being only part-human, is already a walking epitome of that monstrously artificial and glamorised self-performance, which the *Miss Bosnia* women are expected to strive for. Survival through masquerade becomes the privilege, and the burden, of the Feminine.

Two political fakes

The paradox of the real fake assumes politicised and confronting coloration in *The Temple* and *The Incorruptible*, Nowra's topical parables of Australian public life wherein the 'fakes' retain their masculine social identities. The Frankenstein theme is used as a metaphor for those national phantasms to which we have been, and continue to be, enthralled. In both plays there is a double movement of teaching and surpassing of the teacher. Laurie, already an upwardly mobile 'self-made' man, enlists as his Sorcerers' Apprentice the ambitious Nick, seducing him with power, Porsches and playmates. Crashing the Porsche cripples Nick and lobotomises his humanity. Now on crutches and full of metal plates, he resembles a lurching B-movie cyborg crawling snake-like on the floor.[39] 'Quite literally', he tells Laurie, 'I'm an iron man' (37). He is remade as Laurie's creation: 'Instead of screwing girls, you'll screw companies' (39). Animated by pain and drugs rather than by bolts of Tesla electricity,[40] Nick's mind works overtime, promoting him from apprentice to tutor through orchestrating a series of audacious take-overs which brings Laurie to the top of his heap—Australian of the Year. This coke-stoked Mephistopheles proves an over-reacher and Laurie's South Sea Bubble bursts, taking the savings of 'Mr and Mrs Australia' with it. Laurie and Brenda, fakes with attitude, do their own moonlight flit from an economically devastated Australia with what's left of their stolen loot. Even in ignominious Libyan exile when planning their next assault on the luckless pre-capitalist economy of Vietnam,[41] Nick remains Laurie's henchman and symbiotic son, an obsessed Creature on the verge of self-destruction and bound forever to his beer Baron Frankenstein. By contrast, *The Temple*'s true autonomous hybrid—the pupil who outstrips his creator—is Terry Macarthur, who ultimately transfers his fascinated allegiance from

The rewards of the feminine masquerade. Khristina Totos,
Russell Dykstra and Nicholas Papademetriou in *Miss Bosnia*,
La Boite, 1995. (Photo: Justine Walpole)

Laurie back to his hated dead father. On a treacherous mission to lure his exiled mentor into the grasp of the Australian Securities Commission, the playboy Terry pays apt tribute to what Laurie has taught him: 'You created me... You got me when I was vulnerable. You've taught me to be ruthless' (89).

Though compelled by an undercurrent of compensatory needs, Laurie himself remains an essentially comic character and anti-hero of black farce; a Jonsonian obsessive who continually bounces back, cushioned by an optimism as inflated as Alan Bond's airship. While the character can be performed with darkly psychologised intentions (see Chapter 1) in generic terms he is of the company of Alfred Jarry's clown-monster Ubu in his 1896 puppet farce *Ubu Roi*. As clownish grotesques, Laurie and his tacky retinue are simultaneously menacing and comically indestructible.[42] His consort Brenda is the epitome of nouveau-riche kitsch, Lady Macbeth in faux leopard lycra. While driven by survivor competitiveness and the need to humiliate the old money which has kept him out, Laurie is as blissfully unaware as Mrs Malaprop of his significant clangers: 'I'm the Jesus Christ of entrepreneurs—I smash temples!' (57) His characteristic misremembering of what exactly Christ smashed is typical of Nowra's comic subversion of the eighties greed ethos.[43] Laurie is however not just a self-made survivor, but also monetarist Australia's own deregulated Creature. 'You encouraged me—you created me' he accuses the audience, rounding on his supposed persecutors in the traditional monster-movie *scène à faire*, 'Now you're turning on me—like a nation of cowards' (85). In theatrical terms the working-class survivor Laurie is a real fake: what the audience sees is just what they get and in the recent past what they lauded: a cowboy with a mobile phone. Laurie can, however, manipulate his larrikin persona as conscious performance, in strategies designed to bluff and confuse his supercilious foes: 'You know how Australians play the professional larrikin', muses the New Zealand patrician Lorna St John (44). The stage larrikin—a demotic social persona assumed as camouflage by the masculine middle-class male on the make— has a significant history as an easy acceptance and self-validation icon for audiences of New Wave Australian drama. Nowra's Laurie Blake—like Bob Hawke, everybody's 'mate'—throws both our political and our theatrical Creatures back in our faces.

It is less easy, however, to celebrate Ion Stafford of *the Incorruptible* as Australia's Creature, though he undoubtedly is. 'I'm not your

Frankenstein's creature: Nick as iron man. Paul Goddard in
The Temple, Sydney Theatre Company, 1994. (Photo: Stuart
Campbell)

mate,' he coldly reprimands the minority leader he is about to expel from the coalition (16). The phrase 'self-made man', indispensable to the petit-bourgeois fantasy-narrative of individualistic striving in an asocial jungle world, becomes in Ion's case infused with sinister gothic resonance. In theatrical terms, Ion's polio limp and the bizarre electrical contraption he uses on his legs suggest the conventional wired-together Frankenstein's monster, but one who blindly disowns his discursively constructed nature. In cultural, or indeed ontological, terms, self-made men are oxymorons, monsters. Ion pulls the national confidence trick in a different register to the larrikin Laurie, by offering Australia the political oxymoron of a united community of rugged individualists.

As a character, Ion hardly presents as an obvious fake like Laurie or Baby Face. Neither clownishly grotesque nor forgivably entertaining, he compels attention and respect. Ion knows his scriptures better than Laurie, and his own self-comparisons with Christ are disturbingly sincere: 'You are either for me or against me' (69). His mode of audience interpellation is in moral terms more troublingly seductive since, while his vision is as monochrome as the automaton Betty's, he turns back on his audience their own hybrid intellectual and emotional relativity through gambits of menace and seduction. He advances plausible half-truths as revealed dogma and extrapolates partial or conditional assent as total agreement, and thus as legitimation, for divisive populist policies. If we assent to the validity of his examples of wrong-righting, we are expected to swallow the entire fallacy. Ion continually solicits complicity through moments of reasonable appeal which recoil in our faces, as when he protests to the patrician Simon about the early release of a rape-murderer and then bribes him with a blatantly politicised appointment as Chief Justice (39-42). Refusing to understand the logical, political or ethical limits of his homespun philosophy, Ion is a fake who doesn't know he is one. He is Albert promoting himself as plausible Prime Minister material. 'I am the real thing', he tells the Police Commissioner who hesitates at applying police violence to break up a strike. 'Imitations like you always have to be on guard because it knows imitation. It doesn't know the real thing.' (28)

The inclusion in the play of Ion's alter ego, the cynical and comically appalling political fixer Gabo, lends tonal and structural balance. When dressing down Ion in the play's *scène à faire*, Gabo even fakes quoting the Bible back at him:

Your incorruption has corrupted the entire State. In order to service your vision, you have created a sewer of such magnificent proportions that it has become the unofficial government. You have dug that noxious pit as surely as if you had used the space yourself. And you know what the Bible says: he that diggeth a pit, shall fall into it. (71)

'The argument between purity and impurity', Rushdie says, 'is also the argument between Robespierre and Danton.'[44] Impurity incarnate and a shameless fake, Gabo is a classic amoral political survivor who, like Danton, doesn't survive Robespierre-Ion's systematic assassination of his erstwhile mentors, but at least has the virtue of knowing what he is. By contrast, the 'self-made' millionaire Ion is blind to the relative nature of his populist political certainties, which he inevitably presents in terms of immutable moral absolutism. He elevates childhood's partial perceptions and fancied emotional betrayals into pastiched evidence of heaven-sent 'revelations' of Damascus road proportions. He recalls for Louise seeing his young cousin Denise having sex with a farmhand:

I knew, like I was hit by lightning, like it had cleaved me in two, that people were like Denise and the farm-hand, that they would suddenly change and turn on you. And with this revelation, because it was a revelation, came an awareness of my strength. That I need only to be told something once, that I need only to be shown something once in order to learn the lesson it was imparting to me. (63-64)

For this character there is no question of rehearsing or relativising such experiences as material for a developed or dynamic understanding of life's complex praxis: received insights must be preserved with the authority of their pure primal authenticity. Ion's island-clinic of cancer patients, run by a charlatan in whom he has total confidence, appears a sinisterly entropic 'isle of the dead' (46) which nobody leaves alive, a static counter-image to the transformational island of Cythera.

Just as Laurie's ratty vitality seduces and destroys the top-drawer art specialist Miranda, who has coached him in the rapid acquisition of art knowledge (and indeed bankable artworks), the inflexible Ion morally seduces and destroys his own tutor, the emotionally vulnerable public relations expert Louise. Ion plays

Creature to her Frankenstein, letting himself be tutored and remade through the arcana of media self-presentation. Even authenticity is performative, assumable as a mask like any other, but Ion can't see this paradox.

> LOUISE: You're blinking.
> ION: The lights are so bright.
> LOUISE: Blinking means you're lying.
> ION: I'm not lying.
> LOUISE: I know that, but the viewers don't. (24)

Louise, angry with her father over his sexual betrayal of her mother, and bearing a fairly average burden of complex private pain, eludes the discomfort of ethical relativity by becoming the captive of Ion's serene asexuality and asceticism. Through aiding Ion's political suppressions and legal coercions of those citizens discerned as too messily negotiating the ethical impurities and social contingencies of their hybrid society, Louise abjects her own guilts. Only by destroying Ion, 'her' creation, can Louise ultimately possess its artificial perfection; while surviving in a physical sense, spiritually she is as destroyed as Juana mouthing Lynch's words.

Ion as Australia's post-imperial Creature has suppressed his own necessarily hybrid origins within countless preceding and competing social narratives. At bottom, his self-taught philosophy and uncompromising politics are essentially comfort-seeking and sentimental, demonstrating that simplistic aestheticising of contemporary political complexities which characterises populist fascism. As moral mentor or political saviour he proves but the naïve artifact of his own wilful bricolage: a *Readers' Digest* Mussolini, a mulga-wood messiah. In the ultimate irony, through imagining himself supra-historically validated as the uncompromising 'real thing' of Australian public life, the austere bush Robespierre is revealed as the very epitome of sinister kitsch.

Chapter 4

Performing histories

Cultural performances

Whether formalised or spontaneous, embedded performances in Nowra's theatre are the principle means by which outlines of past, future or alternative histories are placed to the forefront of his 'detached' theatrical structures. Bodies in the act of performance become transfigured with significance beyond their narrative plot roles, and inscribed with repressed public and private histories, whether utopian or dystopian. When Nowra's characters desire to impose dreams or to engage for their survival in acts of counter-theatre, they will typically mount a seductive, subversive or compelling performance, co-opting their fellows and even their spectators into a process of which the outcome is ambiguous and mutually transformative (see Chapter 2). Much is at stake in these performances, where the body is the vehicle for painful, intense and sometimes inarticulate bids for self-proclamation. Identity is not revealed as already complete but created within the process of responding to outside scripts and challenges. Insistence on the theatricality of theatre and the performativity of self renders these plays both dramatically compelling and typically 'detached'—estranged in a Brechtian sense.

In a clear example of the condensed theatricalising of repressed history the ergot-infected soldiers of *Inside the Island*, besides being possessed by private enthusiasms, become also phantoms of empire: seers of the imperial past and prophets of its future (see Chapter 3). But even in Nowra's post-1985 scripts, which appear more realist in

dramaturgical texture than the formal and musical structures of the
early plays, metaphors of performance still carry a large burden of
complex meanings. Metatheatrical self-presentation as a drive
towards survival, for example, is evident in *Miss Bosnia*'s audition
sequences and beauty contest performances, where the contestants
must excel in creating a fantasy or dream persona transcending both
their everyday selves and their grim situation. *Radiance* will be
examined below as an example of such performative complexity at
work in a realist-seeming script. The processes of theatre as a
metaphor for self-invention will be demonstrated through analysis
of *Così* with its structures of audition, rehearsals, improvisation and
performance.

Culture and dreams are communicated in Nowra's theatre by
self-conscious performative acts on the part of his characters, and
comedy or catastrophe may ensue when the sometimes bewildered
onstage audience seeks (or fails) to comprehend the full meaning of
the performance enacted for them, or to respond appropriately. *The
Golden Age*, in particular, is insistently structured around its
characters' attempts to exchange and conserve communal rituals of
which the meanings become alien when undertaken before new
onstage audiences. Pantomimic acts of sympathetic magic also occur
in this play, like Betsheb and Mac's rainmaking dance (25-26) or their
energetic if frustrating fertility ritual (19-20). While Francis is ill at
ease witnessing the formal Greek tragedy performed by the Archers
in Hobart, he responds with energetic improvisation to the forest
people's own performative style. Francis performs for Betsheb his
athletic football routine (23), a Melbourne version of a masculine
mating dance, which complements Betsheb's scene with Mac. This
mime functions as his own cultural vision, and operates as ceremonial
exchange for the 'King Lear' play through which his hosts have
expressed their sacred mythology.

Music and verse are indispensable to Nowra's concept of non-
naturalistic theatre, as is a wide range of theatrical devices:
metamorphic shape-shifting, carnival disguising, impersonations,
recitations, rituals and internal plays. Consciously undertaken
performances by dramatic characters are a traditional structural
method of communicating obscured or latent meanings significant
to the larger plot; and in Nowra's work some kind of formalisation
via performance or self-display appears intrinsic to the characters'

interaction. Such playlets may also serve to elucidate a society's cultural values, drawing attention to their ideal or prophetic importance through a marked change of dramatic style. For example, the Shelton family of *Sunrise* consolidates their romantic family mythology through their performances of the Orientalist fable 'The Blind Singer and the King'. But the fullness and waywardness of meanings in these metatheatrical performances may exceed their authorised textual encodings. Venice, who witnesses the performance of her family's mythology, interprets the 'tiger' character of 'The Blind Singer', a consuming force who must be destroyed for reasons of love, to be the demon of guilt haunting her beloved grandfather Clarrie, and so she shoots him so that he may gain release. Some Nowra performances are private idiosyncratic rituals like the Shelton family's pageant, some may be brief dances, songs or recitations, and others are more elaborate and formal 'translations' or appropriations of canonical dramatic texts.

Crow's family possesses two social rituals. Her husband Patrick has taught them familial and historical continuity via the handshake, thus clasping 'the hand that shook the hand, that shook the hand, that shook the hand of Napoleon' (18). Her son Boofhead transfers this continuity to Mrs Gavin (14), indicating their kinship as outsiders. When bullying and seducing her lawyer Thompson into aiding her quest for legal rights, Crow tries the same gambit on him, and then varies it to a different ritual:

[*She advances on* THOMPSON *and strokes his cheek.*]

These fingers have touched the cheek of my mother, who in turn has touched her mother's cheek, who in turn touched her mother's, stretching back and back, for thousands of years... Where we're standing was where mothers touched the cheek of their daughters for thousands of years. Now it's gone. This land belonged to us but was taken... I'm not turning the other cheek. They can slap my cheek all they like, but I'm not going to turn it... I'm not gonna be forced to be a wanderer in my own land.

What Thompson then receives, besides a kiss on the cheek, is a stinging slap, Crow's payback for his discarded daughter 'Lily in the Compound' (60-61). Crow is tough and relentless in trying to arrange her children's lives according to her family script, nearly estranging her son Vince and 17-year-old Ruth in so doing. Ruth in particular, whom Crow magics and bullies into a doomed marriage with Vince, is the object of her particular severity and vigilance. At the play's conclusion this mother-daughter bond, stretched almost to breaking point by the disruptions of colonised life, is restored as Crow learns to accept help:

> [*To* RUTH] Over here...
>
> > RUTH *comes closer.*
>
> Closer.
>
> > RUTH *comes closer.* CROW *raises her hand.* RUTH *flinches, thinking she is going to be hit. Instead* CROW *touches* RUTH's *face with her fingers.*
>
> Remember these fingers on your cheek. (72)

Even the most recessive Nowra characters may do a party piece indicative of their needs and beliefs, the energy of which surpasses the comedy of a sometimes erratic, imperfect or naïve expression. Albert sings '*Frère Jacques*' in fractured French (he doesn't understand what it means) and proudly recites to Edward his childhood poem about Smokey the Dog (81, 92). Sergeant Collins of *Inside the Island* does a ventriloquist routine with a sock puppet to amuse Susan Dawson: being all of seventeen years old, she disdains this childish entertainment. Andy the idiot child loves recitations of 'Little Black Sambo', while as prelude to the doomed cricket match Lillian Dawson recites her muscular-christian poem 'Pure at Heart', proclaiming it 'eternally true'. Tocky in *Capricornia* is unimpressed with Norman's reading of 'world-famous' passages from the *Rubaiyat* of Omar Khayyam, and even less so with his own poetry: what she likes is Lewis Carroll's 'Jabberwocky', which while seeming 'bloody stupid' to Norman holds considerable emotional importance for Tocky (53-54). At the Act One curtain in *The Temple*, Laurie Blake leads the cast in regaling the audience with an inspirational corporate motivational anthem 'Blakey's Dream':

> Everything not nailed down
> is there for you to take
> every day you'll reign supreme
> living example of Blakey's Dream (35)

'We'll take on the world and Blake it!', he concludes. Later as an ebullient Australian of the Year, proclaiming to the audience 'private enterprise works!' Laurie sings us his own advertising jingle 'Expand or Die!' (58-59). Laurie is a typical 'real fake' sincere performer (see Chapter 3) unabashedly celebrating his self-referential axioms: 'Why will I inflict my voice on you? Because I believe every single word. I wrote them!' No matter how kitsch or derivative their expression, Nowra's autodidact characters do believe their own 'every word', and as vehicles of thematic import their jingles and recitations must be taken seriously. While formal recitation or song are lacking in *The Incorruptible*, Ion's blood-and-soil election speeches are impressively sincere as self-performances; by contrast his rehearsed television presentations appear less so.

Self-performance can also bring to attention suppressed or inarticulate meanings and energies at the edge of the dramatic action which question or resituate its principal transactions. In *Sunrise* the linguistic outsiders Eva and Ly surprise the Sheltons during their cultivated party by the disruptive power of their performances. The Czech-speaking Eva, trying perhaps to communicate emotional caution to the romantically besotted Tristan, sings in English a provokingly bawdy ditty she claims she learned from a sailor. The Vietnamese refugee Ly astounds and embarrasses his liberal audience by reciting in 'rude English' his 'poem of exile' about 'communism destroying [his] home' where his rage and pain burn through the surface of the words: 'As he recites it, his body grows stiff with anger and his voice louder. He loses sense of where he is, only the words and emotions now exist for him' (36-37). In order to announce the outbreak of war a jubilant Cho in *Capricornia* interrupts the social dance tunes of the humid Territorian Christmas party by changing the record to loud Chinese music. 'We will beat the Japanese! This is a song of war. You are next! Japan will take over you too' (44e). These embedded formal recitations, songs and tunes form the repertoire through which characters variously enact their self-presentations and/or deep emotions, their dreams and memories (true and false), their social claims and their drives towards transformation.

Spectacles within spectacles: Iphigenia in Tasmania

The embedded performance, or formal play within a play, is a traditional theatrical alienation device used insistently in Nowra's theatre: indeed it is almost his dramaturgical trademark. Writing of

Summer of the Aliens, Joanne Tompkins sees its mirror-box performance structure as 'not designed to imitate *a* play, rather... it imitates *play,* rehearsal of identity and self.'[1] Where actual playlets are not present, formal embedded rituals may take the form of a carnival costume ball, a cricket match, a dinner party or such para-theatrical displays as the slide-show of paintings in *The Temple* produced by Miranda to instruct Laurie in the mysteries of the art which appreciates. Ironically it includes Arthur Boyd's 'Half-caste Bride' in which 'the two men play cards to see who gets her' (27)—Miranda's own situation as one of Laurie's trophies. Beyond their alienating function, these various spectacles and performances further the plays' dialectic and complicate our readings of the frame action. In post-colonial theatre 'metatheatre... is often a self-conscious method of re-negotiating, re-working—not just re-playing—the past and present.'[2]

The Golden Age contains the most extensive examples of what Tompkins calls 'counter-discursive' metatheatre; the reworking and taking possession of canonical texts in order to perform the history and meanings of a subjected group. The forest people's communal myth is enacted in their energetic and pantomimic 'King Lear' playlet, a hybridised romance version of Shakespeare, itself the hybridised redaction of countless other 'Lear' narratives with varied outcomes.[3] The immediate dramatic uses of the 'King Lear' playlet have been discussed in Chapter 2, but citations of another ambivalently tragic myth also contextualise and modify the action of *The Golden Age.* The story of the lost people's return is itself framed as an interior play through a recital of Euripides' tragi-comedy *Iphigenia in Tauris.* By situating the socialite Archer family's rather comically solemn recitation of the Greek text as its prelude, Nowra invites us to read his story through the textual medium of Euripides' play. The 'Lear' material and the Iphigenia myths used in *The Golden Age* exist in dramatic form in both tragic and romantic versions. Their selective re-working and quotation in a modern Australian play destabilise genre and render narrative closure provisional, suggesting the open-ended nature of cultural outcomes and their metamorphic and transitional encodings. Behind each version, whether tragic or romantic, is always visible a generic shadow of the path not taken.

The plot of *Iphigenia in Tauris* concerns a lost Greek princess, the youngest daughter of a shattered family, who has been spirited away by Artemis from a grim scene of sacrifice. Her father Agamemnon has offered her life at Aulis in exchange for a wind to carry his fleet to the Trojan war. In this alternative tradition, Artemis has substituted an animal for the sacrifial victim and removed Iphigenia from her homeland Argos, where she is believed dead. Now she lives exiled on the savage land of Tauris ruled by the barbarian king Thoas, as the unwilling slave-priestess of a savage cult which sacrifices strangers. Accompanied only by his faithful friend Pylades, her brother Orestes is cast onshore at Tauris, an exile who must flee the maddening furies who continually torment him for the murder of his mother Clytemnestra, who had herself slain Agamemnon to avenge the sacrifice of Iphigenia. The priestess prepares to perform the customary sacrifice, but the lost siblings recognise each other just in time and escape from Tauris towards 'home'.

Generically, this frame text is a tragi-comedy with an impact dependent on strong intertextual relationships. It is Euripides' romantic reworking of his own better-known tragedy *Iphigenia at Aulis*, in which the Homeric story is adhered to and no goddess intervenes to avert the princess's sacrifice to imperial military ambitions. The Archers' opening declamation of the 'happy ending' Iphigenia text leaves the narrative outcome of *The Golden Age* suspended but does have some proleptic agency. Elizabeth Archer as the princess declaims to her husband, playing the exiled and maddened matricide Orestes, 'You will never return home. You will die in pain and lie in an unmarked grave' (2). This foretells William's fate, since his engagement with the mystery of the imprisoned tribe, and his attempts to decode and 'capture' their language and mythology, so exile him from his family and his former self that he suicides through guilt and despair. He has fallen under the spell of Betsheb, the imprisoned but still powerful princess, and let himself become a willing sacrifice.

At the play's second last scene (2, 17) the Archer's Euripides performance resumes, with the part of Orestes now assumed as a dynastic duty by Elizabeth's son Peter. 'When a man dies a house, a name, is lost. When a woman dies it means nothing' (73) recites Elizabeth; yet in her own family, as in Betsheb's, the reverse would appear to be the case: men are replaceable and women are the real culture-bearers and survivors. On the metatheatrical level, the Archers' ritualised performance of the private family myth frames the partial return from exile, not of the cultivated patrician Iphigenia/ Elizabeth, but of her abjected double Iphigenia/Betsheb. Nowra's partial and suspended closing of the Euripides frame-text immediately signals Betsheb's final release from her enforced duty in the Hobart asylum of presiding as lonely priestess over 'scientific' rituals which sacrifice her own kin. In the Archers' recitation, Iphigenia recognises her exiled brother Orestes just as she is about to sacrifice him, and together they will escape the land of Aulis. However this pattern is reversed in the main plot, since it is now her exiled brother Francis/Orestes who is about to kill Betsheb, but realises he is trying to kill his own pain and instead effects their escape from the asylum. In the forest, Peter prophesises to Francis, 'She destroyed my father just as she'll destroy you' (76); hence Betsheb's destructive potential is perhaps only suspended.

This myth of Iphigenia in lonely cultural exile immediately connects with the historical story of white convict Tasmanians exiled by imperial dictates on their own savage shore, making it an appropriate vehicle for Australian re-fashioning. The exalted 'princess' status of the Greek heroine is split and refracted between various female characters: the Hobart matriarch Elizabeth Archer; Ayre, the forest people's cultural repository and mother-figure; and Betsheb, their charismatic but vulnerable last survivor. As we have seen in the analysis of gothic motifs in Chapter 3, Francis and Betsheb are the separated brother and sister of this Tasmanian story wherein images of both black and white Australia's historical abjections are cross-read and intertwined. Francis, tormented by the furies of war on the savage shore of Europe, and by remorse over his shamed rejection of his mother, is an appropriate reworking of his Greek prototype: a neo-convict Australian Orestes. Orestes says, 'I live nowhere and everywhere. I am an outcast, hated by the gods' (4). Francis assumes guilt for his participation in his culture's madness: confined in a German military prison for shooting a rocket scientist, he grimly recognises the justice of his convict status. 'This prison perfectly suits my state of mind; I have been bred for it, just as I have been bred to kill' (69). He and Betsheb both encode hybridised aspects of a fragmented and brutalised white imperial history, while Betsheb and her family carry in addition superimposed histories of both invaded Aboriginal peoples and white convict 'exiles'. *The Golden Age* selects for attention two canonical dramas which deal with separated families, persecuted princesses, exile in savage countries, imperial war and the guilts of 'civilisation'. Within a post-colonial reading of the play, various indeterminate resonances are mobilised.

Is the fearsome Tauris, country of madness, exile and pain, to be read as wartime Crete, wartime Europe, or convict Tasmania? Is the savage heath of 'outcastin' of the 'Lear' story to be seen as the Tasmanian forest or the Hobart prison-asylum? And if we read the forest people's story as a metaphor for aspects of Tasmanian Aboriginal history, who indeed are the 'civilised' Greeks and who the 'savage' Taurians? In this drama of intertextual hybridising which both utilises and exceeds its canonical sources, cultural readings remain richly complex and ambivalent.

Musical theatre

Thanks to the collaboration of Sarah de Jong, Nowra's early scripts are more properly seen as music theatre, even as quasi-musicals in the old J.C. Williamson's sense. Their original songs and musical passages frame mood, ironise events and enhance characterisation. *Visions* has five songs and five pieces of mood music, to be played by the disaffected band of Paraguayan musicians who accompany Lynch on her presidential progress. De Jong's instrumentation is simple and deliberately naïve, written for two musicians using such instruments as 'a portable harmonium, a guitar, a basic drum kit... three or four glasses and any other instruments suitable: for example, tambourine, tin whistle, claves, guiro etc'. (83) Since the principal dramatic function of these mute musicians is to express the occulted meanings of the suppressed indigenous Paraguayan culture, their interventions are theatrically important. 'You wouldn't know anything from *Tristan and Isolde*, would you?' Lynch sceptically asks the performers playing their native music. 'Weber? Bizet?' (8)

The musicians' hybrid or dutifully imitative music frames and ironises the dominators' own spectacles: for example, a waltz forms the overture to Lynch's well-rehearsed humiliation of Lopez's crass sisters, undertaken with joke props from a novelty shop (1, 5). The same tune recurs in more sinister context during the 'Bal Masqué à la Paraguay' (1, 7) when after the brutal fight staged by Lopez to demonstrate the declaration of war, he calls to the musicians for a waltz and sweeps Lynch into the dance. The naval encounter with the Triple Alliance, when the Paraguayan flagship (like the HMAS *Melbourne*) rams its own fleet, is generically framed as Offenbachian opéra-bouffe through the sprightly waltz and march which act as overture and incidental music to the ladies' cliff-top viewing of this spectacle through opera glasses (1, 9).[4] Three songs and an instrumental overture occur during Lynch's battlefield pageant (2, 3), where the story of Paraguay's intended future is enacted in childishly naïve style. Even when defeat and disaster overwhelm the dictators and their ragged armies (2, 6), Lynch's largely mute Maid introduces a subversive and quirky comment and counterpoint through her song 'She Likes to Roll Cigars'—not exactly *Carmen Jones* but still a recognisable burlesque of *Carmen*. It appears the natives have in fact learnt something of Bizet, for their own purposes.

The most organic fusion of music and theme arising from the Nowra-de Jong collaboration is the 1980 radio play *The Song Room*, which can be performed theatrically. Pat, the traumatised returned soldier, has for years been in a hospital with other aphasics unable to communicate his wartime experience to anyone, even his daughter and grand-daughter. When Mary, a bossy music therapist, organises a group of patients to play toy instruments, Pat discovers a rhythmic medium through which he can after so many years express his thoughts in erratic verse and song:

> I can talk my name.
> My name is Pat,
> My name is Pat,
> Pat is my name. (137)

At his grand-daughter's children's birthday party Pat seizes his chance and arranges the small guests into a music group, through which at last he is able to speak to his estranged daughter Jane:

> Jane, my only Jane
> Only five.
> You are in your cot,
> I can't tell you.
> Mum is dead,
> The blood is in my head.
>
> Listen, my baby,
> Mum can't tell you
> What's wrong with my head.
> She is dead
> And blood is in my head. (146)

Jane is embarrassed and cuts him short. Mary too is horrified as her rigidly structured lesson is taken over by Pat's outburst of communal repressed experiences, out of place and literally unsayable in peacetime Australia:

> The dead are in
> My broken head
> Hear them!
> I'm talking
> For us all.
> I'm talking to
> The living dead.
> Listen to what
> Is in my head. (155)

Although the music has 'set [him] free' (156), Pat's verbal outpouring of his mental torment is his last, and as Mary wrestles for control of the class he relapses into silence. The play's final aural image is of Mary leading her reduced class in singing a resolutely cheerful 'Row, Row, Row Your Boat' (159). *The Song Room* is an oblique species of Gallipoli play, a 'perfect chamber piece'[5] in which Albinoni's 'Adagio in G', to which Pat listens on the radio, seems to forecast its insistent use as tragic leitmotif in the Peter Weir/David Williamson 1981 film *Gallipoli*.

Dressing 'up'

The volatility and metamorphic potential of the theatrical subject within specific histories can be externalised and suggested through costume. Frequent in Nowra's theatre are incidents of costume change by which a character dresses 'up'—upwards in a class sense—externalising an ideal or potential self which has been obscured through historical or racial marginalisation. As Helen Gilbert explains of vestimentary codes in post-colonial theatre, they do not merely '[deliver] as self-evident particular gender, racial, social and national identities and then [recede] into the background as mere clothing' of the verbal text. Rather, a 'garment is a problematical signifier because the paradox of its transparency conceals a rhetorical power.'[6] Costume textualises those narratives by which holders of strong visions attempt to clothe the bodies and imaginations of those with whom, willingly or unwillingly, they are collaborating to make history. It can also encode the 'rhetorical power', resistance and dreams of transcendence of the colonised or degraded 'half-caste'. Boofhead in *Crow*, a dreamer, clown and seer, appears in resplendent cross-cultural motley wearing the 'Jesse James' cowboy hat he won in a mouse-swallowing bet, and one-lensed sunglasses which fell off a drunken 'Yank' (22). These shreds of the signifying costumes from the popular movieland cultural icons of Australia's powerful new 'allies' constitute not mere mimicry, but are worn as self-inventing trophies signalling small triumphs of appropriation of white-held property. So too the sisters of *Radiance*, whose home is now an 'international' tourist resort, carnivalise and re-inscribe Japanese costume.

Capricornia, an epic of occulted histories disguised as open secrets, commences with an impressive ritualistic mime piece, seducing the audience with a glamorous lie that obscurely tells a truth:

> *Darkness. Gradually a figure emerges: a beautiful woman. She wears a huge, swinging dress. She speaks gibberish, though it could be Indonesian. It is* NORMAN's *mother, the* JAVANESE PRINCESS. *From out of her huge dress* NORMAN *emerges in a white 1930s suit.* (1)

The Javanese Princess embodies Oscar Shillingworth's desperate lie about Norman's birth, a well-meant concealment fantasy which he 'stole' from Constance's dying white father, whose 'little Javanese princess' he begged Oscar to raise 'like a queen' (47). Constance, the half-caste mother of Tocky, instead became pregnant in the compound to the misnamed 'Protector' of Aborigines and died of venereal disease. This 'Princess's' ritualised 'birthing' delivers a living oxymoron; from the rich textured canopy of the dress emerges a black prince clad in immaculate tropical whites, bearing himself with all his assumed caste's consciousness of innate superiority. This is in one sense a false identity, but the high-caste clothes suggest its dimensions of truth: as an Aboriginal person in a racist society Norman is granted rare access to that serene consciousness of self-worth of those who take utterly for granted their privilege. While being himself fitted for a new suit for his courtroom performance in Norman's defence ('up here they'll expect a lawyer from the south to look the ant's pants'), the lawyer Bightit advises Norman to try to 'look humble' in court': both characters must put on an act. Coerced into the 'theatre' of the murder trial ('Port Zodiac's got no wireless or entertainment') Norman still disdains discarding this 'prince' identity for his 'real' one or performing 'the poor blackfella routine' (78).

Norman's various stages of self-discovery involve costume changes; the Javanese Prince costume is last seen at the chaotic Christmas party which appropriately frames the (re)birth of another 'real' Norman. This new identity, at least to the whites, now seems the original and irreducible truth—the chained half-caste dog-boy 'No Name' who crawls on all fours and eats dirt. Oscar remembers with guilt the stubbornly surviving baby dumped on him by his feckless brother: 'You should have seen him... like a blowfly. Caked in dirt, snot everywhere. Hair so matted we had to cut it off' (47). In his imprisonment, again chained by the neck like a dog, Norman is a hybrid of all his identities and can discard none of them. Fat Anna performs a ritual which rebirths him as Nawnim, explaining the significance of the name his mother gave him: 'That's not a dog's name. That's a dingo's name. Dingos are important to your people. You be proud of it' (95). These abrupt somatic metamorphoses through costume signal Bakhtin's 'spasmodic' or 'crisis-type' narration.[7] Norman is an on-going accretion of all the names or costumes he has worn; his naked skin as a newborn 'the colour of honey' (84); the mud-caked infant; the white sahib in tropical costume; the hard-working station-owner in jackaroo costume acting like a 'proper little King of Siam' (74); his dog-like prison chains; and even the Javanese Prince. 'Identity... can be added to, but it does not add up to a final sum or solution.'[8] This shape-shifting via costume and gesture indicates a solution to what Gilbert and Tompkins discern as theatre's dilemma as an iconic art-form; 'to avoid essentialist constructions of race and gender while recognising the irreducible specificity of their impact on subject formation'(206).

Beautiful gowns and ball dresses are the mode by which women characters reach towards the social respect and sexual homage from which their class, ethnicity or historical oppression preclude them. In an ambivalent masquerade prefiguring, in utopian mode, their country's liberation, the *Miss Bosnia* contestants fabricate images of ideal glamour in order to transcend their own and their nation's plight—beautiful female figures being conventional symbols of national identity and sovereignty. Tocky in *Capricornia*, the racial and linguistic hybrid, likewise begins to transform herself, wearing an incongruous combination of ballet tutu and an old men's shirt, when she re-discovers the book *Alice in Wonderland* from which her adoptive father read poems to her and which contains '[her] memories' (66-67).

However, when pregnant and wearing one of Marigold's more stylish dresses, she is presciently fearful that it will be Mrs Hollower's Calvinist reading lessons which will prove ultimately decisive: 'an eye for an eye' (70). Despite Tocky's carnivalising readings, and her social self-invention through the purloining of increasingly beautiful costumes, these clothes do not, in her case, signal immunity from the colonisers' deadly scripts. By contrast, Peggy the maid in *Sunrise* gets away with her cross-class masquerade, which briefly accords her the social privileges and romantic immunity of the high comedy soubrette. Looking lovely in one of the Shelton women's ball gowns, she relishes her transfiguration and survives her night of illicit comic passion with the also class cross-dressed refugee Ly. The latter courts her with mimed Daffy Duck and Fred Astaire routines, since he has been advised that the way to get (or get rid of) a woman is to make her laugh (18).

All the *Sunrise* household are graciously costumed for the performance of 'The Blind Singer and the King', Venice being gowned like a 'fairytale princess' while the adult Shelton siblings are resplendent in Oriental attire. Peggy's husband Albert in his stationmaster's uniform (41), like the gauche schoolmaster Kulygin of Chekhov's *The Three Sisters*, remains a class and temperamental outsider. Sensing that his wife is moving out of his orbit and that counter-action is required, Albert attempts to join the carnival mood by putting on a pair of joke spectacles with goggle eyes on springs, but this act of transformation meets only with embarrassed incredulity. He is further enraged at catching Peggy with a tuxedoed Ly; the latter quickly assumes his protective clown persona, proving his harmlessness by '[walking] like a penguin and [making] duck noises' (42). Vince, the brilliant scientist and stroke victim, demonstrates through costume his fall from eminence and his disorientation and despair at his mind's deterioriation. 'Dressed in a tuxedo but [with] bow tie... undone', he is alarmed and mystified at producing a handful of crushed flowers from its pockets (30); a clownish routine with tragic implications. Evening dress sits equally uncomfortably on the working-class Francis of *The Golden Age* but appears innate to the Archers, whereas when the forest people are dressed up for the welcome 'home' dinner in the Hobart garden they appear at once incongruous and appropriate. The refugees of *Displaced Persons*, their clothes burnt in the cause of quarantine, are incongruously re-dressed in discarded society evening dress, which nevertheless celebrates their survival and prefigures the social validation they may yet achieve in their new country. 'Costume functions as the woven surface on which are negotiated signifiers of past and present, of person and place, and by implication, of self and other.'[9] Cross-class dressing 'up', in clothes either appropriated from the wardrobe of the privileged or bestowed by them, appears a theatrical signal reclaiming the agency and obscured social status of marginalised groups, while suggesting also their provisional grasp on social, as distinct from spiritual or sexual, power.

Transvestisms

Transvestism in general can function, as Marjorie Garber demonstrates, as a device signalling all kinds of 'category crises' and flagging the crossing of more than purely gender borders: those between black and white, for example, or master and servant.[10] Transvestism from female to male indicates transitional social status as well as indeterminate sexuality or, more usually, cultural gender role. Roma of *Byzantine Flowers* must dress as a boy in order to get a job sweeping the mill floor. The upward progress of her social identity is flagged by costume changes; first purloining the dead Mrs Harris's dress, then wearing her own catalogue frock specially ordered from Brisbane, and finally the golden Byzantine wreath of flowers with her white wedding dress. These social-gender shifts signal accretionary rather than transitional identities. Since it is as a substitute for his dead son that she finds her initial place in Tom Harris's life, this masculine potential survives even with the last 'princess' costume. Roma appropriates and retains masculine social status through becoming his heir, the colonial property-owner.[11]

But masculine clothing need not necessarily socially empower its female wearer. In *Spellbound* the young girl Annie dances an erotic tango with her sister-in-law Sylvia, dressed as a man in evening clothes. Sylvia's cross-gender costume shows her performing for Annie a rehearsal of richer emotional and imaginative interactions possible outside this constricted community. It moreover manifests Sylvia's unexpressed and unrequited tragic love for Annie, who finally leaves for Sydney and an appropriate career as a dress designer. Dulcie, the abused child of *Summer of the Aliens*, also tries dressing as a boy to arouse some show of interest from Lewis, whom she thinks might 'really prefer boys', since his conventional adolescent homo-sociality excludes girls as friends, much less as love objects (64). She forces Lewis to steal feather cushions to make the angel costumes in which they gleefully trash the Returned Services League hall, orgiastically revenging themselves on this national symbol of all kinds of imposed social sanctions. This angel guise externalises Dulcie's desire to transcend the sexual abuse she suffers: 'I think life is only a dream. We're the dream of a mentally ill angel' (63). Prophetically, the costume indicates that in Lewis's life she will remain the ideal: 'I did love her, though I didn't understand this until years later when I saw her in the face of my lovers and wished they were her' (83).

An interesting example of male to female transvestism is *Crow*'s Mrs Gavin, the Darwin publican who in the South Australian première was played by Edwin Hodgeman as a man in drag. Nobody comments on Mrs Gavin's transvestism and she is treated as culturally feminine: 'Boofhead swallows the mouse. Some of the onlookers groan in distaste. Mrs Gavin faints, no one takes any notice' (1). Nowra comments that this gender-hybrid character, an outcome of immediate casting exigencies, served to build up the theatrically transformative world of Darwin where 'you experience the extreme of your personality'. Boofhead visits Mrs Gavin who is 'dressed exotically but with some style' (13): 'this sexual outcast [...bonds] with Boofhead—the two outcasts.'[12] Boofhead dreams of metamorphosis like the Irish folk figure 'Sweeney' who can transform into a bird, flying off to escape his enemies; Mrs Gavin prefers to '[fly] off to Lameroo Baths to watch the soldier boys frolic' (18-19). Both characters are exotics and hybrids, dreamers and shape-changers. By contrast, when Terry in *The Temple* cross-dresses as Cleopatra at Laurie Blake's Monte Carlo costume ball, his exotic costume both projects subversive glamour and is used for proleptic purpose: this dynastic patrician intends to confuse and seduce the usurper in order to retrieve his inheritance.

Social transvestism more eclectically carnivalises costume signifiers from class attires and from traditional theatrical characters. In *The Temple* such shape-shifting as Nick's transformation into Frankenstein's 'creature' signals a core thematic relationship, while Laurie Blake's rapid costume transformations dramatise his harlequinesque metamorphoses and suggest the clown's buoyant impunity. His various 'disguises' via costume lie by telling the truth, presenting the audience with double-bluff images to decode. His

Rampaging angels. Damon Herriman and Sara Zwangobani as Lewis and Dulcie in *Summer of the Aliens*, Sydney Theatre Company, 1993. (Photo: Robert McFarlane)

first appearance is in blood-spattered overalls, disconcerting Nick with a handshake that transfers blood to his hand: the Faustian pact is sealed. Laurie then strips off the abattoir overalls to reveal a smart business suit (3-4), a hybrid image of butcher and businessman. At his fashionable restaurant, the nerve-centre of the takeover enterprise, Laurie initially presents an appropriately harlequinesque spectacle costumed in a shredded suit with a trouser leg cut off at the knee and a missing sleeve (44), a result of Brenda's vengeance for his affair with Miranda. However this 'clown' has no trouble buying a replacement suit from a diner who proclaims himself honoured to sell the shirt off his back to one who embodies 'what makes this country great' (49). Laurie assumes his mark's costume while the bedazzled patron leaves the stage in his underpants.

Performing the self and acting up

When a Nowra character wishes to impress his or her agency upon the world, a performance will typically be the result. This is true of the culturally marginalised no less than the powerful, who (as we have seen in Chapter 2) will not only verbalise their visions but entrepreneur performances in which subordinates are expected to learn their roles, but which will rarely run entirely according to script. 'Democracy is foreign to theatre', Roy lectures Lewis in *Così*, since through accepting cast suggestions 'sometimes a vision is destroyed' (63). But there are few genuine auteurs in Nowra's theatre. Not even the most autocratic of Nowra's 'directors', Lynch, Lopez or Lillian Dawson, can make the enactment of imperial scripts merely reproduce their interior 'visions'. The energies and competing needs of their performers will seduce, subvert and translate the performance into something hybrid, open-ended and generically promiscuous: perhaps catastrophe, perhaps farce. The most brutally suppressed or muted characters—Andy, Stef, Juana, Vince (*Sunrise*), Olive (*The Jungle*)—resist total inscription through the intensity of their pain or else, locked in a private world, remain innocent in the face of the coercive desires of others. These visionary or comic characters engage and intrigue the audience.

Performance of the self can take the guise of rehearsal, where a more authoritative persona is assumed as a mode of empowerment: acting 'up'. When as a refugee from the compound Tocky returns to her childhood home Red Ochre, she does a Hopalong Cassidy routine:

'You attempt to take the Bar 20 Ranch, Joe, and you'll bite the dust' (52). This feisty cowboy performance unnerves Norman, since she is using his loaded gun as a prop. Unfortunately her use of the gun in earnest to defend herself from the sexual aggression of Frank McLash leaves Tocky defenceless, and the need to conceal the murder destroys her.

A sly masquerade through self-mimicry of conventional abjection may prove more successful: here the character is acting 'down'. Cherry in *Così* tests Lewis by spinning him a parody of a standard asylum patient's hard-luck story, concerning a childhood spent pointing and retrieving for her father since they couldn't afford a hunting dog. 'Those lakes can get cold when you're swimming with a dead duck in your mouth' (21). Such ironic underdog manoeuvres may also function as devices of intimidating terrorism. When dealing with his class enemy Barry St John, Laurie Blake stages a demonstration of refractory ruthlessness by projecting at his supercilious adversary a magnified version of his own imputed wild cowboy persona—he slashes his prestigious Monet painting. The gesture is theatre, however. Laurie has merely destroyed a reproduction and the real investment is safely in the bank (55-56).

For minority characters in hostile or oppressed contexts, performance as self-parody may prove a compromised strategem of survival. The millworkers' interactions of *Inside the Island* are a prolonged study of the devices by which insolent subordinates project disrespect and non-co-operation while staying just within the permitted bounds of civility. They prey on the young new-chum soldier Higgs and patronise their insecure boss George Dawson. As analysis of the internalised abjection of the colonised—their 'muted' hybridity (see Chapter 3)— these scenes demonstrate the cowardice of survival but show little of its moral or transformative potential. The English millworker Bert complies with the group ethos of his bludging workmates by repeating for George the plummy-voiced routine of the 'bloody British' which buys him group acceptance. '[*Imitating an English upper-class accent*] I went to the Queen's garden party where we ate tarts which made us all break wind—it was a tarty farty party' (53). In this act of sly mimicry it is difficult to situate just who is 'us' and who 'them', or to ascertain the real parodic target of Bert's ambivalent performance: himself as new-chum, George as boss, the anglophile Lillian and women generally, upper-class social pretensions, English condescension or his mates' supine Australian resentment. Mimicry is an ambivalent and 'double-edged' form of articulation, wherein performances of compliance can be menacing and disorienting.[13]

By contrast, Ruth in *Crow* uses her performance of abjection to defeat Vince's rage when he discovers she is pregnant to the white combo-artist Cole. Vince drags her by a length of rope 'like a dog'; since she was 'leading him on' he will do the same. Vince can find no other way to stage his fury and sense of defeat, but his strong physical performance is countered by Ruth's assuming her 'bitch' role and projecting it back at him defiantly and excessively:

> RUTH *starts barking like a dog and howling...*
>
> I'm a dog, you've tied me up like a dog, so I'm a dog.
>
> *She continues to bark, he goes to hit her.*
>
> VINCE: Shut up!
>
> *She barks, howls, grunts like a pig, etc.*
>
> I said, shut up.
>
> *He takes out a knife and cuts the top of her dress.*
>
> RUTH: Kill me, go on, cut me open like a pig.
>
> *She grunts like a pig.*
>
> VINCE: I will, I fuckin' will!
>
> RUTH: Do it, I'm a pig!
>
> *She barks like a dog.*
>
> I'm a dog. I'm a dog! (51)

Ruth's parodic assumption and performance of her victimisation is unnerving in its very danger, excess and metamorphic energy. Rather than being apathetic and self-validating, her risk-taking compliance with Vince's script, accepting and pushing to the limit his theatricalising of their situation, releases energies which are potentially clarifying and transformative. Self-parody here is double-edged and defiant, performing and externalising Ruth's and Vince's common abjection so that it may be confronted.

'The young Lewis [in *Summer of the Aliens*] learns that the way to survive is to rehearse roles: he mimics adults as they mimic other adults, scenes from their childhood, and their fantasies.'[14] As an incest victim, his young friend Dulcie has come to regard her vulnerable

Defiant mimicry. David Ngoombujarra and Claudia La Rose Bell as Vince and Ruth in *Crow*, State Theatre Company of South Australia, 1994. (Photo: Hugh Hartshorne)

body as something instrumental and detached from her spiritual being. She uses her body, her only resource, to stage spectacles of her anguish and defiance, adopting and parodying imposed abjecting scripts to demonstrate her own meanings. When she pulls a knife on Lewis, telling him that's what 'aliens' need to do to protect themselves when they're found out (36), Dulcie is simultaneously performing, concealing and transforming her relationship with her stepfather. She is disgusted with Lewis's compliance with Brian's request to entrepreneur a look at her tits for sixpence (17-18). Upon collection she demonstrates to the boys her own control of the spectacle: 'For two tits, twice the money'(21), she demands, 'You don't buy me, I sell me' (23). After a brief look she accepts Brian's challenge to withstand burning her arm with a magnifying glass. Despite her pain she defiantly endures the torture, using it to elucidate for Lewis his compromised role in the transaction: 'How does it feel like to be a hoon?' (22).

The risk Dulcie runs in her exhibition of tough endurance is that spectators of the somatic displays of the oppressed characteristically prefer to read symbolic and parodic self-punishment as chosen and 'natural'. 'She's enjoying this, aren't you?' says Brian. Like many an Emperor of Darkness, he disclaims responsibility for the acts of his fellow-players and decodes their suffering as innately chosen: 'pain is all they understand'. Lewis is unable or unwilling to decode the nature of Dulcie's acts of desperation or to understand what kind of self-performance she is staging for him. Eventually the doubled consciousness of the Narrator, the audience's onstage mediator surveying a younger self, physically forces Lewis to witness the unambiguous spectacle of Stan's abuse (74).

The brothers Vince and Boofhead in *Crow* use their bodies as ambivalent mediums of survival. Boofhead is a skilled performer, a regurgitator swallowing live mice and money for bets; clown-like acts of somatic magic which echo the spiritual magic with which he is in touch. Eventually the legal codicil rejecting Crow's property claim is similarly dispatched: 'Eat it and make sure it stays down there' (62). Through his tent-boxing career as the Ebony Prince, his brother, in a more extreme and self-punishing fashion, also parodically plays into and exceeds white perception of the 'blackfella' persona. Vince narrates how when racist bushies urge some luckless or hubristic mate to enter the ring to 'punch that black bastard out', he will let him land a few punches until the challenger begins to comprehend that this will be no easy kill and that Vince is playing with him. The hapless challenger, urged on by his mates, understands himself to be playing a novel and doomed role in a performance he can neither stop nor control. 'For the first time he's got The Fear of a blackfella.' Vince dwells on how he will toy with his sweating victim and finish him off painfully and at leisure, controlling the knock-out blow so that the crowd will continue to be suckered into participation by imagining it 'just a blackfella's lucky punch.'

Vince uses his physical skills to seduce and punish his white tormentors, reclaiming his own purposes by enacting the scripts of his entrepreneurial controller and playing up to the 'blackfella' stereotype of the whites. Within the spectacle he must enact, his satisfaction is to use his courage and strength to ensure its continuance so that more 'yahoos' will be educated with 'The Fear'. Vince's degree of control over the meanings of his tent-show demonstrations, in which his body is the skilled giver and receiver of punishment, remains, however, relative and ambiguous: 'I make the Boss a fortune' (24). Simultaneously the revenge of the marginalised, fervent self-expression and abjected self-objectification, Vince's didactic physical spectacles demonstrate the 'double-edged' nature of colonised self-performances, as Bhabha and Tompkins explain. He can, however, vary the dominant script when its continuance doesn't suit him. When Cole challenges him to a score-settling fist fight, Vince merely whips out a bayonet and stabs him: 'Yeh, life's unfair', he tells his dying rival. 'I learnt it really early' (68).

Performing hidden history in *Radiance*

Radiance is the story of a mother's homecoming to heal her estrangement from the daughter she has not been allowed to know or acknowledge. Behind this story lies the Australia's haunting by the disruption of several generations of Aboriginal families through decades of government policy. 'Who is she?' is the refrain of the dead mother's song, and the question is asked by all the characters as they seek the meaning of their dislocated history. On the day of her mother's funeral, the internationally famed opera singer Cressy returns to her childhood beachside home in Central Queensland. To Cressy this house is alive with dread and trauma, since she was brutally raped underneath it when a child by one of her mother's many gentleman callers. In a gesture echoing that of the white authorities, Nona, the daughter of this rape, was taken from Cressy by her mother and raised as her own daughter, while both Cressy and her sister Mae were removed by the authorities to remote institutions. For Cressy and Mae the house is haunted by their mother and electric with the charge of emotion and silences that she bequeathed them. Mae had been her nurse and eventually jailer, enduring her dementia and rage, and has now received a notice of immediate eviction from the house's real owner Harry Wells, the most permanent of her mother's clandestine white lovers. Unlike Nona, Mae and Cressy have no reason to love this house, which was never their home, either emotionally or legally. Once outside on the tidal mudflats, the older women recall their fragmented heritage of spiritual identity: 'Mum once said that those stars were our spirits. Sister stars—for sisters'. 'But there's only two', Nona objects, closer to the truth than she knows (37). During the course of the night Nona discovers who her mother really is, and takes her grandmother's ashes 'home' to Nora Island where their people came from, now a Japanese-owned private resort: 'First the whites, now the Japs' (51) sums up their history of dispossession. 'We're scattered, like Mum, like her mum. But we'll take her home. And we'll have to do that for each other' (50).

A play theatricalising a shattered family's haunting by historical secrets and shame, *Radiance* displays a conventional two-act structure with the retrospective exposition and culminatory revelations appropriate to the gradual unfolding of family secrets. In such naturalistic structures the 'truth' is conventionally positioned as the ultimate disclosure which exhausts the secrets. However such patterns of closure cannot be expected of this 1993 post-Mabo play, performed in a political climate in which the Aboriginal right to 'home' yet remains provisional and dependent on the fluctuating goodwill of powerful whites. The 'secret history' of Australian race relations—the sexual exploitation and humiliation of legally powerless black women and the fragmentation of black families—to which many contemporary Aboriginal people are heirs, is at once occulted and evident. This history is staged through a series of impersonations and narratives which simultaneously reveal and conceal dispersed identity and painful mysteries.

As one might conventionally expect, Cressy is given two expository monologues concerning Nona's origins. The first at the end of Act One is a partial, masked truth, a desperately improvised bricolage, claiming that their mother was raped and bashed by a visitor while Cressy hid under the house in fear. When she went upstairs, Cressy elaborates, her mother tried to protect her by acting normally: 'She was putting on an act for me, pretending everything was all right and so I went along with it' (34). Here Cressy is not exactly telling the truth but perhaps rehearsing her ability to eventually speak it, but the speech at least does perform for her daughter that act of protection which Cressy's own mother failed to perform for her. The audience also hears a vivid and pitiful depiction of the mother in the role of sexual victim: a fantasy cover-story which concentrates and focuses Cressy's own rage at her mother, while facilitating her identification with the dead woman through articulating her intuition of a crucial common experience. As Crow remarks, 'sometimes bullshit is the pathway to truth' (11). Cressy's second story finally identifies Nona's real mother as herself, the actual rape victim rejected as a slut when her pregnancy could no longer be hidden. 'You know what happened when I told her—she hit me. She said I was lying. That it wasn't her boyfriend—that is was one of the local boys and I was blaming him. She didn't believe me' (52). Nona's reaction is to replay to Cressy her grandmother's vehement rejection: 'You're a liar... I'm going to scatter my mother's ashes... I was not born from dirt!' (53). 'No more secrets and lies', Cressy insists (53). However Cressy's seeming culminatory explanation still leaves many secrets unspoken, particular those concerning the paternity of each of the three women. The play's only named men are Harry Wells and Father Doyle, whose voice is heard pontificating on the radio which Mae angrily buries in the tidal mud. Only their mother knew the identities of the fathers of the two older girls, and paternal origins remain, like herself, an enigma.[15] The only thing she taught all her daughters is the song 'The Belle of Dublin (not 'Belfast') City'; maybe a clue, maybe not.

Interpretation of the play's historical and post-colonial context depends on this being a fictional black family at a particular moment of Australian social history; and the sisters' childhood being coeval with the end of that period of government policy which separated both black and white children from their mothers for reasons of forced assimilation or perceived moral danger. A single black mother of part-white children, doubly vulnerable on racial and sexual grounds, had little chance. Cressy and Mae, though placed in institutions, at least knew who their mother was and where they were born, but she is their only known kin and her own family connections are a mystery, perhaps as much to herself as to her daughters. 'Mum said our relatives were scattered across the whole country' (10). Although the island from which her people were displaced can be seen from her house, the mother would appear to have been completely exiled from the rest of her family, as was the official practice. She has depended on promiscuous sexual relations to gain a precarious tenancy of a house where she could at least look across the water to her unattainable home; a survival priority to which everything has been sacrificed and which has damaged her children. The heritage they really craved was precisely the one the mother was unable to give them.

> [MAE] I came here because I wanted to know. I wanted to know where I came from, how I ended up the way I did. I'd take her down to the beach and I'd point to the island. I'd ask her: what happened, how did my great great grandparents get thrown off the island? She wouldn't answer. I wanted to know about my father. My relatives. About her. (43)

Cressy sees that her mother's silences, no less than her stories, have perpetuated this estrangement, particularly between herself and Nona: 'That stranger. That selfish woman. Look at us, we're strangers because of her' (26). The sisters' heritage is 'scattering' and numbing silence. The scattering of the family is realised when the mother's ashes fly through the air during an attempt to transfer them to a Radiance liquorice tin. The sisters have a hard time retrieving the ashes and what they replace is well mixed with vacuum cleaner contents. Although all the sisters have the dramatic function of performing the dissociated fragments of the dead mother's experience (see Chapter 3), their reunion and revelations can restore no primal pre-traumatic purity or unity: there is no 'home' to which they can return. These 'lost selves' can never simply re-unite.[16] The pain and 'scattering' are now part of their heritage, as are enigma and potent silences. The three sisters are caught up in a difficult but open-ended process of re-invention. Post-colonial identity is not

The scattering of the mother. Deborah Mailman, Roxanne
McDonald and Lisa Maza in *Radiance*, QTC/Kooemba Jdarra,
1997. (Photo: Paul Aurisch)

locatable within a concealed past which dramatic narrative can uncover and exhaust, but perpetually created in the present. The eruptions of history and the volatile process of self-renovation are typically coded in this play, less by formal techniques of exposition than through the costume changes and the embedded performances through which the women 'try out' those shreds of the past and future which may fit.

Madama Butterfly and the Polynesian princess

Nona is the play's comic shape-shifter, arriving with a suitcase full of outrageous wigs and fashionable costumes which gradually transfer to her sisters, carnivalising their sombre dress and hybridising images of ethnicity and sexuality. Black dresses are worn by all the women, but the distinction of class and social register between Mae's country-town genteel poverty, Cressy's European haute couture elegance, and Nona's in-your-face youthful stylishness will be made evident through differences in these garments' cut and fabric. Nona's first tussle is with the respectable nurse Mae, dressed for the funeral in 'a dowdy black frock' (1). Mae is disconcerted at Nona's proposed funeral attire of a skimpy black party frock redolent of urban nightlife. To Mae her sister looks like a 'slut' and Mae has had enough of her own mother in that role. Nona is equally disgusted that Mae has no matching black knickers she can borrow. Mae gives her one of her dead mother's dresses to wear, which goes on over the abbreviated party dress. Wearing the old-fashioned frock and her fashion-victim high heel shoes, Nona presents a hybridisation of herself masquerading as the dead woman—the first of the theatricalisations of the enigmas of identity and of the mother's sexual and moral roles. Cressy's appearance fresh from the London flight in 'a stylish and expensive black dress' brings metropolitan glamour to the humble seaside house. 'I'm no ghost' she says (6), but the 'ghost' is before her incarnated in this bizarrely double-imaged Nona. Cressy has her own chic hat, while Mae again produces 'mega daggy' hats for herself and Nona to wear. At the last moment Nona peels off the mother's dress and drags out of her suitcase vermilion and strawberry blonde wigs, settling for the latter. She goes to the funeral 'as herself'—a sexy black blonde with no knickers, white ones having been rejected as beyond the fashion pale. 'If brevity is the soul of wit then your dress will be worth a few laughs at the gravesite' Cressy caustically observes (8-9).

Signifiers of identity and ethnicity are further hybridised after the funeral in a prolonged mime sequence commencing in Scene 3, when Cressy, whose famous operatic role is Madama Butterfly, maternally tidies Nona's chaotic suitcase and tries on her red wig (22). This reminds us that the severe Cressy is in her own way a 'fake', a professional performer. Nona's one recent contact with the singer she thinks is her sister was after a *Madama Butterfly* performance in Adelaide:

> She was fantastic. You know, dying at the end, singing her heart out, killing her kid. So I ask to go backstage... And there she is. In her dressing room. Like a florist shop. She's sitting in her chair, the mirror lights around her like some sort of halo. She's still got her make-up on—Jap eyes, white skin, like a mask. (5)

Now Nona decides to do her own version of Cressy's performance, throwing on a black wig and a red kimono, a souvenir of a 'stingy' Japanese lover. In a strangely effective performance in nonsense Italian Nona enacts for Cressy the opera's last scene. Her mother finds deeply moving this spectacle which offers affiliation through an exchange of performances, particularly as this particular one rehearses and hybridises a myth of particular relevance to their common situation; that of stolen children. In Puccini's opera the powerless colonised mother of a mixed-race child contemplates killing him rather than surrendering him to his white father; but instead of killing the child (as Nona mis-remembers) Butterfly kills herself, preserving honour in the face of defeat and shame. This embedded performance both conceals the past and points to it: reversing the sacrifice Cressy's mother made of her, and reflecting what Cressy herself has had to do by killing her maternal identity to spare Nona the truth. 'You gave her [Cressy] your voice', Nona tells the box of ashes (23). Cressy in turn sees something of her own talent in Nona, criticising her 'professionally' and bewildering her daughter by kissing her 'as if thanking her for the performance' (24).

Cressy's own performance skills are in part self-creating reactions to the pain of abjection; her desire for transcendence over her shamed misery as a young girl abandoned without visitors in the Brisbane convent:

> There we were, us girls in the steam and stink of the laundry, with its smell of starch and dirty clothes... one day I saw a picture in one of the nun's magazines. It was a film star playing a Polynesian princess, wearing a sarong, hibiscus in her hair. She looked so beautiful, so exotic, so far from the laundry. And so I pretended to be her. I'd wrap a table cloth around me, put a hibiscus in my hair and sing to the other girls. They'd applaud me and I'd do it again and again, until I thought I was the princess, pretending the copper steam was the steam of a volcano I was about to throw myself into and sacrifice myself to the gods. But of instead of throwing myself in, I won a singing scholarship. (27)

Cressy's solution to her exiled fate is a career of performance, fabricating such trans-cultural identities as a heroic doomed white-skinned Japanese mother in an Italian opera, or a sacrificed 'Polynesian princess'. This latter is, however, a Hollywood travesty of the exotic which (if the magazine star was Dorothy Lamour) is itself already a bizarre accretion of fake ethnic signifiers. *Radiance* plays with these culturally shifting performative codes of identity; for the colonised such bricolage becomes a tool of self-creation and exorcism. Identity is chosen, fakes are real, and the role-playing of theatre images the serious intention of these investments.

After her 'Butterfly' playlet, Nona produces a pair of Doc Martens from her suitcase, insisting that after the storm they will walk across the mudflats and take their mother home to her island. Mae then effects her own significant costume transformation, appearing with her hair loose and wearing the wedding dress her mother had put aside for that fictitious white wedding to Harry Wells, 'the man she truly loved'. To Nona she appears the 'spitting image' of her grandmother, but Mae, never having known her mother in any carefree mood, merely laughs at what she thinks is Nona's nonsense (28). Mae, the most repressed and angry of the sisters, both theatricalises her own sacrificed romantic longings and ironically impersonates her mother's futile dreams. All three sisters, now in some form of hybridised costume, are sprayed with their mother's ashes when the tin explodes all over them. The sense of haunting is built up with thunderstorm effects, and is concentrated in Cressy's muted anguish when Nona rushes under the house, the site of her conception, uttering joke spooky noises and maniacal laughter. She then emerges with a false clue to the paternal past; a battered black cowboy hat which she insists belongs to the fantasmatic Black Prince: 'Mum said he wore a cowboy hat' (32).

The journey across the mud flats is undertaken in various forms of hybridised gender and ethnic drag: Nona in her kimono and the blonde wig, Cressy red-wigged and barefoot with her designer dress rolled up, and Mae in the wedding dress and Nona's Doc Martens. Mae sways to dance music on the radio, drowning out the town boys' distant chanting of derisory songs about the 'old witch' who lived in the house. She relates the story of her mother's collapse into violent dementia, when she 'began to yell out obscene things, demented things' in church. Mae and her mother became each other's prisoners and town pariahs, even from the revivalist church where her mother screamed in tongues until 'eventually even they understood she was possessed by madness, not by God'. In an ecstasy of pain Mae re-enacts the mother's last moments, 'possessed by the devil, her eyes on fire' screaming in tongues and refusing to the end to tell her daughter where she came from or 'just once' that she loved her (44–45). 'Who is she? Who is that Mae? I've got nothing', she concludes. The completion of Mae's identification with, and furious exorcism of, the mother is appropriately undertaken in wedding dress as she resolves to burn down Harry Wells' non-connubial house. 'Get my own back on this town. Get my revenge on Harry—Mum's revenge' (46). Cressy enthusiastically joins in the plan.

As the fire rages '[burning] it all away' (54), Cressy reappears with her dress torn and smouldering and her hand burnt: the rape narration is evoked and foreshadowed through costume. The sisters join in a 'joyous, loud version' of 'The Belle of Dublin City', 'dancing wildly, almost possessed, the energy reminding us of how they must have been at their happiest when they were girls' (50).[17] This song, 'the only thing [the mother] taught them all', seems to have become their unifying family ritual, but only momentarily. Nona reasserts her intention to pursue the seductive Black Prince fantasy bequeathed her by her grandmother. So the anguished Cressy forces her to hear her final story—or is it another protective and partial truth? While only Cressy knows for certain the identity of at least one of the sisters' fathers, she like her own mother isn't telling everything. It is left an enigma what Nona's incest fantasies might be concealing, and whether paternal origins are ever knowable, or even significant.

Above: Transcultural self-performance: Nona as Madama Butterfly. Rhoda Roberts. Below: Possession: Mae speaks in tongues. Rachael Maza. *Radiance*, Company B Belvoir production, Sydney, 1993. (Photos: Elise Lockwood)

While the Black Prince phantasm has been exorcised, the sisters' business of renegotiating and re-dressing the fragmented images of their mother will forever remain unfinished. In their 'scattered' world this kinship between black women is the only connection really worth fighting for.

Così: 'The more real it is...'

Ever since Aristophanes' comedy *Thesmophoriazusae*, in which Euripides' tragic style and themes are comprehensively burlesqued, audiences have relished the deconstructive function of paratheatrical references; and writers have used them to celebrate the conventions of theatre or to mount critiques of, or homages to, the art and political opinions of their contemporaries and forebears. *Così* is the most comprehensive example in Nowra's theatre of characters' self-construction and renovation through the agency of performance—which, as we have seen, is his constant stylistic and thematic signature. Mozart's 1790 comic opera of the volatile nature of sexual attraction among the aristocracy is rehearsed and performed in the 1970s by mental patients in a burnt-out theatre; the action offstage embraces the mass theatre of the anti-war marches engaged in by Lewis's friends Nick and Lucy. This historical frame points to larger imperial violences and situates Lewis's enterprise as 'reactionary' according to his friends' harsh judgements: 'Love is an emotional indulgence for the privileged few' (70). Nick is rehearsing Brecht's *Galileo*, and Lewis initially proposes to his inmate cast a performance of the learning-play *The Exception and the Rule*, about 'how a man sacrifices himself for the good of his mates' (8). But this Anzac-flavoured plot arouses little enthusiasm and Roy's vision prevails—they will perform what appears to be the bizarrely inappropriate *Così Fan Tutte*.[18] That this is an opera and nobody can sing or even speak Italian does not dishearten Roy, to whom generic constraints and the stringent demands of performance disciplines are mere details.

Arguments about aesthetic value and political agency thus set Brecht against Mozart (Da Ponte's humble contribution as librettist is typically discounted), and wild claims for their pre-eminence are made by the adherents of both camps. For Roy, in a Lynch-like colonising grand gesture of erasure, their *Così Fan Tutte* would be a national première and act of cultural mission. 'We'll be making

Above: Rehearsal time. Anna Mercer, Jeremy Callaghan, Edgar Metcalfe, George Shevstov, Kelton Pell, Peta Toppano and Kathryn Hanlon in *Così*, Black Swan, Perth, 1995. (Photo: David Dare Parker) Below: Mozart in the madhouse. Kerry Fox, Barry Otto, David Field, Ben Mendelsohn, Elspeth MacTavish and Bob Baines in *Così*, Company B Belvoir production, Sydney, 1992. (Photo: Stuart Spence)

history. Australian history. We'll bring culture to this place' (11). His claims for the work's inherent value are as personally invested and inflated as any high-culture chauvinist's: 'Without this opera having been composed, there would be just a clanging, banging, a bedlam all around us. The music of this opera keeps the world in harmony' (13). Nick and Lucy's aesthetic preference and personal motivations receive little textual validation (particularly in the revised version which cuts back material in the household scenes of the 1992 script in order to impose unity of place).[19] As Murray Bramwell remarked in the *Adelaide Review*, 'If the Moratorium movement was made up only of heartless, lecherous Brecht directors we'd still be in Danang.'[20] Nowra has never been a fan of Brecht, here the scapegoat for all manner of political and aesthetic tyrannies. In 1983 he described him as 'boring, preachy, inhumane and obvious in his symbolism'.[21] This play sets out to settle some old scores with seventies dramatic orthodoxies. Opera and music, however, remain abiding inspirations for dramaturgical models and alienation devices:

> The great plays to me are operatic—*Lear, Hamlet*. There is a sense of the enclosure of an emotion within the tableau of a particular scene, rather than the emotion growing through a continuum as in a naturalistic play... singing creates a detachment.[22]

The structural parallels implied by the comic changes of heart of Da Ponte's lovers and their Melbourne student counterparts survive in the 1994 revision. In the matter of sexual infidelities and undue jealousies, both men and women appear 'like that' and moreover just like each other.

If opera is to be the choice, which school of opera?[23] Zac the over-lithiumed accompanist scorns *Così* as a 'pissy opera' and recommends Wagner: 'he's got balls' (30). He demands the right to play a Wagnerian overture on his piano accordion but on performance night is too pilled to play. He suggests 'the destruction of Valhalla' as appropriate deconstructive curtain music. 'Instead of the insipid happy-go-lucky music of Mozart... Wagner... foreshadows what is going to happen to the couples in the future: a life of torment and adultery' (73).[24] Questions of love and fidelity are passionately argued by the cast, who disagree over genre. The recessive and stuttering Henry is the strongest critic of the text, objecting, moreover, to Lewis's decision to costume the shape-shifting heroes as 'Albanian communists' when Australia is at war with North Vietnam: Lewis has the sense to substitute more topical Australian soldiers. Henry reveals his resistance to what he sees as Mozart's hip 1960s message: 'This *Così* condones the cccorruption of innocence. Women are told to be tramps. Free love. Women are not to be trusted' (48). When Lewis argues that 'whether love is an unswerving emotion and whether women can remain true' is comic material, Henry explodes: 'Whether women can remain true is a ttttragedy' (49). The show must validate his life script, or his reworked version of it: 'My mother only lllloved my fffather, no one else. He died in Kkkorea and she llloved nnno one else but me' (48).

Like many novice actors, the asylum cast measure their understanding of their roles against their experience, fantasies and values. Roy, for whom the performance, in the teeth of all evidence, will realise his dream of the way his orphaned childhood should have been, believes in type-casting. The painfully repressed Ruth is 'the definite if not definitive Dorabella', he tries to persuade Lewis (13); and his stuttering and painfully earnest friend Henry is a cert for the genial worldly Don Alfonso. 'Henry used to be a lawyer, they're all cynical, like Don Alfonso' (14). Cherry corners Lewis about the libretto's 'Arabian Phoenix' view of female fidelity and disavows it in her own case: 'With someone like you I could be true and faithful' (34). Ruth, for her part, achieves an aesthetic breakthrough by comparing the role with her perception of herself. Initially, Ruth rejects the theatrical concepts of impersonation and of virtual space. Is the coffee in the onstage coffee shop real or pretend? 'I can handle something being an illusion or real but not at the same time' (26). A 'real illusion', thus defamiliarised, suddenly appears as surreal to us as Ruth finds it. 'The theatre is no place for metaphysics', Roy snaps, but the question once raised remains. 'Shall I pretend I'm acting?' she persists later (29), exasperating Lewis by wanting to know exactly how many steps she should take—Nowra's seeming joke at the expense of Samuel Beckett's minutely-controlled productions.[25] Like most people Ruth is puzzled by the stylistic distinction between the 'real' and the 'natural':

LEWIS: Where ever you want to walk and as many steps as you like. Just try to make it natural.

RUTH: Real?

LEWIS: No, natural, like anyone walking. Yes, yes, just like in real life. (29)

'That woman is crying out for direction', Roy concludes (30). After learning her own (and everybody else's) lines and moves, Ruth suddenly grasps the concept of character as mask. Dorabella is a bit of a tart, Cherry insists, for giving in so easily to the disguised Ferrando's seductions: 'It wasn't me', Ruth protests, 'it was the character'. Lewis enjoys needling her: 'You were pretending?' She finally admits that this is what she has been doing; she has understood the transformative agency of the real fake. Henry characteristically validates the performance on the grounds of verisimilitude: 'My wife was like Dorabella'—'a ttttemptress' (64-65).

But even Henry, after his fashion, eventually develops Brechtian critical detachment, judging Ferrando and Guglielmo to have got what they deserved by pretending to be other people (66-67). It has taken the founding paradox of performance—pretending to be other people—to show him this. Roy has his own crisis of existential identity vertigo; seized with stage fright, he objects, 'Everyone will be staring at me!' Lewis, by now learning fast, shows leadership and talks him round: 'If they didn't stare at you, I'd be worried... I want you to be noticed all the time' (75).[26] By contrast to these pitfalls in mastering the conventions and practices of representation, Zac readily designs an austere anti-realist and functionally bare set with 'no garden, no seashore', as Cherry remarks in disgust.[27] The fantasist Roy adds 'we may as well be back in our wards' (61). Most of the cast love their rehearsals as an escape from their dreary asylum routine into an alternative and precisely-pictured ideal world; but Zac can see little artistic point in visual verisimilitude: 'If I could put up with reality I wouldn't be in here' (62).

It is Cherry, naïve realist and feminist deconstructionist, who devises the most inventive piece of updated staging 'relevance'. More effectively than the visionary Roy or the pompously didactic Nick, she steps into the role of collaborator/director. For Despina's Mesmerism scene Cherry steals a shock treatment machine and persuades Roy to mimic for Lewis the spectacular somatic effects of this procedure, with which Roy is all too familiar. Mesmer was a fraud and old-hat, Cherry pronounces, and anyhow the shock treatment will aid the women's motivation and make the scene appear 'more real'. 'The women aren't twits, are they? Even though the opera makes them out to be. What if the boys' recovery was really terrible, horrific'? (58). Roy plays along and his histrionic convulsions appear so convincing that Lewis, like the audience, begins to wonder whether Cherry has pulled a double-bluff and brought a live machine. 'Method acting', a complacent Roy explains. Cherry defines her subtextual rationale: 'It makes me less of a fake and you see why a woman's heart would soften towards a man if she saw what was happening to him in shock treatment' (60). The logical Ruth is impressed by this display: 'The more real it is, the more real it is'.

Lewis is initially hijacked into realising not his own but Roy's obsessive vision. The role reversal between teacher and pupil, implicit in Nowra's tutorial relationships from the outset, is in this play completed, hybridised and dissolved. The foundational joke of *Così* is that, while Lewis is nominally the director, in this role he is a 'fake' with little to teach and much to learn; but learn he does. Not an obsessional autodidact like Albert, he accepts rather than imposes. Despite contemporary theatre's insistence on the primacy of the auteur-director, he has tolerated and accommodated the competing visions and eccentric energies of his cast, from Roy's manic enthusiasms to Ruth's shy blossoming as she releases her fears in the madness of performance. Lewis is the least forceful but the most effective of Nowra's visionary characters, compromising and improvising his way through rehearsals and eventually taking over the role of Ferrando in a crisis when Doug's arson attempts land him back in C Ward. As the *Così* cast make over Mozart to express their specific needs and visions, aristocratic European art is carnivalised in the post-colonial madhouse.

Notes

Introduction

[1] *Sunrise.* Sydney: Currency, 1983, p. 17. All further references to this edition.

Chapter One (pages 1–60)

[1] Louis Nowra, 'Indonesia and Me', in *The Precious Woman*, trans. Tuti Indra Malaon, ed. Philip Kitley. Toowoomba: University of Southern Queensland Press, 1997, p. v.

[2] Louis Nowra interviewed by Margaret Throsby, ABC-FM radio, 13 May 1997.

[3] Brief accounts of the Herbert shooting and trial can be found in the *Age* and *Argus* at the appropriate dates. Here they have been supplemented by information from Louis Nowra.

[4] 'Autobiography', in Kelly, ed., *Louis Nowra*. Amsterdam: Rodopi, 1987, p. 30.

[5] 'The two terms... emerged in the response of an élite European culture to the widespread reproducibility of art, to the arrival of the mass media, and to the subsequent invasion of culture by popular tastes and sentiments. Kitsch is a manner of referring to the problem of "taste" in the contemporary world... Everything is reduced to accessible aesthetics: the "classics" translated into cinema and comics, symphonic music into film scores, novels into the *Reader's Digest*. Camp is more complex. It is more removed, more ironic, more refined than kitsch. Unlike kitsch, it is not sentimental but detached. It involves the self-knowledge of artifice and stylization; it is the "lie that tells the truth" (Jean Cocteau).' See Iain Chambers, *Popular Culture: The Metropolitan Experience*, London & NY: Methuen, 1986, pp. 105–106. Hence *Kismet* can be either kitsch or camp, depending on the stance of the observer. Questions of 'authenticity' and camp in both its sexual and aesthetic meanings form the subject of Nowra's comic short story 'The Translator' (see Chapter 3).

[6] 'Autobiography', p. 30.

[7] Lynne Testoni, 'The Rise and Fall and Rise of Louis Nowra', *Harper's Bazaar*, Spring/Summer 1988, p. 84.

[8] Nowra, 'The Father', in Helen Daniel, ed., *Expressway*. Ringwood: Penguin, 1989, p. 146.

[9] 'Autobiography,' p. 30.

[10] Testoni, 'The Rise and Fall and Rise of Louis Nowra'.

[11] 'The Father', p. 146.

[12] Nowra, 'All Eyes', *Independent Monthly*, December 1989/January 1990, p. 7.

[13] 'The Father', p. 151.

[14] 'Anzac and Why I Write', Anna Rutherford and James Wieland, ed., *War: Australia's Creative Response*. Hebden Bridge: Dangaroo Press, 1997, p. 342.

[15] In a recent interview, giving his opinion of official Australian multiculturalism, Nowra declares that the idea of being a 'hyphen-person' (e.g. 'Celtic-Australian') 'sort of stinks of political correctness', and would prefer 'mixed blood' as a solution to racial fantasies of 'pure blood'. See Veronica Kelly, '"More Character-Driven": An Interview with Louis Nowra', *Coppertales: A Journal of Rural Arts* 2, 1995, pp. 89–90.

[16] Chris Beck, 'On the Couch'. *Age* 'Extra', 15 July 1995, p. 2.

[17] Testoni, 'The Rise and Fall and Rise of Louis Nowra'.

[18] Testoni, 'The Rise and Fall and Rise of Louis Nowra'.

[19] See e.g. 'A Summer of Cricket'. *Sydney Morning Herald*, 1 January 1990, p. 8.

[20] 'Autobiography', p. 141.

[21] 'Autobiography', p. 32.

[22] 'Video Interview with Louis Nowra' in Kelly, ed., *Louis Nowra*, p. 134.

[23] 'Autobiography', p. 32.

[24] Candida Baker, 'It's All in the Imagination', *Age*, 2 July 1988, p. 12.

[25] 'Autobiography', p. 38.

[26] 'Author's Preface', *'Inner Voices' and 'Albert Names Edward'*. Sydney: Currency, 1983, p. viii. All other references to this edition.

[27] Paul Makeham, 'The Black Hole of Our History: A Conversation with Louis Nowra', *Canadian Theatre Review* 74, 1993, p. 30.

[28] Martin Portus, 'Nowra Reminds us of What We Want to Forget', *Sydney Morning Herald*, 8 August 1987, p. 50.

[29] 'Autobiography', p. 40.

[30] 'At the Crossroads', *Australasian Drama Studies* 2: 2, 1984, p. 110.

[31] The postman Joseph Ferdinand Cheval commenced in 1879 the building of his *palais idéal*, a splendid piece of naive architecture, at his home in the small town of Hauterives in south central France. He worked on it for decades, intending it to be his mausoleum, but the authorities prevented his burial in this unregulated site.

[32] Pollyanna Sutton, 'Adventure Seeker', *Age* 'Tempo Magazine', 1 April 1992, p. 2.

[33] Virginia Duigan, 'Louis Nowra: The Annals of the Cheated', *National Times*, 6–11 December 1976, p. 42.

[34] Suzanne Spunner, '*Sleezee* a Banal Flop, But Don't Miss *Ravages*', *Melbourne Times*, 9 March 1977.

[35] Margaret Jones, 'Obscure, Realistic', *Sydney Morning Herald*, 4 March 1977, p. 7.

[36] The Paris was floated on grants totalling $40,000 from the Sydney City Council and the State Division of Cultural Activities, and an auction of donated artworks by Martin Sharp, John Olsen, Charles Blackman and Brett Whitely. In *Patrick White: A Life*, Sydney: Vintage 1991, David Marr reports White as having donated $10,000 of his own money (p. 586). Bob Ellis's riposte to Marr, who coolly reviewed *Pandora's Cross*, was 'Nice one David. Shave carefully.' See Marr, 'Dull Theatre, Beautifully Boxed', *National Times*, w/e 15 July 1978; and Ellis, 'Sydney, Paris and Critics', *Nation Review*, 28 July–3 August 1978.

[37] White, Letter to the Editor, *Australian*, 24 August 1978.

[38] *Visions*. Sydney: Currency, 1979. All further references to this edition.

[39] 'Video Interview with Louis Nowra', p. 135.

[40] Nowra, 'The Short, Nasty, Brutal Life of the Playwright', *Island Magazine* 63, Winter 1995, p. 5.

[41] Makeham, 'The Black Hole of Our History', p. 28.

[42] See Nowra, '*Inner Voices* and the First Coil', *Australian Literary Studies* 9: 2, 1979, pp. 188–199. Reprinted in Kelly, ed. *Louis Nowra*, pp.46–55.

[43] E.g. Dean George, 'A Vision for the Future', *Courier Mail*, 23 April 1979, p. 4. The Anglican Dean of Brisbane's political and salvational reading of *Visions* is under the by-line 'A Christian Point of View'.

[44] See e.g. John McCallum, 'The World Outside: Cosmopolitanism in the Plays of Nowra and Sewell', *Meanjin* 43: 2, 1984, pp. 286–296.

[45] *The Cheated*. Sydney: Angus & Robertson, 1979, p. 82, Item 33: A Cornish postman horded over 20,000 letters which he tired of delivering because of flat feet.

[46] Katrina Iffland, 'Cosying up to Nowra', *Canberra Times*, 3 July 1994, p. 47.

[47] 'Patrick White Replies' (advertisement), *Sydney Morning Herald*, 6 September 1980 and other dates, p. 19.

[48] H. G. Kippax, 'Louis Nowra's Best Play', *Sydney Morning Herald*, 13 November 1980, p. 8; John Moses, 'Louis Nowra's Brave Failure', *Australian*, 17 November 1980, p. 8; Brian Hoad, 'Questions But Too Few Answers', *Bulletin*, 25 November 1980, p. 76. The latter two critics both objected that the play should be giving answers to Su-Ling's final question 'Why?'

49 For a detailed discussion of *The Song Room*'s production processes, see John Hillel, 'Screenplays for Radio: The Radio Drama of Louis Nowra', *Australasian Drama Studies* 30, April 1997, pp. 68–70, where Andrew McLennan cites it as the first major Australian radio drama to use location recording and to involve the writer in production.

50 The same was noted in its 1986 Adelaide revival by the Stage Company, where Murray Bramwell described the Beast (played by the comic mime Glynn Nicholas) as like Rin Tin Tin 'loping around looking for his plate of Good-Os.' See 'Dramatic Beauty Unrealised', *National Times*, 14–20 February 1986, p. 37. See also Bill Courcier, 'Best Little Fight in Town', *Sydney Morning Herald*, 29 December 1980, p. 7; John Moses, 'The Beast—But Not a Beauty', *Australian*, 29 December 1980, p. 8.

51 Nowra, 'At the Crossroads', p. 109.

52 The Lighthouse ensemble consisted of twelve actors and three musicians. The personnel remained fairly stable over the two years and consisted of Robynne Bourne, Peter Cummins, Melissa Jaffer, Alan John, Gillian Jones, Melita Jurisic, Russell Kiefel, Stuart McCreery, Robert Menzies, Jacqy Phillips, Geoffrey Rush, Kerry Walker, John Wood. Robert Grubb and Belinda McClorey also performed with Lighthouse.

53 Robert Milliken, 'Nowra Carves into the Upper Crust', *National Times*, 18–24 November 1983, p. 34.

54 Nowra, Lecture on *Sunrise*. University of Queensland, Department of English, 18 August 1987. Audiotape.

55 Leonard Radic, 'Louis Nowra Learns to Adapt', *Age* 'Saturday Extra', 25 August 1984, p. 14.

56 Portus, 'Nowra Reminds us of What We Want to Forget'.

57 Jo Litson, ' The Wicked Ways of Louis Nowra', *Weekend Australian Magazine*, 18–19 April 1987, p. 9.

58 Martin Portus, 'The Victims of a Messiah Complex', *Sydney Morning Herald*, 30 April 1988, p. 74.

59 Jo Litson, 'A Newer Nowra', *ABC Radio 24 Hours*, September 1993, pp. 60–61.

60 Kelly, 'More Character-Driven', p. 91. The article referred to is probably Portus, 'Victims of a Messiah Complex'.

61 Radic, 'Louis Nowra Learns to Adapt'.

62 See Nowra, 'A Flying Pig and an Erotic Diversion Are Part of the Package', *Sydney Morning Herald* 'Good Weekend', 29 June 1985, pp. 39–42.

63 Makeham, 'The Black Hole of Our History', p. 30.

64 Litson, 'The Wicked Ways of Louis Nowra'.

65 Jeremy Eccles, 'Displaced Persons', *Look and Listen*, September 1985, pp. 23–24, which refers to 'Red Knights'.

[66] 'The Short, Nasty, Brutal Life of a Playwright', p. 3. In 1987 he classified his degree of control over work in different genres: 'Novels are your children, plays are your step-children and telemovies are an orphan on your doorstep' ('Wicked Ways of Louis Nowra').

[67] Portus, 'The Victims of a Messiah Complex'.

[68] See Hillel, 'Screenplays for Radio', pp. 72–73.

[69] Sally MacMillan, 'Nowra's Golden Rage', Australian 'Weekend', 16 December 1989, p. 11.

[70] David Hough, 'A Harmony of Composition on a Grand Scale', Times on Sunday, 29 November 1987, p. 31.

[71] Litson, 'The Wicked Ways of Louis Nowra'.

[72] ibid.

[73] Nowra, 'The Shrinking Vision', Island Magazine 39, 1989, p. 13.

[74] Murray Bramwell, 'Journeying to Capricornia', Advertiser, 8 September 1990, p. 12.

[75] Bramwell, 'Journeying to Capricornia'; Louise Nunn, 'A Première Feeling', Advertiser 'Weekend Magazine', 7 May 1994, p. 18–19.

[76] MacMillan, 'Nowra's Golden Rage', p. 11.

[77] See e.g. Joanne Tompkins, 'Celebrate 1988? Australian Drama in the Bicentennial Year', Australian and New Zealand Studies in Canada 11, 1994, pp. 103–112; and Helen Gilbert, 'Monumental Moments: Michael Gow's 1841, Stephen Sewell's Hate, Louis Nowra's Capricornia and Australia's Bicentenary', Australasian Drama Studies 24, 1994, pp. 29–45.

[78] Nowra, 'Wine, Women and Thongs', Sydney Morning Herald 'Guide', 25 April 1988, p. 1.

[79] Philip Adams, 'Watch This as a Last Resort', Weekend Australian 'Magazine', 30 April–1 May 1988, p. 13.

[80] As noted by Paul Makeham in his review of Radiance, Australasian Drama Studies 25, 1994, p. 190.

[81] John Carmody, 'Cythera to Whitsunday: The Making of an Australian Idyll', Sydney Morning Herald, 25 September 1987.

[82] Roger Covell, 'Tropical Love Story', Sydney Morning Herald, 5 September 1988, p. 18.

[83] Pollyanna Sutton, 'Adventure Seeker', Age, 1 April 1992, p. 3.

[84] Litson, 'A Newer Nowra', p. 61.

[85] See Hillel, 'Screenplays for Radio', pp. 74–76 for account of production and reception of Summer of the Aliens.

[86] 'Soap opera' and 'best-sellers' were evoked, see e.g. Brian Hoad, Bulletin, 16 January 1990; Rosemary Neill, Australian, 1 January 1990; Paul Le Petit, Sunday Telegraph, 7 January 1990. Jeanny Brown in the Daily Telegraph, 6 January 1990 compares it with the television miniseries, Fields of Fire, but understood Roma's dilemma as

contemporary: 'whether to remain true to her people or sell out to white society'. See *ANZTR* 3: 12 December 1989, pp. 21–24.

[87] Nowra, 'The Shrinking Vision', pp. 11–13.

[88] Peter Davis, 'Defiant Visions from the Outer', *Canberra Times*, 14 October 1990, p. 28.

[89] Beck, 'On the Couch'.

[90] Geraldine O'Brien, 'From New Zealand, Heavenly Murderous Creatures', *New York Times* 'Arts and Leisure', Section 2, 13 November 1994, pp. 15–16.

[91] Nowra, 'Rex Cramphorn', *Australasian Drama Studies*, 20 April 1992.

[92] Sutton, 'Adventure Seeker', p. 3.

[93] Helen O'Neill, 'Autobiographical Nowra Names Tax Man his Muse', *Sydney Morning Herald*, 16 April 1992, p. 14.

[94] Visual and descriptive material on the productions of *Love Burns* by the Seymour Group and by the Lyric Opera of Queensland can be found in John Jenkins & Rainer Linz, *Arias: Recent Australian Music Theatre*. Melbourne: Redhouse Editions, 1997, pp. 116–118, 139–140.

[95] James Koehne, ' The Story and the Music...', program of *Love Burns* by Graeme Koehne and Louis Nowra, Adelaide Festival, Playhouse, 28 February [1992], p. 5.

[96] Nowra, 'The Story...', program of *Love Burns*, p. 4.

[97] O'Neill, 'Autobiographical Nowra Names Tax man his Muse'.

[98] Alison Croggon, 'Act of Revelation', *Bulletin*, 21 April 1992, p. 101.

[99] Nowra, 'The Short, Nasty, Brutal Life of the Playwright', p. 6.

[100] For an analysis of the varied theatrical and curriculum uses of *Così* see Helen Gilbert, 'Theatre and Cultural Commerce: Louis Nowra's *Così*', *Southerly* 57: 3, 1997.

[101] At the time of writing in early 1998 this remains true of *Inside the Island*, *The Precious Woman*, *Sunrise*, *Spellbound*, 'Byzantine Flowers', *Crow* and the still-developing *Deceit*. *The Watchtower* has had no professional production after its NIDA première, and, apart from its STC complete production, one scene only from 'The Jungle' has been performed alone (by STC and Black Swan). The first two plays have however seen use as performance texts in Australian tertiary institutions. *Precious Woman* was performed in 1990 by the Chung Ying Theatre Company of Hong Kong, but a planned production in Jakarta by Teguh Karya of the Indonesian-language translation in the early 1990s was aborted through adverse governmental attitudes towards culture with any kind of Chinese content (see Philip Kitley, 'The History of the Dual Language Text' in the published translation by Tuti Indra Malaon. USQP 1997, p. vii.). *Inside the Island* received a reading directed by Peter Kingston at Government House, Sydney, on 31 May 1997, as part of the

Government House Cultural Program in association with the Australian National Playwrights' Centre. Plans to produce *Crow* in Canada with Native Canadian actors are afoot at the time of writing.

[102] John McCallum, 'New Voices Unheard in a Dramatic Tragedy', *Australian* 'Weekend Review', 20–21 June 1992, p. 11.

[103] Litson, 'A Newer Nowra', p. 61.

[104] Litson, 'Wicked Ways of Louis Nowra'.

[105] Nowra, 'The Short, Nasty, Brutal Life of the Playwright', pp. 7–8.

[106] Rosemary Neill, 'The Secret of Success is in the Script', *Australian*, 23 July 1993, p. 11. In 1995 in a talk to the Salamanca Writers' Festival in Hobart Nowra assesses his relationships with actors during rehearsal; and how a writer should judge the pressure of contradiction—hating actors trained in psychological realism to alter lines and characters in favour of linear development. He still rejects workshops which can 'make a better play, but it's a smoother play. Early drafts may have been more interesting because they contained the weirder things, the rougher, the unique view of the world.' Even so, rehearsal can present a similar smoothing out: 'my relations with actors and directors [is] a closer, more empathetic one, but are the plays less personal and more generalised?' 'The Short, Nasty, Brutal Life of a Playwright', p. 5.

[107] *ANZTR* 6: 10 October 1992, p. 141.

[108] Nowra, 'Indonesia and Me', p. iv.

[109] See e.g. Robert Macklin, 'Australia Council "Decrepit, No Vision"', *Canberra Times*, 7 April 1993, p. 3; [Anon] 'Swimming Against the Tide', *Age* 'Lifestyle', 23 May 1993, p. 2; [Christopher Bedloe, Domenic Mico, Peter Robinson] 'Louis Nowra on "Whingeing Artists" at the Press Club on 6th April 1993', *Muse* 119, May 1993, pp. 19–21; 'Revenge of the Baby Boomers', *Bulletin*, 20 April 1993; and Nowra, 'Whingeing Artists, Money, Political Correctness and Bureaucracy', [Address to the National Press Club, Canberra, 6 April 1993], Oral History Collection TRC 4365, National Library of Australia.

[110] 'Swimming Against the Tide'.

[111] Makeham, 'The Black Hole of our History', p. 28.

[112] Nowra, 'Whingeing Artists, Money, Political Correctness and Bureaucracy'.

[113] Richard Meale's opera *Voss* with libretto by David Malouf premièred at the Sydney Opera House in 1986. Its first scene, used in *Sydney*, contains a piano medley of 1840s tunes played at a colonial society party while the chorus sing of 'golden Sydney'. In 1994 Nowra was working on a film adaptation of White's novel which was subsequently abandoned due to problems with funding the film of a book whose rights are American-owned ('More Character-Driven', pp. 91–92).

[114] Hillel, 'Screenplays for Radio', p. 78.

[115] Litson, 'A Newer Nowra'.

[116] Nowra, 'The Chaos of Greed', *Age* 'Saturday Extra', 24 July 1993, p. 11. For analysis of the fortunes and media construction of Alan Bond, see Graeme Turner, *Making It National: Uses of Nationalism in Australian Popular Culture*. Sydney: Allen & Unwin, 1994, pp. 15–40.

[117] John Larkin, 'Nowra's Hard Look at the Eighties', *Sunday Age*, 25 July 1993, p. 7.

[118] Ad-libbing actors invariably swear, Nowra believes. See 'The Short, Nasty, Brutal Life of the Playwright', pp. 5–6.

[119] Kelly, 'More Character-Driven', p. 84.

[120] Kelly, 'More Character-Driven', pp. 85–86.

[121] Carmel Dwyer, 'Medal Puts Nowra on Top', *Sydney Morning Herald*, 6 July 1994, p. 24.

[122] Pamela Payne, [Review of *The Temple*], ANZTR Vol 8 No. 1, January 1994, p. 23.

[123] For Rosemary Neill he 'bristle[d] with bad energy and an sense of bottomless appetites'; Pamela Payne judged that he 'walk[ed] confidently a tightrope between larrikinism and monstrosity'; Stephen Dunne found him 'too much of a nice guy'; while Ian Phipps praised his 'chillingly ferocious energy and magnetic attraction' and considered 'he becomes truly the monster Louis Nowra envisaged.'*ANZTR* 8: 1, January 1994, pp. 22–23.

[124] Portus, 'The Victims of a Messiah Complex'.

[125] Kelly, 'More Character-Driven', p. 84.

[126] Nunn, 'A Première Feeling'.

[127] James Roy, 'Sharing Cultures: An ABC/CBC Radio Drama Exchange', *Canadian Theatre Review* 85, 1995, pp. 19–21.

[128] Hillel, 'Screenplays for Radio', pp. 78–80.

[129] *Così: The Screenplay*. Sydney: Currency, 1996. See also Nowra, 'The Lunatics That Run Hollywood', *Sydney Morning Herald* 'Metro', 22–28 March 1996, pp. 8–9; and Jo Litson, 'Cosi's Cossies', *Australian* 'Weekend Review', 23–24 March 1996, p. 10. At one stage Alfred Molina was a possible cast member ('More Character-Driven', p. 79).

[130] Richard Waller, 'Search for Humanity in the Bosnian Tragedy', *Courier Mail*, 22 July 1995, p. 20.

[131] Tim Robertson, [Review of *The Incorruptible*], *Age*, 14 July 1995, in *ANZTR* 9: 7, July 1995, p. 6.

[132] Jack Hibberd, [Review of *The Incorruptible*] *Australian*, 14 July 1995, in *ANZTR* 9: 7 July 1995, pp. 6–7.

[133] Peter Robinson, 'Nowra's Picture of the North', *Canberra Times*, 2 September 1996, p. 10.

[134] 'Peter Robinson, 'The Siege of Sarajevo on Stage', *Canberra Times*, 15 June 1996, p. 11.

[135] Mark Naglazas, 'Survival Instincts Put Bosnia on the Stage', *West Australian* 'Today', 28 November 1995, p. 4.

[136] Waller, 'Search for Humanity in the Bosnian Tragedy.'

[137] Kathryn Favelle, 'Beauty Pageant from Hell', *Muse* 152, June 1996, p. 20.

[138] Nowra, 'Meat Marketing', *Sydney Morning Herald*, 3 October 1994, p. 11.

[139] John Mangan, 'Controversial *Miss Bosnia* Divides the Audience at Perth Festival', *Age*, 1 March 1996, p. A17.

[140] Kelly, 'Video Interview with Louis Nowra', p. 142.

[141] Robinson, 'The Siege of Sarajevo On Stage'.

[142] For an account of the generic characteristics of 'serio-comic' Menippean satire see Mikhail Bakhtin, *The Dialogic Imagination*, pp. 26–27. These include powerful and course laughter, 'the liberty to crudely degrade', intellectual enquiry, unmasking of ideologues, utopian fantasy, freedom to move from 'heaven to earth, from earth to the nether world, from the present to the past, from the past into the future', parodies and travesties, multilingualism and autobiographical approaches, enabling (as with Petronius); the 'offering [of] a realistic reflection of the socially varied and heteroglot world of contemporary life.' Since Bakhtin characterises Menippean satire as an 'autobiographical' genre, '[permitting] the author, in all his various masks and faces, to move freely onto the field of his represented world' (p. 27), the stage *Summer of the Aliens* might claim to be Nowra's first literal Menippean satire, but generic features of Saturnalia and rogueish adventures through a cynical and culturally hybrid post-imperial society are more evident in 'The Jungle'.

[143] See Vicky Roach, 'A Movie Rated PC', *Daily Telegraph*, 12 September 1997, pp. 1–2; Lynden Barber, 'Flap Over a Burning Question', *Australian*, 31 October 1997, p. 14.

[144] Wal Eastman and Felicity Plunkett, [Reviews of *Deceit*] *ANZTR* 10: 8, August 1996, p. 37.

[145] Davidson, 'Interview with Louis Nowra', in Kelly, ed. *Louis Nowra*, p. 86.

Chapter Two (pages 63–98)

[1] *The Golden Age*. Rev. ed. Sydney: Currency, 1989, pp. 9–10. All further references to this edition.

[2] Veronica Kelly, 'Louis Nowra' in Bruce King, ed., *Post-Colonial English Plays: Commonwealth Drama Since 1960* . London: Macmillan, 1992, p. 55.

3 See Helen Gilbert, 'Dressed to Kill: A Post-Colonial Reading of Costume and the Body in Australian Theatre', in J. Ellen Gainor, ed. *Imperialism and Theatre: Essays on World Theatre, Drama and Performance*. London & NY: Routledge, 1995, pp.104–131, which analyses costume coding in *Inside the Island* and *Visions*.

4 See e.g. Jim Davidson, 'Interview with Louis Nowra', p. 80.

5 *Op. cit*, p. 78: 'There's a wonderful piece of graffiti that I see on the way to the Sydney Theatre Company every morning: it says "Our Culture is Produced by Your Minds"'.

6 For an understanding of how Harris' idea is applied to contemporary Canadian and Australian drama, see Joanne Tompkins, 'Infinitely Rehearsing Performance and Identity: *Africa Solo* and *The Book of Jessica*', *Canadian Theatre Review* 74, 1993, pp. 35–39 and '"The Story of Rehearsal Never Ends": Rehearsal, Performance, Identity in Settler Culture Drama', *Canadian Literature* 144, 1995, pp. 142–161. The latter article discusses *Summer of the Aliens, Così* and *Radiance*.

7 See e.g. Elinor Fuchs, *The Death of Character: Perspectives on Theatre After Modernism*. Bloomington: Indiana UP, 1996. She sees the two principle streams of modernist theatre as the Zolaesque naturalistic mimetic project, and the post-Symbolist self-consciously theatrical cosmic and quest narratives.

8 Jeremy Ridgman, 'Interview: Louis Nowra, Stephen Sewell and Neil Armfield talk to Jeremy Ridgman', *Australasian Drama Studies* 1:2, 1983, p. 122.

9 Some of this material is more fully expounded in Kelly, 'Louis Nowra', in Bruce King, ed., *Post-Colonial English Plays: Commonwealth Drama Since 1960*, pp. 50–66.

10 *Post-Colonial Drama; Theory, Practice, Politics*. London & NY: Routledge, 1996, p. 205. For discussions of *Visions* and *The Golden Age* in this context see pp. 221, 224–226.

11 Makeham, 'The Black Hole of Our History', p. 29.

12 Quoted in Bill Ashcroft, Gareth Griffiths and Helen Tiffin, *The Empire Writes Back: Theory and Practice in Post-Colonial Literatures*, London & NY: Routledge, 1989, p. 35. Their paraphrase of Wilson explains his novelistic style of 'mixing past, present, future, and imperial and colonial cultures' as rejecting 'the apparently inescapable polarities of language and [deploying] the destructive energies of European culture in the service of a future community in which division and categorization are no longer the bases of perception.'

13 Makeham, 'The Black Hole of Our History', p. 30.

14 In 'At the Crossroads' Nowra pays tribute to Neil Armfield, director of the Nimrod première of *Inside the Island*: 'Armfield has been able to counter my metaphors and detachment with a humanness and sense of the reality of the events onstage' (106).

[15] Lynch, the poor Irish *demi-mondaine* with cultural aspirations, is referring to the French poet Charles Baudelaire, whose poetry she uses in song form. His 'nigger' is his creole mistress Jeanne Duval, his 'black Venus' and inspirer of many poems in his famous (and banned) book *Les fleurs du mal*.

[16] 'Director's Notes', in Nowra, *'Inside the Island' and 'The Precious Woman'*. Sydney: Currency, 1981, p. 94. All further references are to this edition.

[17] Alison Croggon, 'Act of Revelation', *Bulletin*, 21 April 1992, p. 10. Alyn Brodsky's book *Madame Lynch and Friend* was a source for *Visions*. Brodsky portrays the indomitable but limited Lynch as a self-appointed cultural missionary to Paraguay who bore many studied insults from Paraguayan high society and particularly from Lopez's repulsive and ignorant family who refused to acknowledge his 'whore'. It was many years, and many children, later that Lynch turned into the vengeful tyrant and ruthless looter in the war in which she and Lopez imposed genocide on Paraguay more thoroughly than their enemies. Nowra treats humiliations inflicted on Lynch, such as the spattering of her dress with mud from the carriage of the Lopez sisters, to create scenes in which, seemingly gratuitously, she inflicts this punishment on them (I, 5, see Brodsky p. 70). The historical Lynch's past history is buried in the text of *Visions*, but even her most appalling acts have their reasons.

[18] *The Incorruptible*. Sydney: Currency, 1995, p. 13. All further references to this edition.

[19] *Albert Names Edward*, p. 78. Albert is possibly remembering in typical mishmash fashion Alfred Hitchcock's 1945 thriller *Spellbound*, where a war-traumatised Gregory Peck's amnesia is cured by the psychological sleuthing of Ingrid Bergman.

[20] *The Cheated* contains a section 'Wall Within Walls' with news accounts of incidents where old people, lovers or children were self-imprisoned through dread of a uncontrollable world outside, or incarcerated by their families through shame and twisted protectiveness. Nowra's drama contains many examples of such 'cheated', notably feral children from Ivan in *Inner Voices* to Olive of 'The Jungle'.

[21] Nowra, 'Instructions to a Painter', *Southerly* 45: 2, 1985.

[22] The interactions of *The Golden Age*'s eroded family are complex on the realistic level. Stef is Angel's son (36–37) yet Betsheb takes over as his mother while Angel clings to Melorne. While Angel has been fertile, Betsheb seems not to be. If in the 'King Lear' performance the family play 'themselves' it is an inverted ritual which substitutes emotional preferences for genetic relationships.

[23] *The Temple*. Sydney: Currency, 1993, p. 11. All further references to this edition. The published text has the name 'Burchett' for this declining dynasty; it was changed during rehearsals for the Playbox première to one more redolent of 'old' Australian money and Sterling snobbery.

Their family brewing business, says the patriarch, was started by 'a free settler, not a convict or emancipist' (9).

[24] 'Shall We Dance?' (Scene 7) in 'The Jungle'. Unpubl. The MS (p. 5) adds the line '... I hope it was because only a father could kill with so much hate'.

[25] Makeham, 'The Black Hole of Our History', p. 30. In the *Tales* of Nahman of Bratslav, from which comes the epigraph of *The Precious Woman*, is found a woman who can burn out a man's brain with a lens: 'The King and the Emperor', p. 75.

[26] *Whitsunday.* Sydney: Australian Opera, 1988. Program. n.p.

[27] *Palu.* Sydney: Picador, 1987, p. 221.

[28] 'Byzantine Flowers'. Unpubl TS, p. 62.

[29] This argument is developed further in Veronica Kelly, 'Staging Mabo: The Recent Theatre of Louis Nowra', in Irmtraud Petersson & Martin Duwell, eds. *'And What Books Do You Read?' New Studies in Australian Literature.* St Lucia: UQP, 1996, pp. 112–125.

[30] 'Such organic metaphors [trees], and others like "parent-child" and "stream-tributary" acted to keep the new literature in its place. The plant and parent metaphors stressed age, experience, roots, tradition, and, most importantly, the connection between antiquity and value. They implied the same distinctions as those existing between metropolis and frontier: parents are more experienced, more important, more substantial, less brash than their offspring. Above all they are the *origin* and therefore claim the final authority in questions of taste and value'. Ashcroft, Griffiths & Tiffin, *The Empire Writes Back*, p. 16.

[31] Testoni, 'The Rise and Fall and Rise of Louis Nowra', p. 85.

[32] Nowra, '*Inner Voices* and the First Coil', in Kelly, ed., *Louis Nowra*, pp. 51–52.

[33] This is the octet of sonnet 121 of *Les fleurs du mal*.

[34] The war left Paraguay a nation of women, having killed three quarters of the male population. Brodsky (258) gives the prewar 1864 population as 525,000, reduced by 1870 to 221,000 of whom 28,700 were male, mostly aged over 80 or under 8. Woman and children fought the invaders with unfailing determination and appalling courage.

[35] In his lecture on *Visions* at the University of Queensland on 3 June 1985, Nowra explained his reworkings of the text for the 1985 MTC production. He saw that Valera should have been Juana's brother, not her cousin, since he wanted a closeness between them which Valera exploits, trading off his sister's abilities to gain money. He added more affection between Lynch and Lopez in the swamp scenes, but made it clear that Lopez is angry at the play scene, seeing it as patronisingly naïve and a slur on his culture. In the MTC production Juana gave the last speech in a French accent, which Nowra approved as it stresses that her last 'vision' derives from Lynch, not from her own internal life.

[36] Jean Baudrillard, *Seduction* trans. Brian Singer. London: Macmillan, 1990, pp. 54–55.

[37] See Veronica Kelly, '"Who's the Bigger Dill?" The Madhouse in Recent Australian Drama' in Leigh Dale & Simon Ryan, ed., *The Body in the Library: Post-Colonial Representations of the Body.* Amsterdam: Rodopi, forthcoming.

[38] Boofhead's encouragement to the failing Crow as they struggle across the tidal beach from the bombing of Darwin. *Crow.* Sydney: Currency, 1994, p. 71. All further references to this edition.

[39] Nunn, 'A Première Feeling', p. 19.

[40] *Radiance.* Sydney: Currency, 1993, p. 26. All further references to this edition.

Chapter Three (pages 99–140)

[1] This Bugs Bunnyish image derives from hints in the stories of the careers of the historical Francisco Solano Lopez and Eliza Lynch. When the latter tyrannised over the provincial *haut monde* of Asunçion she gave masked balls where attendance (and financial contribution) were compulsory and the hostess dictated the costumes of the guests. In the *demi-monde* of Louis Napoléon where Lynch hoped to establish herself, transvestite *bals masqués* are reported, including one where half the Garde Impériale attended dressed as nuns. See Macintyre, *Forgotten Fatherland*, p. 23; Brodsky p. 25.

[2] See Peter Brooks, *The Melodramatic Imagination: Balzac, Henry James, Melodrama and the Mode of Excess.* New York: Columbia UP, 1984. This important study argues the social significances of melodramatic repertoire and performance idioms—rhetoric, gesture and music—and the vital function of muteness as melodrama's characteristic physical deprivation (p. 57). 'The text of muteness in particular suggests expression of needs, desires, states, occulted imperatives below the level of consciousness' (p. 80).

[3] Gerry Turcotte, '"Perfecting the Monologue of Silence": An Interview with Louis Nowra', *Kunapipi* 9: 3, 1987, p. 58.

[4] See Gerry Turcotte, '"Speaking the Formula of Abjection": Hybrids and Gothic Discourses in Louis Nowra's Novels', *Westerly* 36: 3, September 1991, pp. 61–72; and Jim Davidson, 'Tasmanian Gothic', *Meanjin* 48: 2, 1989, pp. 307–324 which deals with *The Golden Age.*

[5] Rosemary Jackson, *Fantasy: The Literature of Subversion.* New York: Methuen, 1981, p. 177.

[6] Mary Shelley's volubly philosophical autodidact anti-hero is termed the Creature. In Richard Brinsley Peake's first dramatisation of the novel, *Presumption: or, The Fate of Frankenstein*, performed in London in 1823,

he was renamed the Demon, and rendered mute in the then-prevalent melodramatic style where physical signs held equal importance to verbal ones in the performance intertext. This nameless monster, as created by the leading mime T. P. Cooke, was a powerful and ambiguous pantomimic part of the type which Nowra characteristically writes, e.g. Ivan, Betsheb, Stef, Olive.

7 In her reading of the 'Frankenstein' myths, Jackson differentiates them from the vampire group, although both stories involve the initiator in strong and transgressive acts of will. While I am concentrating here on the Frankenstein metaphor, Jackson's analysis of the communal effects of power incursions contained in the Dracula prototype is a fruitful one for post-colonial analysis. 'In the Frankenstein type of myth... self becomes other through a self-generated metamorphosis, through the subjects' alienation from himself and consequent splitting or multiplying of identities... In the Dracula type of myth... otherness is established through a fusion of self with something outside, producing a new form, an "other" reality... This second type centralises the problem of *power*. Dracula... collects conquests, collects victims to prove the power of possession, to try to establish a total, self-supporting system' (p. 59).

8 See Tony Thwaites, Lloyd Davis and Warwick Mules, *Tools for Cultural Studies: An Introduction*. Melbourne: Macmillan, 1995, p. 182. 'Bricolage' is a term for informal cultural improvisation, using whatever appropriate or inappropriate materials are immediately to hand. The term originated in anthropology, describing social (and by extension literary) practices which take 'social givens and [deflect] them towards other ends, investing them with other meanings'. Bricolage may originate 'on the fringes of received practice, and then either [become] absorbed into, or [force] a rupture with, the official version.'

9 'I Was a Teenage Alien' in *Summer of the Aliens*. Sydney: Currency, 1992, p. 6.

10 Chambers, p. 107.

11 'The Translator', *Overland* 101, pp. 2–6.

12 The ergot episode of *Inside the Island* is based on the famous 1951 outbreak in the small French town of Pont St Esprit. See John Tittensor, 'The Town That Went Mad', *National Times*, 16–22 August 1985, and subsequent correspondence with Nowra about the nature of the contaminant (ergot, mercury, alkaloid etc) and the motivation for the cover-up by the authorities. One symptom of 'St Anthony's fire' amplified in *Inside the Island* is the hallucination of being on fire and the body emitting flames. Blackened limbs (an image used in the play) are clinically the first sign of the gangrene which frequently ensued; in Nowra's context they suggest hybridisation between the black indigene and the white settler experiences.

[13] See Kelly, '"Lest We Forget": *Inside the Island*', in Kelly, ed. *Louis Nowra*, pp. 99–113.

[14] See Mikhail Bakhtin, *Rabelais and his World* trans. Helene Iswolsky. Bloomington: Indiana UP, 1984, for the category of Carnival, which validates and sacralises the 'lower bodily stratum' and its functions.

[15] See Helen Gilbert, 'Post-colonial Grotesques: Re-membering the Body in Louis Nowra's *Visions* and *The Golden Age*', SPAN 2: 36, 1993, p. 629.

[16] Nowra in an interview rejected the category of 'hyphen-person' or 'Irish-Australian' and some recent constructs of official ethnically-based 'multi-culturalism' (see Chapter One): 'I think that eventually all the human races should interbreed. I'm a great believer in mixed blood. Like in *Miss Bosnia* when they mention the dogs of Sarajevo now being mixed breeds... This nineteenth-century fantasy about pure blood is such a shocking fantasy because, yes, it's still with us.' See Kelly, 'More Character-Driven', pp. 89–90.

[17] Salman Rushdie, 'In Good Faith', in *Imaginary Homelands: Essays and Criticism 1981–1991*. London: Granta, 1991, p. 394.

[18] This scene takes place in Macarthur's obsession, an aviary of tropical birds which demonstrate their own good breeding by shitting on visitors. The moral and sexual ambivalances of the term 'mongrel' within Australian poplar usage are interestingly explored in Nick Enright's 1991 play *Mongrels*.

[19] Robert J. C. Young, *Colonial Desire: Hybridity in Theory, Culture and Race*. London & NY: Routledge, 1995, pp. 8–9. All further references to this edition.

[20] Young (180). The empirical refutation of the sterile 'hybrid' through the proliferation of mixed-race people caused the nineteenth-century supremacists to shift their grounds: 'As so often with racial issues, instead of being abandoned altogether, the scientific arguments in support of racial prejudice moved elsewhere, to the theory of "types", to questions of psychological, intellectual and "moral" difference, to the terrifying ideas of social Darwinism and eugenics, and the adaptation of evolutionary theory to the ideas of racial supremacy and the extinction of races' (13).

[21] Nowra describes references to the 1st-century BC elegaic poet Ovid, and to the rock group the Velvet Underground, in his novel *The Misery of Beauty* as 'examples of the trash and highbrow mixture I fondly juggle'. See '*Inner Voices* and the First Coil', p. 54. For example, Ovid's grotesquely bloodthirsty battle between the Lapiths and Centaurs (*Metamorphoses*, Book 12) appears to be referenced in the novel's description of the Rabelaisian mêlée precipitated by Earl in Baltroy's nightclub (66–73). The precise function of Ovidian moods in Nowra's plays has received no attention to date.

[22] Michael Holquist, ed., *The Dialogic Imagination by M. M. Bakhtin: Four Essays*. Austin: University of Texas Press, 1981, pp. 113, 115 passim. Bakhtin's complex argument about the differing historical valencies of the metamorphosis trope is contained in his development of the idea of the novelistic chronotope (111 ff.). He finds Ovid himself typical of a cultural moment wherein metamorphosis becomes a private, dehistoricised experience, although he allows that the structure of his poem retains the image as part of 'the whole world of cosmogenic and historical process' (114).

[23] Nowra in his article '*Inner Voices* and the First Coil' speaks of the references to Ovidian metamorphoses and flux running through *Inner Voices* and *The Misery of Beauty*. In *The Watchtower* the character Nell reads from Ovid's poem with its many bird transformations. Typically these narratives of the internal experience of metamorphosis emphasise loss of human speech, e.g. the transformation into bats of the daughters of Minyas: 'They had no feathery plumage with which to fly, but they did raise themselves into the air on transparent wings. When they tried to talk, they uttered a thin sound, in keeping with their changed bodies, and continued their complaints in faint squeaks.' *The 'Metamorphoses' of Ovid*, trans. Mary M. Innes. Harmondworth: Penguin, 1955, p. 105.

[24] Dulcie in *Summer of the Aliens* is played as a black character in the stage version. In the radio original there is no indication of Dulcie's race; in the theatre version she is rendered Other both by her race and by her experience of sexual abuse.

[25] *The Dialogic Imagination*, p. 360.

[26] 'Bakhtin: Linguistic Hybridity', in Young, pp. 20–28. See also Homi Bhabha, ed. *Nation and Narration*. London: Routledge, 1990. Bhabha's theory of hybridity and mimicry are developed through his essays collected in *The Location of Culture*. London & NY: Routledge, 1994.

[27] Helen Gilbert & Joanne Tompkins, '*Post-Colonial Drama: Theory, Practice, Politics*, p. 210.

[28] Cressy's narrative of her experience on tour with a 'poltergeist'— actually her sleepwalking, which externalises her old terrors and attempts to protect herself from them—suggests that her childhood experiences have given her the incest survivor's typical ability to detach from her body and to perform superhuman feats indicative of intense psychic power (25–26). As she says of her burnt arm, '*gazing at it as if it belongs to someone else*', 'It's only flesh' (49). Cressy and Dulcie of *Summer of the Aliens* are similar sexually abused survivors who try to protect their spirit from their ravaged bodies.

[29] See Rex Cramphorn, '*Inner Voices*' in Kelly, ed. *Louis Nowra* pp. 42–45. Cramphorn reads the play intertextually with Peter Handke's *Caspar*

and Calderon's *La Vida es Sueno* (Life is a Dream), notable reworkings of the theme of the moral education of the prince and the immateriality of glory. To these comparisons can be added Friedrich von Kleist's *Prinz von Homburg*, which Nowra translated in 1982 for Lighthouse, in which the Prince's learning experience of action, disgrace, condemnation and pardon may or may not be a dream.

[30] See David Williamson, *The Coming of Stork*. In *Three Plays*. Sydney: Currency, 1974.

[31] John Bell, 'Director's Note', *Inner Voices*, p. xiii.

[32] 'Louis Nowra on *Visions*', (audiotape).

[33] The question of faking is also significant for the unperformed 'Dreamhouses', where George, locked into agonising mutual dependency with his schizophrenic daughter, in exasperation accuses her of being 'a fake' like her mother, of putting on a performance of madness in order to drive him mad. 'Dreamhouses' [1974] unpub. TS, p. 65.

[34] Frank Gauntlett, *Daily Mirror*, 2 January 1990, and Bob Evans, *Sydney Morning Herald* (1 January 1990), in *ANZTR* 3, December 1989, pp.21–23.

[35] 'Byzantine Flowers' [1989] unpub. TS, p. 83.

[36] In the STC première these roles were doubled by Susan Prior.

[37] 'Metzger's Siege', Scene 12 of 'The Jungle' [1995], unpub. TS.

[38] In the context of 'The Jungle' Nicolae evens the score by refusing to be on his 'best behaviour'. In the subsequent Scene 13 'Dissecting *King Roger*' he stages his own performance by outrageously monstering those of Sean's friends who have warned him about Nicolae's motivations, running amok in the mansions of the top people in the best B-movie Creature tradition.

[39] This imaged derives from accounts of the polio victim, President Franklin D. Roosevelt.

[40] Nikola Tesla was the Croatian-born American electrical scientist whose vivid skeins of electric currents are utilised as visual motif in countless 1930s horror movies.

[41] The published script has the irrepressible trio of Laurie, Brenda and Nick plotting to invade Russia: 'It's the beginning of capitalism. No stupid regulations like in the West. This is the new frontier. This time capitalism will work for us. This time we'll get it right!'... They'll be like babes in the wood' (91). During the rehearsal period of the Playbox première the more topical Vietnam was substituted for Russia.

[42] See also Veronica Kelly, 'Smashing Temples: Cultural Symptoms of the 1980s in Australian Mainstage Comedy and Farce', *Modern Drama* 38, 1995, pp. 97–108.

[43] 'And Jesus went into the temple of God, and cast out all them that sold and bought in the temple, and overthrew the tables of the moneychangers, and

the seats of them that sold doves, And said unto them, It is written, my house shall be called the house of prayer; but ye have made it a den of thieves.' Matt. 21: 12–13.

44 Rushdie, p. 394.

Chapter Four (pages 141–178)

1 Tompkins, "The Story of Rehearsal Never Ends", p. 155.

2 Joanne Tompkins, '"Spectacular Resistance": Metatheatre in Post-Colonial Drama', *Modern Drama* 38: 1 (1995), p. 42.

3 For a discussion of the use of Shakespeare within the counter-discourse of postcolonial theatre, see Joanne Tompkins, 'Re-citing Shakespeare in Post-Colonial Drama', *Essays in Theatre/Etudes théâtrales* 15: 1 (1996), pp. 15–22, which discusses *The Golden Age*.

4 Brodsky (36) relates how Lynch and Lopez toured on their 'honeymoon' to the Crimea, where it was a fashionable entertainment to picnic for an hour or two on a safe promontory overlooking the battle.

5 Jeremy Ridgman, Review of Rodney Fisher, ed., *Seven One-Act Plays* (Sydney: Currency, 1983), *Australasian Drama Studies* 2: 1 (1983), p. 128.

6 'Dressed to Kill', p. 104.

7 *The Dialogic Imagination*, pp. 113, 115.

8 Tompkins, 'The Story of Rehearsal Never Ends', p. 158. This comment occurs in the context of a discussion of Canadian and Australian post-colonial theatre, including an analysis of rehearsal of national identity in Nowra's recent plays.

9 Gilbert, 'Dressed to Kill', p. 118.

10 Marjorie Garber, *Vested Interests: Cross-dressing and Cultural Anxiety.* New York: HarperPerennial, 1993, p.16.

11 Tompkins calls the Canadian play *Afrika Solo* by Djanet Sears (1990) 'a play about the accretion—rather than the discarding of identities' ('The Story of Rehearsal Never Ends', p. 145). The same can be said in a gendered sense about 'Byzantine Flowers' and much of Nowra's theatre generally.

12 Kelly, 'More Character-Driven', p. 88.

13 'Spectacular Resistance', pp. 47–48. Arguing from Bhabha, Tompkins shows that colonial mimicry is double-edged since it 'becomes the vehicle for ironic comment on the original', and menace is always present because 'reflection' is never merely just 'homage'.

14 Tompkins, 'The Story of Rehearsal Never Ends', p. 156. This is the most thorough analysis of the stage version of *Summer of the Aliens*.

15 'The new knowledge of re-ordered kinship at the end of the play does not resolve anything since the identities are confused and composite at

the beginning of the play and remain so at the end' (Tompkins, 'The Story of Rehearsal Never Ends', p. 158). Describing Brian Thomson's set and Fiona Johnstone's lighting design for the Belvoir Street première, Tompkins notes the imaginative amplification of theme by the flooding of the stage for the tidal mud flat scenes: 'the lighting produced endlessly changing and swirling patterns on the wall and ceiling' which conveyed 'the forever unanchored answers to the question they sing, "Who is she?"'

[16] Jackson, *Fantasy: The Literature of Subversion*, p. 178.

[17] The music track for the QTC/Kooemba Jdarra co-production of early 1997 (Brisbane and Queensland tour) was devised by John Rodgers with the vocalist Christine Johnson. The director Wesley Enoch wanted it to be 'about voice. The voice of the mother, the call of the island, the voice of an opera singer.' Characteristic music was devised for the funeral, the fire (in Italian opera mode), with crickets, 'wind, mud and star sounds', with distinctive bird calls for each sister. Mae's speaking in tongues was suggested through music, as was Cressy's operatic voice, and the 'Belle of Dublin City' tune was arranged and transformed. 'John Rodgers on *Radiance*', *OnQ* [Newsletter of the Queensland Theatre Company], Autumn 1997 [p. 3].

[18] The title *Così Fan Tutte* can be translated as 'all women are like that'.

[19] In a review in *Theatre Australasia*, June 1994, of David Bell's Zootango production of the revised script, Richard Bladel regrets the loss of political relevance caused by the excision of the home scenes showing Lewis's 'own private Vietnam', created allusively via such devices as the exploding ginger beer bottles, the squealing pigs at the abattoir, and the burning cat. See *ANZTR* 8: 5, May 1994, p. 96.

[20] Review of *Così* by the Red Shed Theatre Company, *Adelaide Review*. *ANZTR* 7: 7, July 1993, p. 46.

[21] 'Interview: Louis Nowra, Stephen Sewell and Neil Armfield Talk to Jeremy Ridgman', p. 110.

[22] Jim Davidson, 'Interview with Louis Nowra', p. 83.

[23] The most extended textual comparison between Nowra and Mozart/Da Ponte is found in Russell Walsh's review for *Theatre Australasia*, June 1994. He finds that while Mozart (or Wilde, or Orton) make profound statements out of trivial plots, *Così* reverses the process. The character of Doug, whom he finds underused, is an exception in his interrogation of Lewis about his sex life 'with irresistible Bracknellian force'. See *ANZTR* 8: 6, June 1994, p. 44.

[24] In the 1992 text Zac has his last word, ending the play by playing 'Ride of the Valkyries' on his piano-accordion, 'a cheerful maniacal grin on his face' joined by full orchestra at high volume, followed by a blackout and silence (1992, 81). The 1994 conclusion is Lewis's narration of the

fate of the characters and his returning the stage to its pre-performance state of darkness on the line 'Time to turn out the lights' (89). This endings create the most metatheatrically resonant (as well as functional) of Nowra's blackouts. As Angela Bennie comments, 'life and light come from the theatre; anything outside is darkness'. Review of *Così* in the *Sydney Morning Herald*, 23 April 1992, rpt. in *ANZTR* 6: 4, April 1992, p. 41.

[25] Ruth's obsession with exact numbers of steps in a casual stage cross can be paralleled by more sophisticated practitioners: Beckett as director of *Endgame* changed Clov's steps from nine to eight. See S. E. Gontarski, ed. and intro., *The Theatrical Notebooks of Samuel Beckett* Vol. 2. London: Faber, 1992, p. 50.

[26] This detail was borrowed from an incident when the accomplished actor Geoffrey Rush was seized with stage fright and unable to go on in his acclaimed one-man show *Diary of a Madman*. Nowra hoped that Rush would create the role of Roy, but it was assumed by the comic virtuoso Barry Otto.

[27] The La Boite production of 1994, directed by David Fenton and designed by Andrew Raymond, added a period in-joke through Zac's set model. It reproduced the white box and red feather set of Peter Brook's famous 1970 production of *A Midsummer Night's Dream*, making Zac's abstract design concept cutting-edge avant-garde within the play's 1971 setting.

Works of Louis Nowra

(1) Stage Plays (including opera libretti and translations)

Kiss the One-Eyed Priest
Melbourne, La Mama, July 1973. Director Darryl Wilkinson. Unpubl.

Dreamhouses
Written 1974. Not performed professionally. Unpubl.

Albert Names Edward (See also RADIO)
Melbourne, La Mama, 17 October 1976. Director Darryl Wilkinson. Published in *Five Plays for Radio: Nightmares of the Old Obscenity Master*, ed. Alrene Sykes, Sydney: Currency Methuen, 1975. Rev. ed. Sydney: Currency, 1983.

Sleezee
Melbourne, Last Laugh Theatre Restaurant, 19 February 1977. Unpubl.

Inner Voices (See also ADAPTATIONS)
Sydney, Nimrod Downstairs, 25 February 1977. Director John Bell, designer Brian Hocking. Sydney: Currency, 1977. Rev. ed. Sydney: Currency, 1983.

Visions
Sydney, Paris Theatre, 17 August 1978. Director Rex Cramphorn, designer Luciana Arrighi. Sydney: Currency, 1979.

The Lady of the Camellias with Rex Cramphorn (trans.)
Sydney, Drama Theatre of the Opera House, Sydney Theatre Company, 21 February 1979. Director Rex Cramphorn, designer Michael Pearce. Translated from Dumas *fils*. Unpubl.

Cyrano de Bergerac (trans.)
Sydney, Drama Theatre of the Opera House, Sydney Theatre Company, 24 July 1980. Director Richard Wherrett, designer John Stoddart. Translated from Edmond Rostand. Unpubl.

Inside the Island
Sydney, Nimrod Theatre, 13 August 1980. Director Neil Armfield, designer Bill Haycock. Sydney: Currency, 1981.

The Death of Joe Orton
Adelaide, Playhouse, State Theatre Company of South Australia, 4 October 1980. Director Robert Alexander. Playreading. (Written 1973). Unpubl.

The Precious Woman
  Sydney, Drama Theatre of the Opera House, Sydney Theatre Company,
  11 November 1980. Director Richard Wherrett, designer Luciana
  Arrighi. Sydney: Currency, 1981. Published with Indonesian text, trans.
  Tuti Indra Malaon, ed. Philip Kitley, Toowoomba: University of
  Southern Queensland Press, 1997.

Beauty and the Beast (with Rex Cramphorn)
  Sydney, Drama Theatre of the Opera House, Sydney Theatre Company,
  26 December 1980. Directors Rex Cramphorn and Louis Nowra,
  designer Silvia Jansons. Music Sarah de Jong. Unpubl.

Lulu (trans.)
  Adelaide, Playhouse, State Theatre Company of South Australia, 5 June
  1981. Director Jim Sharman, designer Brian Thomson and Luciana
  Arrighi. Adapted from Frank Wedekind. Unpubl.

Spellbound
  Adelaide, Playhouse, Lighthouse Theatre Company, 22 May 1982.
  Director Neil Armfield, designer Wendy Dickson. Unpubl.

The Prince of Homburg (trans.)
  Adelaide, Playhouse, Lighthouse Theatre Company, 2 October 1982.
  Director Louis Nowra. Translated from Heinrich von Kleist, designer
  Mary Moore. Unpubl.

Royal Show
  Adelaide, Playhouse, Lighthouse Theatre Company, 19 October 1982.
  Director Jim Sharman, designer Stephen Curtis. Unpubl.

Sunrise
  Adelaide, Playhouse, Lighthouse Theatre Company, 19 November
  1983. Director Jim Sharman, designer Geoffrey Gifford. Sydney:
  Currency & State Theatre Company of South Australia, 1983.

The Golden Age
  Melbourne, Studio Theatre of the Victorian Arts Centre, Playbox Theatre
  Company, 8 February 1985. Director Rex Cramphorn, designer Shaun
  Gurton. Sydney: Currency & Playbox Theatre Company, 1985. Rev. ed. 1989.

Ghosts (with May-Brit Akerholt) (trans.)
  Sydney, Belvoir Street Theatre, 4 March 1988. Director Neil Armfield,
  designer Brian Thomson. Translated from Henrik Ibsen. Unpubl.

Capricornia
  Sydney, Belvoir Street Theatre, 23 April 1988. Director Kingston
  Anderson, designer Jennie Tait. From the novel by Xavier Herbert.
  Sydney: Currency Press & Belvoir Street Theatre, 1988. Rev. ed. 1992.

Whitsunday (opera)
  Opera with music by Brian Howard. Sydney, Drama Theatre of the Opera
  House, Australian Opera conducted by Stuart Challender, 2 September
  1988. Director Neil Armfield, designer Stephen Curtis. Sydney: Australian
  Opera, 1988 (Text in Program).

Byzantine Flowers
Sydney, Wharf Theatre, Sydney Theatre Company, 30 December 1989. Directed by Kingston Anderson, designed by D4 Design. Unpubl.

The Watchtower
Sydney, Parade Theatre, National Institute of Dramatic Art, 31 May 1990. Director Mark Gaal. Unpubl.

Love Burns (opera)
Opera with music by Graeme Koehne. Adelaide, Playhouse, Seymour Group conducted by Warwick Stengards, 28 February 1992. Director Neil Armfield, designer Brian Thomson. Unpubl.

Summer of the Aliens (see also RADIO)
Melbourne, Russell Street Theatre, Melbourne Theatre Company, 17 March 1992. Director Nadia Tass, designer Trina Parker. Sydney: Currency, 1992.

Così (see also FILMS)
Sydney, Belvoir Street Theatre, 21 April 1992. Director Adam Cook, designer Stephen Curtis. Sydney: Currency & Belvoir Street Theatre, 1992. Rev. ed. 1994.

The Temple
Melbourne, Malthouse Theatre, Playbox Theatre Company, 27 July 1993. Director Bruce Myles, designer Judith Cobb. Sydney: Currency & Playbox Theatre Centre, 1993.

Radiance (see also FILMS)
Sydney, Belvoir Street Theatre, 21 September 1993. Director Rosalba Clemente, designer Brian Thomson. Sydney: Currency & Belvoir Street Theatre, 1993.

Crow
Adelaide, Playhouse, State Theatre Company of South Australia, 14 May 1994. Director Adam Cook, designer Brian Thomson. Sydney: Currency & State Theatre Company of South Australia, 1994.

The Widows (see also RADIO)
Wollongong, University of Wollongong Festival of Creative Arts, 15 June 1994. Unpubl.

The Price of Prayer
Sydney, Wharf 1, Sydney Theatre Company, 7 January 1995. Director David Berthold, designer Kim Carpenter. (Scene from *The Jungle* in 'Sydney Stories', Program 1). Unpubl.

The Incorruptible
Melbourne, C.U.B Malthouse, Playbox Theatre Centre, 11 July 1995. Director Aubrey Mellor, designer Shaun Gurton. Sydney. Currency & Playbox Theatre Centre, 1995.

Miss Bosnia
    Brisbane, La Boite Theatre, Teatar di Migma, 22 July 1995. Director Sue
    Rider, designer Christopher Smith. Unpubl.

The Jungle
    Sydney, Wharf 1, Sydney Theatre Company, 25 October 1995. Director
    David Berthold, designer Peter England. Unpubl.

Deceit
    Hobart, Peacock Theatre, Zootango Theatre Company, 14 August 1996.
    Director Louise Permezel, designer Teresa Lawler. Unpubl.

(2) Radio

Albert Names Edward (see also PLAYS)
    ABC Radio, 15 June 1975. Director Peter Brett. Published in *Five Plays
    for Radio: Nightmares of the Old Obscenity Master*, ed. Alrene Sykes,
    Sydney: Currency Methuen, 1975. Rev. ed. Sydney: Currency, 1983.

The Song Room
    ABC-FM Radio, 18 November 1980. Director and producer Andrew
    McLennan. Music Sarah de Jong. Published in *Seven One-Act Plays*, ed.
    Rodney Fisher, Sydney: Currency, 1983.

The Widows (see also PLAYS)
    ABC-FM Radio, 29 April 1986. Produced by Jane Ulman, Howard Gelman
    and Louis Nowra. Music Sarah de Jong. Unpubl.

Summer of the Aliens (see also PLAYS)
    BBC Radio October 1989. ABC-FM 7 August 1990. Producer Jane
    Ulman. Music Sarah de Jong. Unpubl.

Sydney: A Screenplay for Radio
    ABC-FM Radio, 21 and 28 September 1993. Director Louis Nowra,
    Associate Producer Anne Wynter, Producer Howard Gelman, Executive
    Producer David Chandler. Music Sarah de Jong. Unpubl.

Moon of the Exploding Trees
    ABC/CBC. Recorded 1993. Director James Roy. Music Sarah de Jong.
    Not broadcast. Unpubl.

(3) Television

Displaced Persons
    ABC-TV, 29 September 1985. Director Geoffrey Nottage, producer Jan
    Chapman. Music Martin Armiger. Unpubl.

Hunger
    ABC-TV, 10 October 1986. Director Stephen Wallace, producer Jan
    Chapman. Unpubl.

The Lizard King
  ABC-TV, 28 February 1988. Director Geoffrey Nottage, producer Jan Chapman. Unpubl.

The Last Resort
  ABC-TV, 27 April 1988. 30-part serial. Producer Jan Chapman. Writers Louis Nowra, Gabrielle Lord, Tim Gooding, Bert Deling. Unpubl.

Directly from My Heart to You
  Nine Network, 30 December 1996. Director Catherine Millar, Producers Bryan Brown and Helen Watts for New Town Films. Unpubl.

(4) Films

Map of the Human Heart
  Director Vincent Ward, Writers Louis Nowra and Vincent Ward. Vincent Ward Film Productions, Distributed Miramax 1993. Unpubl.

Così
  Director Mark Joffe. Writer Louis Nowra. Producers Smiley Films in association with Meridian Films, 1995. Screenplay published Sydney: Currency, 1996.

Heaven's Burning
  Director Craig Lahiff. Writer Louis Nowra. Producers Al Clark and Helen Leake, 1997. Producer Duo Art Productions, 1997. Unpubl.

Radiance
  Director Rachel Perkins. Writer Louis Nowra. Producers Ned Lander and Andrew Myers. Distributed Beyond Distribution, 1998. Unpubl.

(5) Novels, short stories

The Misery of Beauty: The Loves of Frogman. Sydney: Angus & Robertson, 1976.

The Cheated. Sydney: Angus & Robertson, 1979.

'Instructions to a Painter', *Southerly* 45 (2), 1985, pp. 157–163.

'The Translator', *Overland* 101, 1985, pp. 2–6.

Palu. Sydney: Picador, 1987.

'The Father', in Helen Daniel, ed., *Expressway.* Ringwood: Penguin, 1989, pp. 144–151.

Edge of the Earth: Stories and Images from the Antipodes by Vincent Ward, with Alison Carter, Geoff Chapple and Louis Nowra. Photos Geoffrey Short & Miles Hargent. Auckland: Heinemann Reed, 1990.

'In the Forest of the Eternals', in Tony Ayres, ed., *String of Pearls: Stories About Cross-dressing.* Sydney: Allen & Unwin, 1996, pp. 137–155.

Red Nights. Sydney: Picador, 1997.

(6) Adaptations of Nowra's writing

Inner Voices
Opera with music by Brian Howard and libretto by Louis Nowra.
Melbourne, Grant Street Theatre, 2 October 1979. Director Peter Jordan,
performed by the Victoria State Opera conducted by Richard Divall.
From his play *Inner Voices*. Unpubl.

The Cheated
Dance theatre with choreography by Kai Tai Chan and music by
Richard Vella. Sydney, Cleveland Street Performance Space,
10 February 1986. Director Kai Tai Chan for the One Extra Dance
Company. From his book *The Cheated*.

The Misery of Beauty
Play. St Kilda (Melbourne), Theatreworks, Lunar Theatre, 25 August
1989. Director Wendy Joseph. Adapted by Wendy Joseph from his novel
The Misery of Beauty. Unpubl.

(7) Articles, interviews, lectures (selected)

Beck, Chris. 'On the Couch', *Age* 'Extra', 15 July 1995, p. 2.

Davidson, Jim. 'Interview with Louis Nowra', *Meanjin* 39: 4, 1980,
pp. 479–495.

Kelly, Veronica. '"More Character-Driven": An Interview with Louis
Nowra', *Coppertales* 2, 1995, pp. 79–92.

Maclean, Alanna. 'Can We Start Doing it Better? Louis Nowra Talks to
Alanna Maclean', *Muse* 118, April 1993, pp. 4–5.

Makeham, Paul. 'The Black Hole of Our History': A Conversation with
Louis Nowra', *Canadian Theatre Review* 74, 1993, pp. 27–31.

Morley, Michael. 'Louis Nowra on Translating and Adapting *Lulu*',
Theatre Australia, June 1981, p. 23.

Nowra, Louis. 'On His Use of Language', *Theatre Australia*, November/
December 1976, p. 11.

—'Writer's View', *Theatre Australia*, December 1978, pp. 17–18.

—'*Inner Voices* and the First Coil', *Australian Literary Studies* 9: 2, 1979,
pp. 188–199. Rpt. in Kelly, ed., *Louis Nowra*. Amsterdam: Rodopi,
1987, pp. 46–55.

—'Translating for the Australian Stage: A Personal Viewpoint',
Australian Literary Studies 10: 3, 1982, pp. 336–343.

—'At the Crossroads', *Australasian Drama Studies* 2: 2, April 1984,
pp. 101–112. Rep. as 'Theatre Turning Point: The Future for Australian
Plays', *Age Monthly Review* 3: 12, April 1985, pp. 3–6.

—'A Flying Pig and an Erotic Diversion are Part of the Package', *Sydney Morning Herald* 'Good Weekend', 29 June 1985, pp. 38–42.

—'Louis Nowra on *Visions*' [Lecture]. Department of English, University of Queensland, 3 June 1985. Audiotape.

—'Autobiography'. In Kelly, ed., *Louis Nowra*. Amsterdam: Rodopi, 1987, pp. 27–41.

—Lecture on *Sunrise*. Department of English, University of Queensland, 18 August 1987. Audiotape.

—'Wine, Women and Thongs', *Sydney Morning Herald* 'Guide', 25 April-1 May 1988, pp. 1, 6.

—'The Shrinking Vision', *Island Magazine* 39, Winter 1989, pp. 11–13.

—'A Summer of Cricket', *Sydney Morning Herald*, 1 January 1990, p. 8.

—'All Eyes', *Independent Monthly*, Dec/Jan 1990, p. 7.

—'Whingeing Artists, Money, Political Correctness and Bureaucracy'. [Address to the National Press Club, Canberra, 6 April 1993], Oral History Collection TRC 4365, National Library of Australia. Audiotape.

—'The Chaos of Greed', *Age* 'Extra', 24 July 1993, p. 11.

—'Is This Guy for Real?', *Sydney Morning Herald* 'Agenda', 20 December 1994, p. 13.

—'The Short, Nasty, Brutal Life of a Playwright', *Island Magazine* 63, Winter 1995, pp. 3–8.

—'The Lunatics That Run Hollywood', *Sydney Morning Herald* 'Metro', 22–28 March 1996, pp. 8–9

—'Anzac and Why I Write', *War: Australia's Creative Response* ed. Anna Rutherford and James Wieland. Hebden Bridge, Yorks: Dangaroo Press, 1997, pp. 342–344.

—'Indonesia and Me', *'The Precious Woman,' with Indonesian Text translated by Tuti Indra Malaon* ed. Philip Kitley. Toowoomba: University of Southern Queensland Press, 1997, pp. iv–vi.

Ridgman, Jeremy. 'Interview: Louis Nowra, Stephen Sewell and Neil Armfield talk to Jeremy Ridgman', *Australasian Drama Studies* 1: 2, 1983, pp. 105–123.

Turcotte, Gerry. '"Perfecting the Monologue of Silence": An Interview with Louis Nowra', *Kunapipi* 9: 3, 1987, pp. 51–67.

Select bibliography of sources

AUSTLIT (the Australian Literature Database) CD ROM.

Australian and New Zealand Theatre Record, 1987–1996.

Ashcroft, Bill, Gareth Griffiths & Helen Tiffin. *The Empire Writes Back: Theory and Practice in Post-Colonial Literatures.* London: Routledge, 1989.

Bakhtin, Mikhail. *Rabelais and his World* trans. Helene Iswolsky. Bloomington: Indiana UP, 1984.

—*The Dialogic Imagination: Four Essays* trans. Caryl Emerson and Michael Holquist. Austin: University of Texas P, 1981.

Bedloe, Christopher et al. 'Louis Nowra on "Whingeing Artists' at the Press Club on 6th April 1993', *Muse* 119, May 1993, pp. 19–21.

Bhabha, Homi, ed. *Nation and Narration.* London: Routledge, 1990.

—*The Location of Culture.* London & NY: Routledge, 1994.

Brodsky, Alyn. *Madame Lynch and Friend: A True Account of an Irish Adventuress and the Dictator of Paraguay, Who Destroyed that American Nation.* New York: Harper & Row, 1975.

Brooks, Peter. *The Melodramatic Imagination: Balzac, Henry James, Melodrama and the Mode of Excess.* New York: Columbia University Press, 1985.

Broome, Richard & Alick Jackomos. *Sideshow Alley.* St Leonards, Allen & Unwin, 1998.

Carroll, Dennis. *Australian Contemporary Drama* Rev. ed. Sydney: Currency, 1995.

Chambers, Iain. *Popular Culture: The Metropolitan Experience.* London & New York: Methuen, 1986.

Core, Philip. *Camp: The Lie That Tells the Truth.* London: 1984.

Davidson, Jim. 'Tasmanian Gothic',*Meanjin* 48: 2, 1989, pp. 307–324.

Duigan, Virginia. 'Louis Nowra: The Annals of the Cheated', *National Times*, 6–11 December 1976, p. 42.

Eccles, Jeremy. 'Displaced Persons', *Look and Listen*, September 1985, pp. 23–24.

Ellis, Bob. 'Sydney, Paris and Critics', *Nation Review*, 28 July–3 August 1978.

Fitzpatrick, Peter. 'Asian Stereotypes in Recent Australian Plays', *Australian Literary Studies* 12: 1, 1985, pp. 35–46. Rpt. (part) in Kelly, ed. Louis Nowra, 1987.

—Review of *The Golden Age*. *Australasian Drama Studies* 7, 1985, pp. 139–144. Rpt. (part) in Kelly, ed. *Louis Nowra*, 1987.

—*After the Doll: Australian Drama Since 1955*. Melbourne: Edward Arnold, 1979.

Fuchs, Elinor. *The Death of Character: Perspectives on Theatre After Modernism*. Bloomington: Indiana UP, 1996.

Garber, Marjorie. *Vested Interests: Cross-dressing and Cultural Anxiety*. New York: HarperPerennial, 1993.

Gilbert, Helen. 'The Dance as Text in Contemporary Australian Drama: Movement and Resistance Politics'. *ARIEL; A Review of International English Literature* 23: 1, 1992, pp. 133–147.

—'Postcolonial Grotesques: Re-membering the Body in Louis Nowra's *Visions* and *The Golden Age*', *SPAN* 2: 36, 1993, pp. 618–633.

—'Monumental Moments: Michael Gow's *1841*, Stephen Sewell's *Hate*, Louis Nowra's *Capricornia* and Australia's Bicentenary', *Australasian Drama Studies* 24, 1994, 29–45.

—'De-Scribing Orality: Performance and the Recuperation of Voice', in *De-Scribing Empire: Post-Colonialism and Textuality* ed. Chris Tiffin & Alan Lawson. London & NewYork: Routledge, 1994, pp. 98–111.

—'Ghosts in a Landscape: Louis Nowra's *Inside the Island* and Janis Balodis' *Too Young for Ghosts*', *Southern Review* 27, 1994, 432–447.

—'Dressed to Kill: A Post-colonial Reading of Costume and the Body in Australian Drama', in *Imperialism and Theatre: Essays on World Theatre, Drama and Performance* ed. J. Ellen Gaino.r London & NewYork: Routledge, 1995, pp. 104–131.

—'GI Joe Versus Digger Dave: Contemporary Australian Drama and the Vietnam War', in *War: Australia's Creative Response* ed. Anna Rutherford & James Wieland. Hebden Bridge: Dangaroo Press, 1997, pp. 293–307.

—'Theatre and Cultural Commerce: Louis Nowra's *Così*'. *Southerly* 57: 3, 1997.

—*Sightlines: Race, Gender and Nation in Contemporary Australian Theatre*. Ann Arbor: University of Michigan Press, 1998.

Gilbert, Helen & Joanne Tompkins. *Post-Colonial Drama: Theory, Practice, Politics*. London & NewYork, Routledge, 1996.

Griffiths, Gareth. 'Australian Subjects and Australian Style: The Plays of Louis Nowra', *Commonwealth: Essays and Studies* 6: 2, 1984, pp. 42–48. Rpt. (part) in Kelly, ed. *Louis Nowra*, 1987.

Halliwell, Michael. '"The Space Between": Postcolonial Opera? The Meale/Malouf Adaptation of *Voss*', *Australasian Drama Studies* 28, 1996, pp. 87–98.

Hillel, John. 'Screenplays for Radio: The Radio Drama of Louis Nowra', *Australasian Drama Studies* 30, 1997, pp. 68–86.

Holloway, Peter, ed. *Contemporary Australian Drama* Rev. ed. Sydney: Currency, 1987.

Hutcheon, Linda. *A Theory of Parody: The Teachings of Twentieth-Century Art Forms.* New York & London: Methuen, 1985.

Jacka, Elizabeth. *The ABC of Drama 1975–1990.* North Ryde: AFTRS, 1991.

Jackson, Rosemary. *Fantasy: The Literature of Subversion.* London & New York: Methuen, 1981.

Jenkins, John & Linz, Rainer. *Arias: Recent Australian Music Theatre* Melbourne: Redhouse Editions, 1997.

Kampfner, Judy. 'Nowra Breakout', *24 Hours* 2: 7, August 1990, pp. 12–13.

Kelly, Veronica. 'A Mirror for Australia: Louis Nowra's Emblematic Theatre', *Southerly* 41: 4, 1981, pp. 431–457. Rpt. in Holloway, 1987 and Kelly, ed. *Louis Nowra*, 1987.

—Review of *Sunrise. Australasian Drama Studies* 2: 2, 1984, pp. 124–126. Rpt. in Kelly, ed. *Louis Nowra*, 1987.

—'"Lest We Forget": *Inside the Island'*, *Island Magazine* 23, Winter 1985, pp. 19–23. Rpt. in Kelly, ed., *Louis Nowra*, 1987, and Rutherford and Wieland, ed., *War: Australia's Creative Response*, 1997.

—ed. *Louis Nowra.* Amsterdam: Rodopi, 1987.

—'Apocalypse and After: Historical Visions in Some Recent Australian Drama', *Kunapipi* 9: 3 1987, pp. 68–78.

—'"Nowt More Outcastin": Utopian Myth in Louis Nowra's *The Golden Age'*, in *A Sense of Exile: Essays in the Literatures of the Asia-Pacific Region* ed. Bruce Bennett. Perth: Centre for Studies in Australian Literature, 1988, pp. 101–110.

—'Louis Nowra', in *Post-Colonial English Plays: Commonwealth Drama Since 1960* ed. Bruce King. London: Macmillan, 1992, pp. 50–66.

—'Smashing Temples: Cultural Symptoms of the 1980s in Australian Mainstage Comedy and Farce', *Modern Drama* 38, 1995, 97–108.

—Review of *Crow. Australasian Drama Studies* 28, 1996, pp.167–169.

—'Staging Mabo: The Recent Theatre of Louis Nowra', in *'And What Books Do You Read? New Studies in Australian Literature* ed. Irmtraud Petersson & Martin Duwell. St Lucia: University of Queensland Press, 1996, pp. 112–125.

—'"Who's the Bigger Dill?" The Madhouse in Recent Australian Drama' in Leigh Dale & Simon Ryan, ed., *The Body in the Library: Post-Colonial Representations of the Body.* Amsterdam: Rodopi. Forthcoming.

Kiernan, Brian. 'Some Contemporary Developments in Australian Drama: Louis Nowra and Stephen Sewell', *Australian Papers: Yugoslavia, Europe and Australia* ed. Mirko Jurak. Lyubjana: Edvard Kardelj University, 1983. Rpt. (part) in Kelly, ed. *Louis Nowra*, 1987.

Kiernan, Suzanne. 'Plots in Search of a Narrative', *Sydney Review* 61, Jan/Feb 1994, p. 14.

Le Moignan, Michael. 'The Strange World of Louis Nowra', *National Times*, 23–29 November 1980, p. 40.

Levey, Michael. *Rococo to Revolution*. London: Thames & Hudson, 1966.

Litson, Jo. 'Wicked Ways of Louis Nowra', *Weekend Australian Magazine*, 18–19 April 1987, p. 9.

—'Romantics on the Outside, Looking In', *Australian Weekend Review*, 25–26 April 1992, p. 11.

—'A Newer Nowra', *ABC Radio 24 Hours*, September 1993, pp. 58–61.

—'*Cosi*'s Cossies', *Australian Weekend Review*, 23–24 March 1996), p. 10.

Macintyre, Ben. *Forgotten Fatherland: The Search for Elisabeth Nietzsche* London: Picador, 1992.

McCallum, John. 'The World Outside: Cosmopolitanism in the Plays of Nowra and Sewell', *Meanjin* 43: 2, 1984, pp. 286–296. Rpt. (part) in Kelly, ed. *Louis Nowra*, 1987.

—'New Voices Unheard in a Dramatic Tragedy', *Australian Weekend Review*, 20–21 June 1992, p. 11.

Makeham, Paul. Review of *Radiance*. *Australasian Drama Studies* 25, 1994, pp. 189–193.

—'"Across the Long, Dry Stage": Discourses of Landscape in Australian Drama'. Ph D dissertation, University of Newcastle, 1996.

Marr, David. *Patrick White: A Life*. Sydney: Vintage, 1992.

Nahman of Bratslav. *The Tales*, trans. Arnold J. Band. NewYork: Paulist Press, 1978.

Ovid [Publius Ovidius Naso]. *The 'Metamorphoses' of Ovid* trans. Mary M. Innes. Harmondworth: Penguin, 1955.

Parsons, Philip & Victoria Chance. *Companion to Theatre in Australia*. Sydney: Currency/Cambridge UP, 1995.

['Pierpont'] 'An Evening of Crime and Culture', *Bulletin*, 15 March 1994, p. 98.

Portus, Martin. 'Nowra Reminds us of What We Want to Forget', *Sydney Morning Herald*, 8 August 1987, p. 50.

—'The Victims of a Messiah Complex', *Sydney Morning Herald*, 30 April 1988, p. 74.

Posner, Donald. *Antoine Watteau*. London: Weidenfeld & Nicolson, 1984.

Radic, Leonard. *The State of Play*. Melbourne: Penguin, 1991.

Ridgman, Jeremy. 'Louis Nowra', *Theatre Australia*, October 1980, pp. 18–19.

—Review of Rodney Fisher, ed, *Seven One-Act Plays*, *Australasian Drama Studies* 2: 1, 1983, pp. 128–130. [*The Song Room*]

Robinson, Peter. 'A Sadly Neglected Playwright Gets a Run at Last', *National Times*, 8–13 November 1976, p. 23.

Roy, James. 'Sharing Cultures: An ABC/CBC Radio Drama Exchange', *Canadian Theatre Review* 85, 1995, pp. 15–18.

Rushdie, Salman. *Imaginary Homelands: Essays and Criticism 1981–1991*. London: Granta, 1991.

Rutherford, Anna & Jim Wieland, ed. *War: Australia's Creative Response*. Hebden Bridge: Dangaroo Press, 1997.

Smith, Margaret. 'Fight for Love in *Hunger*', *Sun-Herald*, 18 May 1986, p. 103.

—'Director Mark Joffe interviewed by Margaret Smith', *Cinema Papers* 105, August 1995, pp. 4–8, 55.

Thomson, Helen. Review of *Summer of the Aliens* and *Così. Australasian Drama Studies* 23, 1993, pp. 175–178.

—Review of *The Incorruptible. Australasian Drama Studies* 29, 1996, pp. 206–210.

Thwaites, Tony, Lloyd Davis & Warwick Mules. *Tools for Cultural Studies: An Introduction*. Melbourne: Macmillan, 1995.

Tittensor, John. 'The Town That Went Mad', *National Times*, 16–22 August 1985, p. 41.

Tompkins, Joanne. 'Infinitely Rehearsing Performance and Identity: *Africa Solo* and *The Book of Jessica*', *Canadian Theatre Review* 74, 1993, pp. 35–39.

—'Celebrate 1988? Australian Drama in the Bicentennial Year', *Australian and New Zealand Studies in Canada*, 11 June 1994, 103–112.

—'"Spectacular Resistance": Metatheatre in Post-Colonial Drama', *Modern Drama* 38: 1, 1995, pp. 42–51.

—'"The Story of Rehearsal Never Ends": Rehearsal, Performance, Identity', *Canadian Literature* 144, 1995, pp. 142–161.

—'Re-citing Shakespeare in Post-Colonial Drama', *Essays in Theatre / Etudes théâtrales* 15: 1, 1996, pp. 15–22.

—'Breaching the Body's Boundaries: Abjected Subject Positions in Post-Colonial Drama', *Modern Drama* 40: 4, 1997, pp. 502–513.

Turcotte, Gerry. '"Speaking the Formula of Abjection": Hybrids and Gothic Discourses in Louis Nowra's Novels', *Westerly* 36: 3, September 1991, pp. 61–72.

—'The Circle is Burst: Eschatologicial Discourse in Louis Nowra's *The Golden Age*', *SPAN* 24, 1987, pp. 63–80. See also *Australasian Drama Studies* 11, 1987, pp. 65–77.

—Review of *Capricornia. Australasian Drama Studies* 15/16, 1989/1990, pp. 189–191.

Turner, Graeme. *Making It National: Uses of Nationalism in Australian Popular Culture*. Sydney: Allen & Unwin, 1994.

Young, Robert J. C. *Colonial Desire: Hybridity in Theory, Culture and Race*. London & NewYork: Routledge, 1995.

Index